HOW

TO

ESCAPE

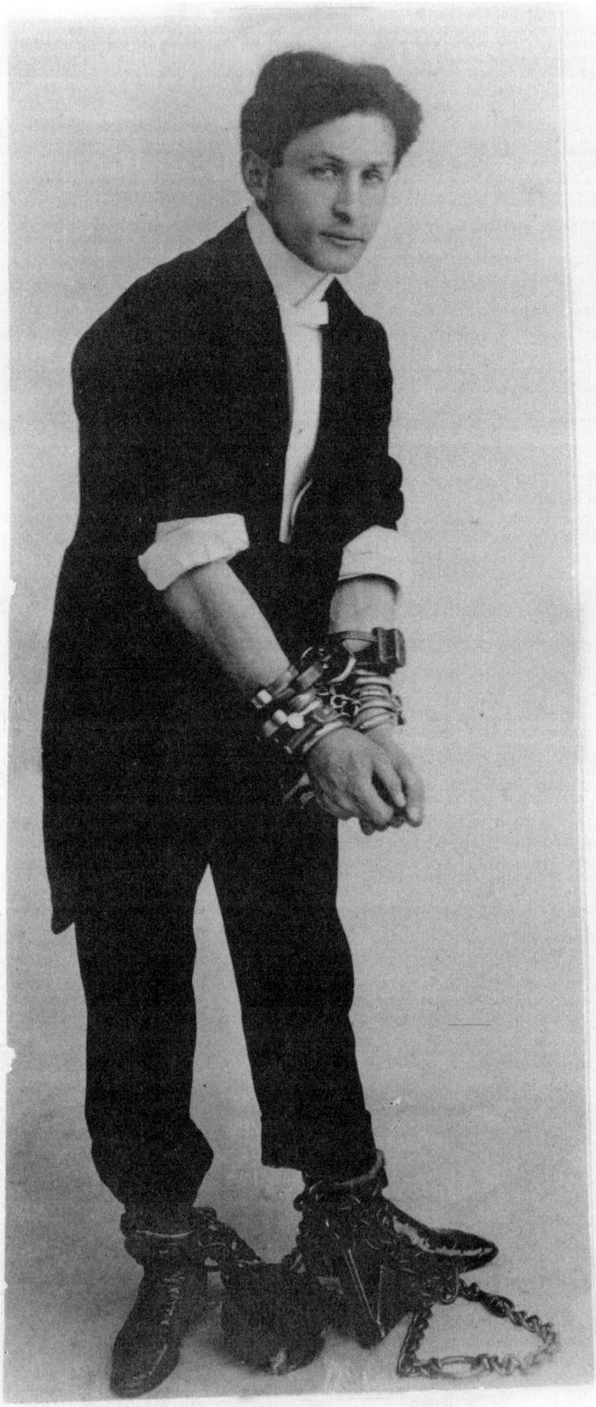

How to Escape

magic, madness, beauty, and cynicism

Crispin Sartwell

excelsior editions

AN IMPRINT OF STATE UNIVERSITY OF NEW YORK PRESS

Published by
STATE UNIVERSITY OF NEW YORK PRESS
Albany

Printed in the United States of America

Excelsior Editions is an imprint of State University of New York Press.
For information, contact State University of New York Press.
www.sunypress.edu

Production and book design, Laurie Searl
Marketing, Michael Campochiaro

Library of Congress Cataloging-in-Publication Data

Sartwell, Crispin, 1958-
How to escape : magic, madness, beauty, and cynicism / Crispin Sartwell.
pages cm — (Excelsior editions)
Includes bibliographical references.
ISBN 978-1-4384-5267-8 (hardcover : alk. paper)
ISBN 978-1-4384-5266-1 (pbk. : alk. paper)
1. Philosophy, American—21st century.
I. Title.
B948.S271 2014
191—dc23
2013034876

10 9 8 7 6 5 4 3 2 1

In loving memory of my father,

Franklin Gallagher Sartwell

Contents

Preface

The items here probably represent the "light" or fluffy side of my authorship, which might be unfortunate, because the light side is also a rather dark side. They range from a personal essay on addiction to a satire on race to an amazing "solution" to the question of the meaning of life itself or, thinking about it from another angle, to the question of the meaning itself of life, or perhaps to the question itself of life's meaning.

The centrality of the arts for understanding historical and contemporary culture, and our coming rapture/damnation by comedy in the cynical ecstasy at the end of history: these are related underlying themes of many of these essays. Often I apply ideas and taxonomies from art history and aesthetics to various sorts of materials, for example to gender and sexual orientation, or to popular music forms, or to the structure of history, and then try to let the material remap those disciplines. I don't insist that any particular one of these essays constitute philosophy or aesthetics or anything else; I've tried to follow from thing to thing, idea to idea, fiasco to calamity, rather than worry about where precisely I was in the disciplinary maze.

Some of these essays reflect engagement with stage and parlor magic and sleight of hand; a number discuss or obviously reflect obsession and addiction; a number display a lifelong love of popular music; a number reflect engagements with my favorite writers and questions about writing. All of these obviously have various autobiographical connections, and I suppose they are all attempts to determine *what you can see from here*, wherever "here" is now: including, white heterosexual middle-aged person; aficionado or enthusiast; daddy, American, me, etc. I'm happy to let these connections emerge explicitly, or not.

As I've gone on writing, I have tried to get less showboaty and more obviously committed to subject matters other than myself, though it might not seem that way. Nevertheless, "I" weaves in and out here, and I do think that even academic writing—which this may be or not—should be more personal insofar as persons, with their passions and pathologies, still lurk behind it or create it in some way. The "I" changes in different essays, but I am not going to be precious about it: by "I" I mean me. I mean me perhaps at different moments or moods; certainly "Detritus" was written at a nadir, and I'm doing better now, and would have something happier to say about myself. I am content even if uncomfortable leaving that essay as a trace of then. It's not, on the other hand, that I'm "a different person" than I was in 2008. If only. But you know how we end up being transformed without meaning to be, under necessity, like ramshackle ships of Theseus.

Most of these texts were read in some form as lectures/multimedia extravaganzas; others were pitched to various sorts of publication with varying success. Thanks to the Theory and Art of Magic Conference, Slippery Rock University, Notre Dame, East Tennessee State, Southern Illinois, Concordia College, Cal State Chico, Oregon State, Gettysburg College, the Nordic Society for Aesthetics, Duquesne, the International Country Music Conference, and others who hosted me on occasions when this material was presented. Parts of pieces appeared in *Harper's*, the *Los Angeles Times*, *The Rolling Stones and Philosophy*, *How Does It Feel to Be a (White) Problem?*, and *Tricksters and Punks of Asia*. All the papers have been at least somewhat revised, though they are still to be taken as representing the time they were composed. For example, "How to Escape" was written before the killing of Osama bin Laden. In some cases, related blog entries from eyeofthestorm.blogs.com or related journalism by me from various sources have been annexed.

Near the end of his life, my father, Frank Sartwell, gave me editions of Mencken's autobiography and Bierce's *Devil's Dictionary* with an air of passing on key bits of family lore. For him, as for his father—both newspapermen in DC—Mencken was the greatest of their own kind, or what they aspired to be: irascible, politically perverse, hilarious, hard-drinking bastards who knew everything, especially about writing. And Dad took me to see the Seldom Scene, Thursdays at the Red Fox Inn in Bethesda, Maryland.

For better and disaster, the effects of Judith Bradford and Marion Winik on the thought and prose style of this book, and the experiences represented, are obvious, at least to me. I think Arthur Danto's influence is pervasive; oh, probably Richard Rorty's too. I read Heinrich Wölfflin's *Principles of Art History* in high school and am still battering my old Dover edition; amazing how something like that can infest your thinking. Throughout, art historical concepts, stylistic characterizations, and terms designating periods (*soul*, for example, or *classical*) should be understood as sketched out in the lexicon, pp. 179–91. Thanks to Andrew Kenyon for collaboration on this volume. The city of Baltimore and the countryside of south central Pennsylvania. The Maryland Institute College of Art and Dickinson College.

As usual, you should blame those people and institutions, rather than the author, for all the infelicities, fatuities, solecisms, barbarisms, contradictions, absurdities, and blunders you find here.

I

How to Escape

2006

In the days after American and Northern Alliance forces took Kandahar, Osama bin Laden escaped from the caves of Tora Bora into Pakistan, handing his cell phone to a decoy and dissipating into the mountainous terrain. Repeatedly after that, the US government came to believe it knew where to find him. He was the target, for example, of the March 28, 2002, raid of a rented house in Faisalabad, Punjab Province, that netted his lieutenant Abu Zubayadh. But he escaped again and again. It quickly reached the point where—until he popped up spectrally on Al Jazeera—he might have been alive or dead, here or there, or, seemingly, both and all at once.

From the point of view of his potential victims, Osama's elusiveness might have been the most dangerous of his achievements because it hinted at something miraculous: all the world's police and intelligence and military, armed with everything from satellites to suitcases full of cash, couldn't nail him down. It's not killing but escaping death that begins to create a cult. The longer bin Laden evaded capture or death, the more dangerous he became, not necessarily as a terrorist but as a symbol.

The association of escape with transcendence is so intimate that saviors and spiritual heroes are always marked by their ability to escape: Jesus from the sealed tomb, Buddha from the cycle of becoming. Indeed, there is a sense that a real hero, or monster, or anyone who seems to have outgrown the mundane—someone who partakes in the divine or satanic—cannot be killed, and so such people are forever being rediscovered after their deaths: Bob Marley, Elvis, JFK, Hitler, Marilyn. There are people who believe that each overcame death and transcended suffering.

Most padlocks have four tumblers at the top of the key chamber. Each tumbler is spring-driven and consists of a driver and key pin housed in a vertical case. When the right key is inserted into the lock, the drivers are pushed up into the hull above the sheer line, while the key pins remain below, allowing the cylinder to turn. There are various ways to pick such a lock, but the classic technique is this: You take a tension wrench, place it into the bottom of the key chamber, and apply a slight torque, enough to "bind" one of the pins. Then, using a hook pick, a half diamond, or perhaps a snake, you "break" that pin, pushing its driver into the hull. When all four pins are broken, the tension wrench turns the cylinder and the lock springs open.

Some pin locks are almost absurdly easy to open. I have a bottom-of-the-line Brinks "Home Security" strong box that I can open as quickly with a pick as with a key. The standard Master Lock padlock—the one that consists of a stack of metal plates and that you used to see on television taking a bullet and remaining closed—is almost as easy to pop. But spend a little more money for a lock with pick-resistant pins, and you have something that's an art project to get open. Still, my view is that if it can be opened with a key, it can be picked.

The event of a lock popping open is small, but it is full. That click feels like a victory of your ingenuity over the security firms of the world. It has a slightly orgasmic quality, enhanced by the sexual symbology of lock and key. But above all, and relatedly, it brings into play the whole metaphysics of escape: the idea that you cannot be held, forced, incarcerated, that you can free yourself, transcend your mundane bonds and the oppressions that hold you, and release yourself into a place of freedom.

Perhaps that's why, like a lot of people, I've been a bit obsessed with escape since I was a child and first read about Houdini. In the early '70s I fancied myself an urban guerrilla, destroying construction equipment that was regimenting forests, or schools that were regimenting minds. I wanted to learn the chemistry of bomb-making and the tactics of concealment. But above all, I wanted to be the sort of person—if indeed there are any such persons—who cannot be held. Handcuff and manacle me and I would free myself. Imprison me and I would be gone . . . like a Houdini.

Our lives bristle with entrapment: legal, spiritual, political, economic. We're locked into institutions, into our schools, jobs, laws, taxes, poverty (or, for that matter, wealth); into our families or aloneness; into our bodies with their flaws or illnesses. And so our lives also bristle with escapes: leaving Pittsburgh for Jamaica, the evening drink or smoke, the darkened theater where, for example, James Bond—the films about whom are constructed almost entirely as a series of fantastic escapes—promises to divert us.

As a child, Charles Julius Guiteau was beaten savagely by his father, who accused him continually of violating God's laws. He ran away from home as a teenager in the 1850s, but internalized the criticism sufficiently to become a religious fanatic. Charles Guiteau published a plagiarized book of religious philosophy titled *Truth*, and eventually fetched up at John Humphrey Noyes's utopian Oneida community in New York, which taught that the second coming of Christ had occurred in 70 AD, and thus that we were all already redeemed and free of sin. Among other things, the residents of Oneida practiced "plural marriage," despite which the conspicuously unattractive Guiteau couldn't obtain a partner. The women of Oneida nicknamed him "Charles Gitout."

Eventually, he broke with the community (or rather, they with him—they accused him of laziness and insanity). He then lived from boardinghouse to boardinghouse, absconding in the middle of the night to avoid payment, while creditors tracked him down repeatedly and repossessed his belongings, if any. Here is a sample of his correspondence with a creditor: "Find $7 enclosed. Stick it up your bung hole and wipe your nose on it." His profession was itinerant preacher, and one of his sermons was described as follows in a newspaper:

> Is There a Hell? Fifty Deceived People [are] of the opinion that there ought to be. The man Charles J. Guiteau, if such really is his name, who calls himself an eminent Chicago lawyer, has fraud and imbecility plainly stamped upon his countenance . . . Although the impudent

> scoundrel had talked only fifteen minutes, he suddenly perorated brilliantly by thanking the audience for their attention and bidding them good-night. Before the astounded fifty had recovered from their amazement . . . [he] had fled from the building and escaped.[1]

Whatever his merits as a preacher, he moved on to politics. Guiteau declared his support of James Garfield in the 1880 election, and gave a series of speeches to that effect. Puzzlingly, he expected Garfield to reward him with the consul generalship in Vienna. When this was not forthcoming, he met Garfield's train at Union Station in DC on July 2, 1881, and shot the president in the back with a .44. The wound was not considered mortal, but like many people before and since, Garfield escaped this mortal coil under the auspices of his physicians. Meanwhile, Guiteau himself believed that Garfield would survive and that he, Guiteau, would be let off due to insanity. And so, still in search of a spouse as Garfield's various infections worsened, Guiteau placed a personal ad from prison for a "nice Christian lady." He spent much of his final year at the United States Jail in Washington, and he received so many death threats (along with a bullet fired by a drunk through his cell window) that a special cell was built for him on death row with a bulletproof oak door. Guiteau was executed June 30, 1882.

Late in 1905, officials at the United States Jail invited Harry Houdini (Ehrich Weiss, the son of a Wisconsin rabbi) to test the security of their death row, and on January 6, 1906, they locked the naked Houdini in Guiteau's cell. There were twenty cells on death row; Guiteau's was ordinarily occupied at that time by a man who had smothered his wife and then slept with her corpse. Each cell was brick-lined with a recessed door, equipped with a state-of-the-art five-tumbler lock. When the officials returned twenty-seven minutes after they'd locked Houdini in, they found that he had not only opened his own cell, but had switched every prisoner to a different cell.

One suspects that Houdini's career, during which he challenged any police department to hold him, in which he successfully escaped from any handcuffs and manacles by which he was constrained, in which he was chained inside trunks and dropped in a river, wriggled free of straitjackets, mail sacks, milk cans, and so on, was concatenated from equal parts skill, trickery, and bribery, though Houdini certainly denied the latter. He said that he had been trained by a German locksmith, and there is ample evidence that he was a master of the art of picking locks as well as an excellent athlete. But no doubt in a pinch he could substitute in a pair of gaffed cuffs, or get a little help from a guard.

But whatever his method, his name became synonymous with the miraculous. Arthur Conan Doyle was sure that, despite Houdini's repeated assertions that there was a perfectly mundane explanation for every one of his performances, he could de- and rematerialize, traveling back and forth to and from the spiritual realm. And a circle of magicians still gathers on the anniversary of his death to determine whether he can manifest himself from the Beyond, despite the fact that Houdini devoted much of his life to exposing fraudulent mediums.

Handcuffs are of necessity rather simple mechanisms. Keyed so that many people can open them and so that the police don't have to carry around dozens of keys, they can in general be opened quickly with a skeleton (say a regular key the bit of which has been filed down slightly). Their security depends on the prisoner not having such a thing about, and, more importantly, not being able easily to get anything into the keyway.

For such reasons, police departments have learned to prefer single-use plastic ties, essentially of the sort that are sometimes used to secure toys inside their boxes for sale. The preferred method of escape here would no doubt be a blade, or better, access to a sharp surface and some time. But again, their effectiveness depends on the thoroughness with which a prisoner is searched, the care with which his environment is controlled, and the surveillance that can be maintained.

Of course, being "handcuffed" has become a figure of speech for any situation in which we are constrained. And we are constrained continually, among other things by our physical limits. Manacles mimic the action of paralysis, but all of us face the constraints on our physical capacities at all times.

In one ferocious jaunt starting in 1876, the great conjuror and hero of Houdini, Harry Kellar, played Boston, Philadelphia, DC, Rio de Janeiro, London, Liverpool, Edinburgh, Gibraltar, Malta, Madrid, Madeira, Cape Town, Kimberley, Mauritius, Bombay, Allahabad, Cawnpore, Lucknow, Melbourne, New Zealand, China,

Japan, Vladivostock, and Bangkok. Then he performed his way across the Pacific and thence back to the east coast of the United States. This and many like tours by many like magicians suggest that magic is universally comprehensible, which in turn suggests that more or less all people everywhere understand the mundane physical limitations under which we all labor, as they (and we) could hardly fail to do. "DECAPITATION FEAT: Or—LIFE IN DEATH. A LIVING HUMAN HEAD suspended on a common Tea-Tray, three feet above the Body. The Head Eats, Smokes, Talks &c." Virtually anyone anywhere would be bewildered by such a demonstration of liberation from gravity, from mortality, and from whatever you were doing that day before you took your seat in the theater. Illusion serves to emphasize the implacable reality of our physical world.

The idea that the body *(soma)* is the prison *(sema)* of the soul *(psyche)* is traditionally attributed to Pythagoras in the sixth century BCE. The factor most responsible for keeping us locked in this prison, according to Pythagoras, was the consumption of beans. Hence the second Pythagorean theorem: "Wretch! Keep thou from beans." What promised to free us, on the other hand, was pure mathematics. The idea that the body is the prison of the soul was probably already ancient when Pythagoras taught it, and has had a venerable history since.

As Socrates prepared to swallow the hemlock, he argued that "those who really apply themselves in the right way to philosophy are directly and of their own accord preparing themselves for death." And he says of death: "Is it [not] simply the release of the soul from the body?" He then argues that the wise despise the pleasures of the body and have been seeking their whole lives to purify their souls of the pollution of the physical: its desires, its transgressions of the moral law, and above all its illusions. After death the soul will freely experience the pure forms of goodness and beauty: "So long as we keep to the body and our soul is contaminated with this imperfection, there is no chance of our ever attaining satisfactorily to our object, which we assert to be the truth."

When Jesus faced execution, he told Simon that "The spirit is willing, but the flesh is weak," and he cursed the cowardice that made him hesitate in the face of his own release from suffering. After the crucifixion they laid him in his tomb and rolled a stone over the entrance. But when Mary and Mary Magdalene came to pay homage, a young man dressed in white told them, "He has been raised; he is not here."

In Augustine's interpretation, mankind was cursed at its inception by original sin (embodiment, more or less) and Jesus came to redeem us, to aid our escape into God's kingdom. And countless Christians have tried to emulate Jesus and so realize the promised transcendence of sin and suffering. The saint yearns above all for transcendence, for a way out, and finds it in an overcoming of and escape from the prison-house of the body.

Michel Foucault in his history of prisons reversed the ancient formula and declared that "the soul is the prison of the body."[2] He argued that our consciousness is shaped by institutions: schools, prisons, families, employers, hospitals, armed forces, in which we are more or less continually under surveillance and subject to punishment. Thus, we learn to control ourselves, to take command of ourselves in accordance with what the institution demands. That is, we become the slaves of ourselves, or our bodies become the slaves of our minds.

His classic example is the Panopticon, the ideal prison designed around 1800 by Jeremy Bentham, on which many later prisons (such as Stateville in Illinois) were based. The arrangement is circular, so that the whole of each cell is visible from a central tower. The guard in this tower is in turn screened from the prisoners, so that they never know whether they're being watched. In such an institution, says Bentham, one learns to be the prison guard of oneself—that is, one gains a conscience, "reforms." All of our modern megainstitutions are devoted to giving us that sort of self-mastery and hence self-enslavement. This creates a pervasive situation of power in which we may well yearn to escape not only from our institutions, but from ourselves.

But perhaps in America, the prison is the prison of both the body and the soul. More than two million Americans are currently incarcerated.

For generations by the 1810s, the Seminoles of Florida had given haven to escaped slaves from the American South, and they were by the early nineteenth century an interracial tribe. The United States made war on the Seminoles—starting with attacks by Andrew Jackson and finishing up with attacks by William Tecumseh Sherman—in order to recover the escapees and their descendants and force the Seminoles onto the Trail of Tears to Oklahoma. Resistance was initially led by the great war chief Osceola. In 1835, when Osceola was visiting the trading post at Fort King, his wife Morning Dew—the mother of his four children—was seized by slave catchers. From that moment, he was an implacable foe. He once reportedly "signed" a treaty by stabbing it with his knife, declaring that "I will make the white man red with blood, and then blacken him in the sun and rain, where the wolf shall smell of his bones, and the buzzard live upon his flesh."[3] Fifty-two of the fifty-five warriors in Osceola's retinue were of African descent. He was captured by the army in 1837 when he came in under flag of truce to negotiate, and died of malaria in a cell at Castillo de San Marcos in St. Augustine.

His two lieutenants Wild Cat and the Black Seminole John Horse were transferred to Fort Marion, where they were held with two dozen others in an 18-by-33-foot cell. Wild Cat later wrote that "We resolved to make our escape or die in the attempt." They spent weeks loosening the stonework in the jail's roof and starving themselves in order to fit through the hole. The band escaped south for five days, surviving on roots and berries, and finally rejoined Wild Cat's tribe near the Tomoka River. They were pursued by Colonel Zachary Taylor, 180 Missouri riflemen, and eight hundred regular army soldiers. Wild Cat and John Horse lured this force into an ambush in the swamp (the Battle of Lake Okeechobee), one of the great victories of the Seminole wars, in which twenty-six US soldiers were killed and 112 wounded, while the Seminoles lost four warriors. Wild Cat and John Horse remained free and for many years prosecuted a successful guerrilla war.

But over the years they were worn down by starvation. Wild Cat's twelve-year-old daughter was kidnapped by the army. Eventually the whole band was sent west under Wild Cat's leadership to the Indian territories. They faced starvation on the way, and then again at their destination, where they were assigned the same territory as the Creeks, a tribe with which they had been at war for decades. Slave traders continued to capture Black Seminoles, despite government pledges of protection that had been the condition of the surrender. In 1849, Wild Cat and John Horse with a band of their people escaped through a gantlet of Creeks, settlers, and slavers to Coahuila, Mexico, where they disappeared.

Most prison escapes do not occur directly from the cell, but from work details or recreation periods. A long period of confinement no doubt acts as a spur to human ingenuity, and it may be that the prisoner has little to think about but the weaknesses in the security system. But the range of techniques mirrors Houdini's maneuvers, from misdirection to fakery to bribery to the actual ability to open locks. And like some of Houdini's stunts, a jailbreak often requires genuine courage and the willingness to risk death. Unlike Houdini's stunts, however, a jailbreak also often involves the willingness to kill other people, and though there is little future in a hostage situation, getting hold of a weapon and shooting your way out is still the direct method.

But often a prison escape, like the perennial illusions of stage magic, relies still on the old standbys of deception: misdirection, diversion—the dummy in the bed, the gun made of soap, the escape that is itself faked and then perpetrated after the search is on. And there are still escape artists who claim to be able to pass through the bars of a prison cell, for example David DeVal, who accepted a challenge from the RSPCA in Oldham, England, to allow police to search him and place him, handcuffed, in a dog kennel, from which he promptly emerged. DeVal markets gaffed locks, handcuffs, boxes, whipping posts, and straitjackets.

Raymond Hamilton was born in a tent on the banks of the Deep Fork River in what had been Indian Territory. His father worked in a lead-smelting plant near Henryetta, Oklahoma. At 5 feet 3 inches and 120 pounds, the younger Hamilton was tiny, but vicious. He grew up in the same rough West Dallas neighborhood as Clyde Barrow and Bonnie Parker. In 1932 he joined Bonnie and Clyde in a rampage of robberies and killings, raiding federal armories, robbing oil refineries, and killing police officers from Missouri to Texas. The gang's ability to escape and survive was remarkable. They shot their way out of a house in Joplin, Missouri, a motel in Platte City, Missouri, and an ambush meeting with relatives in Dallas County, Texas.

Hamilton split with the Barrows, formed his own gang, and was captured in Michigan. Sentenced in Texas to 362 years, he was sent to the Eastham Prison Farm. On the night of January 15, 1934, Clyde Barrow hid guns in a woodpile near where he knew Hamilton would be laboring. Hamilton retrieved his gun the next morning and started shooting at the guards while Clyde Barrow supplied covering fire. Bonnie, in a black Ford V8 about a mile from the shootout, stood on the horn. A bunch of prisoners piled in, and they headed for Fort Worth.

After Bonnie and Clyde were ambushed and killed in Louisiana, Hamilton was apprehended again, sentenced to die, and placed on death row in Huntsville, Texas. Having bribed a guard to smuggle him a gun, he shot his way to a perimeter tower, disarmed the guard there, made his way over the fence, and launched another spree. Recaptured in the Fort Worth rail yards, he was immediately executed at Huntsville.

That was in 1935. The next prisoner to bust out of death row in Texas was Martin Gurule, who had been convicted of killing two people during a robbery in Corpus Christi. On Thanksgiving in 1998, Gurule and six other prisoners colored their thermal underwear black using a magic marker, put dummies in their beds, cut through a fence in their recreation yard, and made their way to the chapel roof, where they were discovered. Guards fired on them, and they all gave themselves up, with the exception of Gurule, who kept going over two ten-foot fences, leaving blood on the razor wire. Cut and wounded, he drowned a few hours later in the swamp.

Philip Brasfield is a writer who has been imprisoned in Texas for a quarter-century and who was on death row at Huntsville at the time for the murder of a six-year-old child, of which he claims to be innocent. Brasfield writes that "I don't know how many times a day I thought of leaving. Most of us entertained fantasies of daring escape. Release from death row was a perpetual prayer." And Brasfield hints that dying free and in defiance in a swamp is preferable to dying as a prisoner, that Gurule's death had a transcendent quality.

Gurule escaped, but he did not escape, if you follow me.[4] And perhaps, in the long run, none of us does. Perhaps there is no way to transcend death or the mundane or ridiculous constraints imposed upon us by our bodies and our lives in them. Maybe there really is no escape from people, from the physical constraints that surround us and the physical limitations that give us shape. Maybe also, liberation from human institutions, from the giant grinding bureaucracies of modernity, is at this point impossible.

Our need to escape arises in the nature of desire itself; once freed into consciousness, it has no necessary limit, but constitutes an infinite series of aspirations, envisions an infinite freedom even from itself. Like that other perverse artifact, the mathematical number series, desire exceeds the possibility of its own calculation and increases indefinitely: it exceeds every bound that could be conceived. The series of natural numbers is mad: it bristles with infinities, which bloom between any two numbers no matter how tight the gap. Every momentary whim entails its own infinity, and the question is whether you pursue it or not. If you do, you will quickly experience the barriers entailed by your own finitude. We can in some sense conceive the infinite infinities of mathematics, but to achieve a comprehension or to actually traverse any given series is impossible, because we quickly find the limits of time, concentration, alertness. And once we start wanting, there is no logically necessary place to stop. The first three of the Buddha's fourfold noble truths: "Life is suffering. Suffering is caused by desire. There is a way out."

The great stoic Epictetus, who was born a slave, taught that the key to freedom was renouncing desire and realizing that there is no freedom in the world, that we must distinguish what is under our control from what is not and surrender the desire to control what we cannot. What we cannot control, for Epictetus, is the way other people act or think, and in general the way the external world is. The world exists exactly the way it must and it unfolds without our having any control over how it unfolds. Nature and culture are our prisons. It is the inner world that is free: for example, we can genuinely choose to accept the world as it is and find peace, or to reject the world and make ourselves miserable.

But as Epictetus recognized, that is no simple matter. We can feel just as imprisoned in ourselves as by our world, and accepting the world just as it is is an immensely difficult discipline, fit for sages and bodhisattvas. The ropes, we might say, always chafe at least a little. The figure of the outlaw or revolutionary is always the figure of the escape artist: someone who ignores our world of commuting, work, bills, debt, housecleaning, cooking—routine. On the same day Raymond Hamilton was executed,* John Dillinger—who had dematerialized from an escape-proof jail in Indiana and who burned mortgages when he robbed banks—was killed in a hail of gunfire at the Biograph Theater in Chicago, though a 1970 book titled *Dillinger: Dead or Alive* asserted that the Biograph operation had killed a double and that Dillinger—like Jesus, like Marilyn—was still going strong. Frankly, I think he didn't escape the bullets and hence became immanent in all things on July 22, 1934.

*That is false. Dillinger was killed about ten months earlier. For purposes of the essay, however, it is perfectly true.

II

Divas, Dudes, Queens, and Studs

Gender and Sexuality as Aesthetic Expressions

2013

Male/female and gay/straight, whatever else they are, are aesthetic vocabularies. They are, we might say, fundamentally systems of the arts. It is important here to take "arts" or "the aesthetic" in their broadest possible scope. I want to include, for example, bodily comportment or movement styles, including dance and sport but also styles of walking, sitting down, and so on; linguistic communication: slangs, informal or formal poetries and polemical strategies, verbal and written styles; personal adornment including clothing and hairstyles and body alteration, as by plastic surgery, exercise, and tattooing; distributions of the environment as in interior design or landscaping, or the design and arrangement of artifacts and styles of shelter: architecture and design arts, painting and sculpture; crafts or ways of making or manufacturing; sound design including musics; scents and deodorizers and cookery; television and film; and so on.

Now, one thing to notice about all these things is that they make use of other things. There's no use calling your outfit merely social code or vocabulary; you'd better have the fabric and then the fabric's making in mind too. One good thing about using the arts is that they are social practices that always obviously make use of things and transform things, so they show our embeddedness in a real physical world. But of course your outfit does also function as a social vocabulary, and you are conveying all sorts of things about your identity by the way you dress, while even what's possibly available emerges from a set of social and economic practices around clothing, even in cases where one intentionally defies or teases the going conventions.

For example, it's not necessary quite to agree with Judith Butler that the man/woman split is a matter of performance rather than biology to note that it is at least in part a matter of performance. The ways we experience the gendering of others and the way we express our own gendering to others are largely contained in things like styles of movement and clothing, hair growth and removal, scents and grooming procedures, and preferences in the arts. There are media (cable networks, internet zones) generally aimed at women, and media generally aimed at men. But then as well as the apparently normative cases, we've got to keep in mind all the crossings, betrayals, and emigrations, all the tiny bits of gender dysphoria: pretty much all media are available to anyone. You have boys who move like girls and vice versa, or boys who move like girls on some occasions in some respects, and so on.

Let's begin by exploring one simplistic set of relations, or grid of four boxes: male and female, straight and gay. First you get the disclaimer: everything is at an absurdly general level; I'm trying to describe a cultural imaginary; no person occupies any point in the taxonomy with perfect centrality—and that goes for male and female as well as gay and straight and the various clusters of taste. Also every interstice is occupied.

I think that popular culture at this moment is dominated by an aesthetic coalition of straight women and gay men. One could sum it up like this: a celebration of artifice, an apotheosis of appearance, an orientation toward spectacle. Now, the appearance/reality split itself needs all sorts of examination; it is ideology as well as a metaphysics. But one way it needs examination is precisely as a gendered and orientated aesthetic pair. It's a complementary system, a yin yang. You can't have one without the other. But I might just sketch: we're classical, you're baroque. You're rococo, we're neoclassical. You're impressionist, we're cubist. You're pop, we're minimalist.

As styles, gender and sexual identities annex material from everywhere; so for example they absorb the appearance/reality distinction, now translated into a series of aesthetic expressions. So, femininity, we might say, involves an administration of appearances, whereas masculinity deploys an aesthetics of reality. What is interesting about this is that it is not exactly metaphysics but not exactly not; femininity/masculinity translates appearance/reality into a series of tropes or symbols or narratives; it is definitely not a revelation of the very nature of truth, nor is it, I believe, its source; rather, it is at play with reality, showing its liquidity as well as its stubbornness. Nor should we regard femininity as the creation alone of straight women or of straight women under pressure by straight men. Gay men have rearticulated femininity profoundly, and hence masculinity as well, but then gay women and also straight women have constant input to the meaning of masculinity, and femininity too: all of these things are in constant interchange, and what is reality at one moment or for one purpose is appearance at the next, or is deployed consciously as an aesthetic repertoire. All poles are being constantly naturalized and then appropriated in self-conscious aesthetic rearticulations.

We might think of ornaments, cosmetics, scents as the witchcraft of femininity: a play with appearance that also signifies frivolity, pleasure, or an autoerotic enjoyment of the appearance of oneself one creates, as well as a seduction of the masculine or a disempowerment of it, an act both of acquiescence and resistance. But then, in relation to the structure of femininity, the aesthetic repertoire of masculinity comes to a certain consciousness, and one learns an ethics of simplicity or straightforward naturalness precisely as an aesthetic repertoire: one learns to move like a man, whether one is a man or not. One learns to move like a man within gay communities, or within lesbian communities, or within heterosexual male communities, or within mixed communities, which is emphatically not to say that masculinity is a primordial character which gets reinterpreted in these contexts; for one thing, it is at stake in each context and always mutating, and what signifies truth or nature or reality at one time and place may not at another.

These roles or identities or aesthetic systems arise in a system of complements, but they are in action in time, like art movements, which they also literally are; they merge and diverge, divide within and coalesce across; the situation at a given time is complex and it's in the middle of reconfiguration. Without touching the biology or genetics at all, the way male and female and straight and gay and masculine and feminine function makes them, I think obviously, interdependent and unstable. Ultimately, the destabilizing element is desire, which constantly pushes and pulls each particle in different directions. The center or eye consists of all the sexual and erotic and aesthetic pairings, all the ways people in different groups are drawn to each other and repelled by each other, all the places and ways they merge and segregate themselves from each other, and each other from themselves, and by which they constantly register one another: psychologically, linguistically, musically, visually, sexually.

The distinctions between straight women and straight men—the immense Venus/Mars differences that supposedly make us incomprehensible to each other—are of course also the center of heterosexual erotics. We want to be incomprehensible to each other, and hence be ourselves. This is actually symbolized in the yin yang, for example: it's a fucking cosmology of difference. Within heterosexuality, the differences become more and more intense because they are the center of the erotic lives of both sorts of people: men get manlier and drive trucks and watch sports; women get girlier and wear frills and sparkles and makeup and stuff. They drink Chardonnay and gossip or whatever. Yo, we can't stand that shit; we don't understand it, pointedly. But what it means to be heterosexual is to emphasize the differentiation and want precisely people who drink creamy lattes and have closets full of incomprehensible grooming products and iPods full of the worst music ever. We are conniving to make ourselves so different that we can't communicate, and so different that we can't not want, can't not be for one another what the other lacks. Then again, precisely because of wanting, we are drawn into proximity. We get to know each other. We want to be friends. We're frustrated that we can't communicate. We try. We oscillate toward similarity, and of course we are massively the same as embodied human beings and as part of the same culture or system of identities, even if our bodies and cultures are a bit different too. We try to approach our heterosexual relationships homosocially.

But and so, I don't think there's any objective normative weight in the eroticization of difference: sameness can also be eroticized (and every nuance in between). So we might call that homonormativity or yin yin or yang yang. But heterosexual men and women are the same in that they are heterosexuals, and gay men and women are both gay. So this dimension is not just in play within gay and lesbian groups. In every combination and in every point in between given nodes, there is both sameness and difference, and either might be used erotically or conceived as repulsive. It's perfectly possible for a straight man and a straight woman to wink at each other in a gay bar and form a coalition of shared experience. Now as, say, lesbians emerge into a kind of erotic solidarity, straight men are migrating to similar symbol systems and erotic configurations, and vice versa: or as the hets push out, they enter into an erotics of identification with the homos of the other gender, scattering outliers throughout the journey. One thing I'm trying not to do here is make the het categories fundamental; or to define the homo categories as parasitic on the het categories: I do think in their contemporary configuration they are mutually simultaneously caused, and inconceivable except as a whole system.

Here's a nice gendered aesthetic pair playing across all the arts: cool vs. fabulous. Cool, I propose, originates as a straight male category: classic examples are Humphrey Bogart and Miles Davis. Coolness suggests simplicity, stillness, dignity, self-containment, or the idea that one is not dependent emotionally on others, a withdrawal in some sense from the social. One of its opposites is the fabulous: an aesthetic of over-the-top display that is a constant reaching out, the obverse or reverse or converse or inverse or something of laconic cool. The history of fabulousness might be as old as the aesthetic coalition of gay men and straight women, something coeval with it in the late nineteenth century, perhaps. In a way it's a feedback loop in which y'all are egging each other on, as in the whole of the way that Katy Perry is styled by a committee of gay men and straight women, as portrayed in the film *Part of Me*. The only definitely straight guy, Russell Brand, is completely invisible, stashed off in a relationship corner somewhere. The Kardashians or the cast of Jersey Shore are in their way fabulous; I'm going to speculate that the straight male audience of such shows is relatively small.

One way into the aesthetics of gender/sexual identity, again, is in terms of natural as against artificial, which is part of the way the male/female yin yang is set up. But I want to say that in this context naturalness is, first, an ideology, and second, it is an aesthetic repertoire or set of conventions, and that it depends conceptually on concepts of the artificial. So, for one thing, heterosexuality's naturalness is rather supported by its reproductive function, so that one conceived heterosexuality as an evolutionary imperative, and homosexuality as a twisted mis-expression of the natural process of human reproduction. Whatever. I think the coolness of a Miles or Humphrey is specifically constructed to contrast with femininity. Also, straightmaleness *is*, precisely, a set of styles of self-ornamentation, of movement, speech cadence, or in short of performance that is no less stylized than its complement, but which by its own ideology must suppress this fact. And it is constantly mutating, partly by contrast to whatever constitutes the feminine or artificial at a given moment; or rather they mutate mutually, season by season. The naturally masculine is a style. It is not supposed to be a style; that is, it is supposed to be natural. Well, that is itself a style, naturally.

Let's start with "laconic"; we straight guys tend to think of other groups as chattering too much. Thus Eastwood's "Man With No Name." Now, I could see a camp reading of the Spaghetti Westerns in which he appears. And what's paradigmatically masculine now looks rather different from what was paradigmatically masculine in 1972. So withdrawn is Clint's character from language that there is no word for him at all, or his name is the fact that he has no name. Or as Miles said: "I always listen for what I can leave out": precisely the opposite of, say, a Liberace or operatic style of excessive expression. Guys are always wanting you to bottom-line the thing, cut to the essence, just recite the plain facts, and the way gay men or straight women chatter fills us with boredom and, possibly, loathing. We want words and other things to be of use: they and everything else ought to be restricted to their utilitarian function.

Now, this may appear to be an antiaesthetic mode of comportment, precisely a rejection of ornament, or whimsy, or excess, or appearance. But it is, I am asserting, just as much an aesthetic as its complement, and, if you will pardon my saying so, just as conscious of itself as an aesthetic, and just as important and excellent as part of the world's aesthetics. You can see this in how compelling the Man With No Name and Miles Davis are as aesthetic icons. I don't think you want to just float free into fabulous appearance with no anchor in reality or restraint: at minimum a rhetorical anchor, Strunk-and-White minimalist plain speaking, commitment to truth, sincerity. Nor would you float up there as you have, I think, if we didn't still sit here signifying the opposite; you need the ballast. In some ways, your fabulousness is a liberation, of course, a beautiful expanding of the authentic self. But it is also made possible and comprehensible by our continuing presence and reassertion of T-shirt and jeans realism. Well, and vice versa of course. And of course, the hetmale point of view feeds back into the look of a Katy Perry, as created by straight women and gay men: her giant boobies are both responsive to what straight men want and hence perhaps what gay men want to be, and they parody what straight men want or hyperbolize it.

So one thing we need to understand is how volatile the aesthetic expressions are over time and how subject to how many inputs. So, for example, having hippie-length hair or new-wavish earrings might at some points have offended normative masculinity, or even gotten you kind of gay-bashed, whatever your sexuality. By the '80s at latest, though, younger redneck guys had adopted long hair, and now you could take a look at a country star like Brantley Gilbert: he is managing to signal masculinity with all kinds of heavy jewelry, though it really matters in detail exactly what the jewelry is like: he favors black and silver, and the rings, for example, would be pretty functional weapons, while the bracelets have the quality of gauntlets. Indeed, one sort of has to infer what Brantley Gilbert looks like under all the decoration, just as Dwight Yoakam or Clint Eastwood hid behind a hat in a way that almost made them into logos. But I would say in the case of country music you see an aesthetic coalition of straight men and straight women, and one thing to look at is the way men get done up in this context; as I say, the affiliations are complex, the crossings continual. For one thing, people consume in pairs and groups, so that if a straight woman and a straight man are coupled up, they have to negotiate about the music, find things they can both stand or stations they can listen to when all else fails, ways to look that keep the other's interest.

It seems to me that, even though straight men still dominate political and economic power, the straight woman/gay man alliance dominates media and popular culture. I think this was plenty true even before gay characters started appearing everywhere, like on *Glee*, for example. The only zone of television where you will reliably find a straight male aesthetic is sports, and here we might be allied with lesbian women. Who really watches, let's say, *American Idol* or the dance-offs or all those fairy tale or vampire-type dramas? I think probably straight women and gay men are the primary consumers of what is usually called straight-up pop music, with its techno-type dance beats and besparkled divas. The fashion industry, I believe, and in particular the way women look in most media—on television, in magazines, on runways—is the product of an alliance of gay men and straight women who have essentially operated as an autonomous aesthetic sphere for decades. This dominance has been building since before sexual identities were quite thematized or set up the way they are now. What we would now call gay men, for example, more or less invented, and did not just appropriate, the Broadway musical, an aesthetic which is currently abroad over the whole culture. *High School Musical*, with its vast audience of tweeny girls, begat *Glee* and a revivification of the movie version, a la *Les Mis.* Or we might think of the development of Warhol, the Velvet Underground, the New York Dolls, Glam.

I want to emphasize again the extreme celebration of artifice in all these items. Sometimes you think you're seeing someone in full-body makeup, or you can't tell where the body ends and the hair extensions begin, where the voice leaves off and the vocoder kicks in, etc. But it's important to regard both artifice and the rejection of artifice as aesthetic vocabularies that vary in relation to one another over time. I think we are in a situation in which artifice has been intensifying through the whole culture for some time, which makes the signifiers of authenticity both more important as touchstones and also more willing to use, or more tolerant of, various forms of artifice, as someone like Brantley Gilbert shows; now authenticity is signaled not in a general way viewable at a great distance, like say Springsteen's jeans and white T-shirt and leather jacket, but in detail precisely as a series of decisions about ornaments, as it were a detailed reply to the sequins and processed hair and voice of a Beyonce or Rihanna or Fergie.

The volatile swirl of sexual/aesthetic identities is an erotic vortex or tornado, in which people are pulled in all sorts of directions by identifications and by disidentifications or disavowals. So the fact that I'm not female, and that I signal that with an entire repertoire—the way I move, the way I dress or groom, the way I adorn my environment, and so on—just is also the fact that I'm male: a complete aesthetic arsenal, but one that makes sense only in relation to its complements. And then the fact that I'm straight: well, that makes use of the same stuff. And so does the fact that you're not a straight woman. And then, with a negation, that you're not a lesbian; then, that you're a gay man; then, with a negation, that I'm a straight man, and so on, on each whirl picking up more debris, the whole thing changing shape as it spins. It gets worse, because you've got all sorts of other social/aesthetic categories involved: race, for example. And each group is always welcoming a new young cohort with different cultural icons, outfits, slangs, and so on, which is one way it evolves over time. And even if Katy Perry is demonstrably inspiring young gay men, their elders have their own icons or their more mature taste, which also ranges up and down class identities, so there are highbrow and lowbrow gay aesthetics, for example.

One point is the connection of the erotic to the aesthetic, proverbial since Plato's *Symposium*: beauty is conceived by Sappho, by Plato, by Plotinus, and—in a different key—by Edmund Burke, as fundamentally opened up by sexual longing, though potentially responsive to longings of all kinds. What tugs or attracts or magnetizes in the experience of beauty is the force of unsatisfied or even unsatisfiable desire, and every identity expresses a different dimension or vocabulary of longing by embodying its vision of beauty.

This is what drives the cyclone round and round, as people re-affiliate and re-express, catch up or hold on.

One thing a diva is likely to be is a sex symbol among heterosexual men: the diva manifests various flavors of extreme femininity. Gay and straight men end up appreciating Beyonce from different angles, but certainly erotically both ways round, or in different registers of the erotic: yearning to identify or yearning to possess, which are not entirely separable ideas. If, say, lesbians at a certain point distinguish themselves from straight women by identifying with masculinity, then part of masculinity is precisely eroticizing femininity: hence, lipstick. Or if gay men are disavowing heterosexuality by disavowing masculinity or identifying as feminine, then part of being feminine is eroticizing masculinity: pretty soon you've got muscle-bound dudes with mustaches everywhere, more masculine than me by a ways. But notice, the categories that gay men and lesbians are putting into play here are not primordial or natural, and what counts as masculine and feminine in the first place is constructed as a norm by the "deviations," and how you code masculine as a male or feminine as a female is partly constructed in contrast to the detailed way gay men defy or fail at or modify or play with masculinity, and the way lesbians do so with femininity.

There are many oppressions embedded in this unfolding situation, long histories of oppression that are also eroticized, as dominance and submission, for example. Also these patterns are complex. For example, if gay men are oppressed as gay in patriarchy, they are also privileged as male in the same system: even in the simplest square each identity is doubled or multiplied. But even with all its weight, we don't want to be without the system of identities, because then we'd stop wanting, and also become incomprehensible to ourselves. There are also many liberations, many zones of liberation, many Stonewalls in this configuration or process. All sorts of loves and all sorts of beauties are opened up as possibilities in the midst of the storm; it's the longings opening up within and across that make the beauty possible or give rise to it or even are it. We might think about the straightmale beauty of a Michael Jordan or a V-8 engine, the gay beauty of a Judy Garland or the exact right outfit: it would not be crazy to look at these as both homo- and heteroerotic, as expressing solidarity and difference at once, or the erotics of identification and the erotics of distinction, volatile across time. There might even be transpositions over time as expressions of yearnings-across.

What I think we should want to do with these identities is not destroy or overcome them: no one really has that power even if they are sheer or mere cultural constructions. What we should do is play with them. We need to try to lighten the weight of these systems, or reduce some of their power to configure hatreds—hatreds of the same and hatreds of the different—even as we try to hold on to the ways they configure loves. For these are also systems of exclusion, of course. What you want to try to do is increase the pleasure they offer and decrease the pain, and I say the best place to focus and celebrate is the art, taking art at its broadest possible sweep, from body presentation to food to music to scent to interior design to cityscape. This is where the play of differences is relatively harmless, but profound. You can't have the identities without exclusions or at least judgments of taste that more or less condemn what is in contrast. But a question is: to what extent can you have these judgments without contemplating destruction? We often actually do pretty well at that, and straight guys in particular need to do it better without abandoning ourselves.

So one thing I am not going to do is just try to disown my male straightness. Perhaps every time I put on a Merle Haggard record I am fending off gayness or expressing homophobia. But on the other hand, no one is really a monster in virtue of their sheer aesthetic preferences. Can it be morally wrong to prefer Flatt and Scruggs to Verdi or to dislike rococo interiors? First off, it's not under my control, exactly; I just do, though of course tastes can be pursued or cultivated. And second, it's not that I can't make actual arguments for these preferences; I do it all the time. At any rate, I propose to criticize my own homophobic tendencies in almost any dimension but the aesthetic. I intend to promote equality and liberty for all God's creatures. But I don't propose to pretend that I think Judy Garland made better music than Muddy Waters. We're in a great gay moment. I propose to approve this politically with all my heart and soul while rolling my eyes at its aesthetic products.

I come here as a spokesman for the awesomeness of straight guys. We have given a lot of great stuff to the world, and we are, in our own way, extremely aesthetically oriented; or, if you could take the oppression out, what you'd have left would be all kinds of interesting symbols and gestures, including all these evolving signifiers of sincerity and authenticity and simplicity, hard work and self-discipline. You might think those are oppressive ideas; you don't actually want to be without them, though. That's how we want to be seen, how we dress, how we want to think, how we want to talk.

As I say, I think the oppression has been taken out of this aesthetic repertoire at least to this extent: a gay male/straight female aesthetics dominates our culture. Now, I say that in your moment of victory you can afford to acknowledge that our various aesthetic expressions and principles constitute a contribution and that you love us for it. And we don't want to lose it partly because of course you do want it.

In short, we should really love each other. Secretly or not, we do. We certainly need each other and depend on each other and want each other. We should stay different and we should yearn and try to appreciate. We should slum in each other's bars from time to time, and smile, etc. I think if you let these things play with you and play with them, the system might become more liquid or improvisational or multidimensional. But who knows? It might even get more extremely differentiated or simplified, which could be interesting too if it doesn't freeze. But you want to start thinking of the gender/sexuality square as an immense set of aesthetic resources, which are also ways to be.

III

Beatles vs. Stones

An Aesthetics of Rock Music

2011

When I was but a wee lad, the Beatles vs. Stones thing was the greatest aesthetic debate of the generation. No doubt it rages still through the halls of nursing homes. Now, first off, I would say that this was a rather unfortunate turn of events. At any given moment, there are many interesting acts in popular music doing all sorts of things, and the idea that it all came down to two was sort of silly. And no pop musician, I assert, can possibly pay off on the adulation accorded, in particular, to the Beatles; in the face of their reception as transcendent, God-touched geniuses, as emblems of an entire era, as strange essences of our collective consciousness, and so on, the actual music is absurdly inadequate.

Well, that itself will tell you where I will come down on the Beatles and Stones. But before I do, let me note that the idea of the essence of a generation or a zeitgeist pressed into the grooves of an LP is borrowed from modernist conceptions in the fine arts and elsewhere. One might think of the figure of Beethoven, or Van Gogh, or Nietzsche, Picasso, or James Joyce: more-than-human forces of nature, transcendent geniuses who foresee the future and take us there by courtesy of the incredible roiling forces contained in their giant heads.

The way we conceive such figures serves a number of functions other than our desire for something—anything, really—to worship. They make telling the story of art or of philosophy or of science much easier: you narrate it as a history of breakthroughs and compelling characters. In the bewildering chaotic welter that is the world of art or of ideas or just the world in general, they provide nodes; they are a way of simplifying experience and history into a shorthand consisting of a few names or biographical sketches. And they are absorbing as character studies, or studies in symbolic pathology, always poised in our imaginations between hypereffectiveness and mental illness. The promotion of any given actual person to this status is—I think—well-nigh arbitrary, but it makes things easier and satisfies our basic impulse to have something or someone to admire unqualifiedly.

This is not to say that everything is just as good as everything else, or that some artists aren't better than others. But I do want to say that no one is as better than everyone else as figures such as Picasso or the Beatles are imagined as being.

We might, to continue the discussion of modernism in the arts, distinguish between traditional and avant-garde art histories, or between traditional and avant-garde arts. The avant-garde arts are peculiar to the West, and Western-influenced cultures elsewhere, since the mid-nineteenth century, or roughly since Manet. They proceed by a series of radical innovations, or looking at it the other way round, through a series of radical rejections of the past: a series of negations. Overcoming or destroying the past is a mark of genius, and avant-garde arts consist of an ever accelerating series of movements, each defined in part by its destruction or negation of the previous movement: impressionism/fauvism/cubism/dadaism, for example, or expressionism/pop/minimalism/conceptualism. In the avant-garde arts, the authenticity of the artist and the work is established by his or its overcoming of the dead weight of tradition; the avant-garde artist frees himself and us from the oppressiveness of what has come before and the rules or restrictions associated with what has come before.

The traditional arts—and here I include crafts such as pottery or fabric arts—establish the authenticity of the work and of the artist through its or her continuity with the past or mastery of the techniques associated with the tradition. They tend to have what we might term a guild structure, in which the artist serves an apprenticeship with a master and absorbs precisely the sort of strictures and skills that the avant-garde artist is dedicated to destroying.

Such practices are characteristic of the arts in almost all non-Western cultures, and in the arts of the West at least until romanticism.

Now let's apply these distinctions and complications to popular music. For example, country music is a pointedly traditional form, and new artists constantly pay their respects to the generations that have gone before. Indeed it is very likely that a country song will be about country music, and it might mention Hank Williams or Patsy Cline. And it will often try to establish its connection to traditional themes, settings, objects: beer, for example, or trucks (which put in an appearance even in many Taylor Swift songs, for example, which are essentially country-inflected pop songs), or small towns. In addition, even in very mainstream or poppy or crossover country music there will often be touches of traditional instrumentation: pedal steel guitar, or fiddle, or mandolin. And of course the basic song structures, or even specific melodic themes, fall into a fairly narrow range. To take another example, the blues is a traditional form. The twelve-bar structure of the blues, with its pattern of recurring lines and the typical turnaround, are identifying features, and though artists have some freedom to alter or depart from these forms, a too radical departure disqualifies the item as a blues song.

Of course, blues and country music have changed radically over time. They have been electrified, for one thing. They have produced virtuosi who introduced various innovations; we might think of the guitar styles of Robert Johnson, B.B. King, Eric Clapton, and even Jimi Hendrix in this light; or the harmonica work of Sonny Boy Williamson and Little Walter. But these innovations also preserve an underlying continuity. If they do not, then the musician no longer counts as a blues or country artist. Indeed, that is obviously in question with regard to a figure such as Hendrix, whose excellence one might take as being in part his poise between traditional and avant-garde forms; he inverts a blues lick, or tears it to shreds, or de- and reconstructs it until it is barely recognizable.

Through the whole twentieth century, American popular music styles cross-pollinated. Country music itself emerged in a mixture of black and white Appalachian and Southern motifs; one might also consider such syncretic forms as rockabilly, or gospel, or the melding of country and swing in Bob Wills and the Texas Playboys. And finally, we might consider rock 'n' roll. The rock of, for example, Chuck Berry or Elvis Presley, is both an eclectic and a traditional style, innovative as combining elements of the traditions of blues and country in a fresh way, traditional as proceeding in a relatively rigid observance of structures that emerge from these traditions. It combined the syncretic/traditional styles of black and white Southern popular music—jump blues, gospel, rockabilly—into something that both captured and pushed forward the traditions of American popular song. American popular music, in short, is a series of traditional forms, but it is always also a synthesis of such forms.

Both the Beatles and the Stones emerged as aficionados of this music and of the streams that led into it, and Keith Richards and Mick Jagger first bonded as young record collectors: always obsessively focused on the obscure blues record they didn't have yet. Like a lot of kids in a lot of eras since the dawn of recorded sound, they were archivists, buffs. And they often deployed a rhetoric of traditional purity (though this was a radical rejection of the culture around them): they wanted the record by the purest, the simplest, the most bluesy blues artist. They peeled back from the eclectic surface of popular rock music to the sources of its form in blues, country, gospel. And they admired the American black artists whom they regarded as the most authentic purveyors of the eclectic style of rhythm and blues, or what would come to be called soul music. Indeed, both the early Beatles and early Stones were essentially cover bands, always on the alert for the latest American black music that they could perform for their British or European audiences.

The Beatles were particularly excellent at this. They took American black pop music—"Twist and Shout," let's say—and stripped it down, cleaned it up, emphasized the big beat at its heart. The early Beatles records are about the best non-black or non-American appropriations of American black pop music ever made: incredibly clear and propulsive, and sung with a delightful tunefulness. Nor do I think they should be condemned at all for their derivativeness: they always paid explicit tribute to their sources, and both the music they took and the music they made were worthy of celebration. Indeed, if we got into the business of condemning out of hand white appropriations of black styles, we'd have to condemn many of the greatest popular musicians of the twentieth century: Bix Beiderbecke, Benny Goodman, Jimmie Rodgers, Hank Williams, Elvis Presley, Janis Joplin, Duane Allman, Eminem etc., etc. No race owns art, even the art it creates, and if white artists sometimes exploited this art and its artists, or made fortunes on styles they didn't invent, they just as often revived the careers of artists they venerated, paid them substantial royalties, and introduced them to new audiences. Many of the Rolling Stones' heroes and sources have toured with them over the decades.

And as innovative and excellent as the Beatles and Stones were as purveyors of the traditional forms of American music, they themselves understood from early on that it was precisely from these traditions that they drew their power and popularity. The traditional forms of American popular music, and especially African-American music, have essentially been the sources of the world's popular music through a whole century, into the eras of disco and hip hop. It would take us beyond our scope to try to explain why that should be. Only let me say that the combination of simplicity and sophistication, the emotional power of the melodies and the lyric themes, the directness of the expression, the excellence of the sound structures as arenas for improvisation (and indeed the very idea of musical improvisation, the sense of simultaneous craft and immediacy), the way the music makes bodies move: all these now underlie the very conception of popular music all over the world. Indeed, a number of these elements have been traced to African sources, and the way an audience behaves at a rock concert—with very active participation—is closer to African festive and ceremonial contexts than to European art music of the nineteenth century.

Nevertheless, though the Stones and Beatles started out in such a similar vein, they diverged fairly quickly in very clear ways. Now, many things might make someone prefer one to the other. For example, they positioned themselves differently on what might be termed the moral spectrum. The Beatles' image—whatever the reality—was of wholesome young men: nonthreatening, charming. This was one reason they could appear everywhere in many media; for example, it was the persona projected in their movies *Hard Day's Night* and *Help!*. In their initial appearance, they were preteen- and teenage-girl crush objects that even many parents could endorse or dismiss as harmless. And this essential wholesomeness continued as they got more hippielike, grew out their hair, joined the peace movement, explored Eastern religions, and so on, though somewhat darker sides emerged as well. Still, in songs such as "All You Need is Love"—the inspiring yet empty soundtrack for a hundred treatments of hippiedom and the '60s in a thousand films—they captured a positive side of '60s youth culture. Indeed, the Beatles always projected a certain childlikeness, and many of their songs can without strain be covered by Raffi: "Yellow Submarine" (and its bright, happy animation) and "Magical Mystery Tour" are essentially children's songs, though mounted like mini-operas amidst a swirl of distortions.

The Stones, of course, projected a darker and more dangerous image, constantly flirting with images of Satan, for example in *Their Satanic Majesties Request* or "Sympathy for the Devil," in both of which they actually identified themselves, albeit with some irony, as the devil incarnate. Whereas the Beatles were loosely associated with the Summer of Love (though they were no longer performing live by the time of Woodstock), the Stones were associated with Altamont, where a Hell's Angels security guard stabbed a concertgoer. The two represented the kind of twinned fantasies of young female lust: the good boy and the bad boy, the wholesome young man you take home to Mom and the delinquent drug abuser you meet in the alley—the equivalent of the madonna/whore complex.

This idea of the Stones as the Beatles' evil twins was probably to some extent conscious. The bands knew each other (members appearing together, for example, in the made-for-TV feature "The Rolling Stones Rock and Roll Circus"), and probably in part defined their personae as complements. But though they both started as rhythm and blues or soul tribute bands, they fairly quickly diverged in their basic musical approaches. And this, I think, is where the real question of Stones vs. Beatles arises. The Beatles developed an entirely new musical vocabulary that drove rock 'n' roll to a large extent for a decade or more. The Stones developed as well—they got much sharper and more focused and also more original as they went along—but they referred constantly back to the basic rock and soul and blues vocabularies they started with. The Beatles developed into what we might think of—at least in the context of popular music with a massive audience—as avant-garde artists. The structure of the Stones' development is much more closely akin to what I have described as the kind that is present in the traditional arts.

The turn in the Beatles' style was gradual, though in retrospect relatively rapid (after all, their entire recording career lasted only seven or eight years). One might date it from *Rubber Soul* in late 1965, or *Revolver* in 1966. Certainly it is fully realized at latest by *Sgt. Pepper's Lonely Hearts Club Band* in the middle of 1967. Here are some of the characteristics of the shift: a change away from a blues tonality to one that is European-oriented or perhaps British (McCartney associated the sound with British music halls of the 1940s); a shift away from basic rock instrumentation (guitar/bass/drums) to much more elaborate setups involving in some cases a full orchestra and experimental instrumentation such as the use of the sitar; a shift of lyric themes from dance-and-flirt to melancholy love and eventually to surrealist ("psychedelic") poetry.

One could think of this development as a radical expansion of the vocabulary of rock music, or (as I prefer) an entire departure from it. In a *Rolling Stone* critics poll, "Yesterday" was listed as the greatest rock song of all times, a claim which might be refuted on the grounds that "Yesterday" can't possibly be the best anything, but which is also certainly a category mistake; if "Yesterday" is a rock song, I am the Walrus. At any rate, the Beatles' turn produced some charming moments and some lovely melodies, such as "Norwegian Wood" or "Across the Universe," but I propose to you that it featured rafts of meaningless hooha: much of their production from *Revolver* to *Let It Be* is absurdly overblown yet utterly trivial. Picasso's *Guernica* or Joyce's *Ulysses*, is one thing; "Being for the Benefit of Mr. Kite!" "Doctor Robert," "Glass Onion," "Maxwell's Silver Hammer" are something else again. And I propose that the shift was a disaster not only for the artistry of the Beatles, but for the whole genre of rock music. In one way or another, we must hold the Beatles partly responsible for the soulless anti-rock of, say, Elton John or Billy Joel, and for the pretentious yet empty art-rock of bands such as Yes or Emerson, Lake, and Palmer.[1]

Here is something that is certainly a bad idea: take a bunch of fairly average lads with their good pop band and abase yourself before them as though they are messiahs. (Lennon: "We're bigger than Jesus." They were, but that wasn't their fault, or Jesus's; it was their audience's.) Several things will occur to such lads: first, that whatever we are, we better be more than just a somewhat better version of Gerry and the Pacemakers or the Dave Clark Five; we must, in spite of all appearances or anything that could be revealed to honest self-reflection, be world-changing artists. So we had better get busy making *art*: something that in some way sustains the reception or makes it comprehensible. And such a reception invites an immense self-indulgence: the idea that virtually anything we think of, our merest whim, our littlest jingle or nursery rhyme, must be world-shatteringly excellent. The shattered world has seemed to support this absurd assessment from 1965 right on up to the present.

Now let me admit that there are elements of taste that are irremediably subjective, and I am not going to make you hate *Sgt. Pepper* merely by asserting that it sucks, though it does. And let me also admit that it is a bad thing to insist that artists of any variety or quality must merely repeat themselves, that they must always do what you first liked them for doing. And of course, no one should be forced to do what some critic thinks they ought to do; the Beatles had a perfect right to make whatever music they wanted, and people have a perfect right to like it. But let me also point out that once you have heard a song a thousand times, it sounds like an inevitable classic. You may associate it with important moments in your life, for example. Once every documentary of the '60s features Beatles songs, even people who hadn't yet been born will associate the music with the era. We are stuck with the Beatles in a way that makes a real assessment of their achievement next to impossible. Nevertheless, the assessments that have actually been made of their late work have been absurd.

Some of the observations made above show some of the problems with the Rolling Stones. It is a familiar point to say that they stopped developing at a certain point (perhaps as early as *Exile on Main Street*), that they stayed too rigidly faithful to their roots in rock and soul, that they have repeated themselves too often for too long. Well, whereas the Beatles played for less than a decade, the Stones have been performing for more than fifty years. And though it's obvious that they're not as good or as important now as they were in 1970, there is also something admirable about the way they have kept faith with their roots and their talents.

The Rolling Stones are a cosmic essence, a Platonic Form, of rock music. The Beatles started as classicists, and soon went through mannerist, baroque, and rococo stages of aesthetic decadence. I think that one reason for their breakup—whatever women or ego-inflations were involved—was that they had reached an aesthetic dead end; there was nowhere else their actual talents or direction could take them. Soon they would have been writing symphonies and fantasias and operas, and then their artistic limitations would have been even more excruciating in relation to their ambitions than they were already. The Stones actually had their moments of trying to ape the developments instituted by the late Beatles, replying to the psychedelic *Sgt. Pepper* with their own quasipsychedelic *Their Satanic Majesties Request*, for example. Brian Jones tried to learn the sitar before getting kicked to the curb.

But the fundamental impulse was always to strip to the essence of the rock song. Where the Beatles added layer after layer of instrumental and lyrical ornament, Keith Richards tried to find the absolute essence of the rock guitar lick, on "Satisfaction," "Brown Sugar," "She's So Cold." Finally on a late song like "Gunface" he stripped the thing down to a single incredibly alive chord. The Stones return again and again to the sources of their own music in the blues, in country, in soul. They have both celebrated these basic structures and pushed them forward.

One might be less than blown away by Mick Jagger the lyricist: there's a lot of celebration of the supposed hypersexuality of black girls, for instance, but also many interesting twists and fresh departures, displayed above all in the Stones' surprising moments of beauty and reflection: "Wild Horses," for example, or "Beast of Burden"—songs that display an admirable artistry and sensitivity even in the midst of a reversion to roots. There are even reflections on being an aging rock star in "You Got Me Rocking": "I was a hooker losing her looks/I was a writer can't write another book/I was all dried up dying to get wet/I was a tycoon drowning in debt." And one thing we can say for Jagger: he did not write "Glass Onion." The art of the Rolling Stones has developed in the ways that traditional arts develop: by simultaneously nurturing the roots and pushing upward.

As Plato conceived his Forms, they were not things invented by himself or other philosophers; they were things that were both remembered and discovered, or that were discovered by being remembered: they were essences that were our origin and our destiny. The Stones have both remembered and discovered the essence of rock music. They revert continually to the origin, but they also strip away the accretions. Their songs push forward by seeking the basis; they move toward a center we might associate with the work of Chuck Berry, Bo Diddley, or Little Richard, and then they expose that center, or show the center of that center.

Once the Beatles had stopped touring, once the Beatles had stopped making rock music, and after the Beatles broke up, the Stones stopped trying to imitate them or compete directly with them, and made a series of roughly perfect rock albums: *Beggar's Banquet, Let It Bleed, Sticky Fingers,* and *Exile on Main Street.* I propose that this sequence of albums just *is* rock music: its very essence, the definition of the form. Discovering the essence of what you're doing is of course only one way of making art. Departing from that essence in various directions—experimentation, originality, innovation—these procedures have certainly yielded important works. And yet the achievement of one's own essence is also a legitimate aesthetic project. It has never been achieved in popular music with more dedication, more focus, or more power than in the work of the Stones.

IV

Reactionary Progressivism

Bluegrass and Political Philosophy

2009

Music is, in its essence, repetition. This is as true of the fugue or theme-and-variations structure as of the verse/chorus, verse/chorus, bridge, chorus pop song. The fundamental forms of popular music deploy repetition not only inside each song, but across songs. Elmore James essentially made a career out of a single riff, which he swiped from Robert Johnson's "Dust My Broom," and I don't doubt that Johnson swiped it from someone else. Hip hop makes use of mechanically generated repetitions, and is constantly returning to its own earlier sounds, and to the sounds, for example, of funk. Reggae consists of a particular, throbbing beat: each song repeats it many times, and in a sense the whole genre consists of its repetition. Rhythm is repetition. Rhyme is repetition. A series of sounds without repetition is unrecognizable as a melody.

Indeed, it would not be too much to say that this fact connects music to human life or to the universe in general, which has its novelties but rests on its repetitions. Day and night, sleep and waking, the cycle of the seasons, eating and excreting, the progress of relationships, what makes a particular personality distinctive, the orbits of the planets, the energy of the pulsar, big bang and big crunch: cyclical or spiral structures. "I watch every day for sunset," Bill Monroe told Lee Rector in 1980. "I've always done that. I love the sunset. You know it's different every day. It always has a different set."[1]

According to information theory, a perfect repetition is redundant: it conveys no information. On the other hand, no repetition is, actually, perfect. Even when you press play on the same digitally encoded song for a second time, you are listening to it in a slightly different context: a context that includes the first iteration; the song gains or loses significance; is experienced as familiar or surprising. Resorting to paradox, we might say that each repetition of the same is different, each return a moving forward.

We might think about this matter in relation to politics. Often the political spectrum is sorted into conservatives, whom we might think of as advocates of repetition, and progressives, who want to take us to someplace new. This makes sense only if time or progress is linear; the picture is that we stand at a certain point and have to decide whether to go forward or back. But putting it mildly, this distinction is impoverished. The politics of Barry Goldwater or the Young Americans for Freedom in the sixties were every bit as radical—were every bit as much critiques of the present and calls for change—as those of the Woodstock generation. Sarah Palin is no less a progressive figure than is Barack Obama, insofar as Palin calls for a pretty radical change in the status quo. Progress is progressive, but so is regress, or rather, the two are not clearly or firmly distinguished, nor ought they to be, and Obama as much as Palin will call for a return to basic American values and teach the lessons of history, though he has a somewhat different interpretation of that history and those values.

Confucius is, by acclamation, the most conservative political philosopher in human history, and he basically uses the concept of tradition to authorize any possible move: his philosophy is continually looking backward, is a kind of worship of the ancestors and their ways. And yet very consciously Confucius was advocating radical reforms in a culture disintegrating into a chaos of small warring states. Confucius was, we might say, a reactionary progressive, and indeed his philosophy became the template by which the Chinese empire was consolidated and administered for thousands of years: a profoundly backward-looking and conservative regime founded by a radical critic of his own present.

In art history, we might think about this in terms of classical and baroque: the classical is always a return to origins; the baroque expresses the need to strike out forward. But by the same token, the rediscovery of the classical in the Renaissance was a radical critique of its own context. The neoclassicism of a David or a Jefferson at the end of the eighteenth century was, explicitly, a revolutionary movement and also a return in a looping structure to the Renaissance and the Roman republic. It was a reactionary progressive movement.

If I were conceiving history, myself, I'd think about it as a line, but also as a scribble, continually working back and forth, whirling, xing over itself at myriad junctures. But perhaps for present purposes we might think of it as a series of loops, moving forward precisely by rolling back on itself. The question is not forward or backward; we're always moving in both directions at the same time.

It is often said that Bill Monroe invented a musical form or genre, indeed that he's perhaps the only identifiable figure of the twentieth century to do so, with the possible exception of DJ Kool Herc with regard to hip hop. That portrays Monroe as a profound innovator. Now on the other hand, Monroe himself said that he invented bluegrass by trying to play music the way it must have sounded in 1880. Before the term "bluegrass" was used to denote the genre, it was termed "old-timey" music. Some of the defining features of bluegrass—for example, that it is played on acoustic instruments, which is more or less a dogma—appear to be hidebound holding to traditions. Others—for example, the way those instruments are played, often with extreme virtuosity, in a series of competitive solos analogous to hard bop—seem to entail continual innovation. Bluegrass music revolutionized the banjo, the mandolin, and the Dobro (or resonator guitar): it reconceived these instruments thoroughly. Neil Rosenberg calls "tradition regarded as innovation" the "seeming paradox" of bluegrass music,[2] and Ricky Skaggs titled one of his bluegrass albums *History of the Future.*

Before I try to apply the notion of reactionary progressivism to bluegrass music, let's consider some of the intellectual resources of the Western tradition for understanding the shape of history as looping, gyrelike, spiraling, tornadic, and so on. One we might mention is Nietzsche's concept of "the eternal return of the same," which I think he regarded as his most profound thought. Sometimes this seemed to be put forward as a serious account of time as purely cyclical or circular, and sometimes as a thought-experiment. In the latter version, Nietzsche asks you to imagine that a demon appears to you and tells you that the life you have lived, you will live again, in every detail, infinitely many times. Now, he asks, would you curse that demon, or could you accept, or ecstatically affirm, this infinite repetition? The answer to that is supposed to show how much you hate or love your life and this world in which you've lived it: whether you can really face reality. Everything bad that's ever happened to you or to people you love, everything you've ever regretted saying or doing, will recur infinitely many times in eternity. Here we have time pictured as a perfect circle. But the moment of affirmation, in which you open yourself radically to the reality of the world is, in each recurrence, an incomparable, transformative moment. The Nietzschean paradox is that by willing the same thing over and over in eternity, you transform yourself into someone who treasures what is real, who renders even the future into an object of nostalgia. In this sense, I suggest, Bill Monroe is a Nietzschean superman.

Jorge Luis Borges wrote a "story," or rather a parody of a scholarly paper, "Pierre Menard, Author of the Quixote," in which he describes the work of Menard. The latter's masterpiece is a modern rewriting of Don Quixote: a word-for-word identical copy of Cervantes' novel. Menard says of his method: "My solitary game is governed by two polar laws. The first permits me to attempt variants of a formal and psychological nature; the second obliges me to sacrifice them to the 'original' text and irrefutably to rationalize this annihilation."[3] Borges observes that though the two Quixotes are word-for-word identical, they are radically stylistically distinct: "The archaic style of Menard . . . suffers from a certain affectation. Not so that of his precursor, who handles easily the ordinary Spanish of his time."[4]

The last station in our loop is Søren Kierkegaard, who wrote a whole book on this topic and titled it *Repetition*. One of the elements in it is the story of a young man from Copenhagen who lives for a while in Berlin and then returns to his native city. In order to see whether a true repetition is possible, he goes back again to Berlin, rents the same room he had before, goes to the same theater, frequents the same restaurants, and so forth. The experience is at once disappointing and stimulating: he finds that a repetition is both impossible and inevitable: that he cannot have the same experiences and that he cannot fail to be the person who had these experiences. Now doing this may strike you as a remarkably perverse exercise, though not as perverse as rewriting Don Quixote word for word. But in fact it is quite typical: we often seek to reproduce experiences we have had before: set out to achieve the same . . . relationship, home, vacation, or whatever it may be. Indeed, the representation of experiences, for example in snapshots or videos, is precisely an attempt to make a repetition possible, to hold on to something that seems to be receding into an incomparable past. In one sense, such a repetition is impossible, but the attempt at it lends our life whatever comprehensible structure it may have or lends us whatever comprehensible character we may have, a music that is our personhood—and though the routine may be tedious, it is also comforting.

Kierkegaard writes, in what may be termed the emblem of our theme: "The dialectic of repetition is easy, for that which is repeated has been—otherwise it could not be repeated—but the very fact that it has been makes the repetition into something new."[5] This, we might say, displays both the reaction in reactionary progressivism and the progress: the possibility of creating something radically new out of a recapitulation—even one as perfect as possible—of the past. And Kierkegaard goes on to say this: "Hope is a lovely maiden who slips away between one's fingers; recollection is a beautiful old woman with whom one is never satisfied at the moment; repetition is a beloved wife of whom one never wearies, for one becomes weary only of what is new."[6] I have no idea what that means. And yet I am committing myself to it with my whole being.

I hope you will hear these ideas echoed as we briefly explore some themes and moments in bluegrass music. Monroe's band was the training ground of many of the best bluegrass players, and Monroe was a stern taskmaster: he insisted that, whoever was playing his music, they first of all master the proper rhythmic structure—which he thought of as the essence of his style—that they play "pure": though there was room for improvisation, the form was already delineated, and though every performance was unique, every performance was a pure repetition. Four decades into his career, he said "I hope [the next generation of bluegrass pickers] will stand up for what's right and play the music as pure as they can play it for the people. There's one thing that I hope: that the people, when the time comes, that there will be somebody that will get in there and will hang on and do it right . . . someone that's got a lot of willpower and can get things done."[7] This is one reason that Monroe could stand not only as a significant musician, but as the founder of a style: he enforced a repetition that was a continual return to the origin: every performance was an affirmation of the life already lived. It was a commercial formula, but ultimately something much more than that, and Monroe was never as concerned with sales as with whether the playing was "right"; he didn't want you "putting things in" that weren't there before.

For Monroe, the power of the music was the power of the origin, which he thematized as "Uncle Pen," the hills of western Kentucky, and so on. Or even as a return to God: a return to the church of his youth and to the hymnal, and a return of the soul to its maker. A, or even the, great theme of bluegrass, from Monroe's "I'm Goin' Back to Old Kentucky" to Alison Krauss's "Heartstrings," is "the old home place," and cultural historians of the form point to the migration of young men from the Appalachian hills to the industrial and commercial centers surrounding the Appalachian region, such as Knoxville, Chattanooga, Roanoke, Asheville, and farther afield to Cincinnati, Baltimore, Atlanta, Detroit, or Washington, DC. One emotion explored in these songs is the loss of the home place and the family of origin, and the yearning for a return. But in many songs—I think of "Weathered Grey Stone" (Johnson Mountain Boys) or "Rank Strangers" (Stanleys), for example—the return, when accomplished, proves impossible, in a perfect instantiation of Kierkegaard's "dialectic of repetition": one returns to find one's parents or sweetheart dead, or the way of life or the land in which one originated disrupted or over.

The return home is a return to the self, and Kierkegaard once said that the most difficult task is to become what you already are, precisely because everyone wants to be something more or different. And it is a return, too, to a cultural identity of rural, perhaps Scots-Irish "mountain folk," an endangered way of life, a dying culture, and so on. I think it is an interesting question, familiar to folklorists, whether this identity is an authentic antecedent reality, or is, in fact, manufactured in being remembered and represented, or represented and remembered. The nostalgic song of home, I think we should say, both describes and creates a shared identity. The Grimm Brothers, for example, in collecting and repeating and rearticulating folk tales, in coming up with written, canonical versions, selecting and deleting, and so on, were describing but also forging a German identity. The same might be said, for example, of Zora Neale Hurston's collecting of folktales and song lyrics of African-Americans in the South: it was both a mimetic and an articulatory representation, both the reflection of an antecedent reality and a remaking of reality in repetition.

Neil Rosenberg astutely proposes that bluegrass, the genre, begins not at the famous moment that Bill Monroe took the stage with Lester Flatt, Earl Scruggs, Chubby Wise, and Howard Watts, but when the Stanley Brothers started performing and recording in the same mode a year or two later, with an overlapping repertoire that included songs such as "Molly and Tenbrooks," a Monroe number drawn from a traditional song that the Stanleys managed to release on record after Monroe recorded it, but before Monroe's record was released.[8] Monroe, of course, was angry about this, and apparently left Columbia Records specifically because it signed the Stanleys. But some years later he understood such things differently: not as plagiarism but as a tribute to the power of his own music. And ever since, bluegrass has been a continual cycle of return, tribute, veneration: a cycle in which innovation and tradition cannot be distinguished or in which they are always in what Kierkegaard would call a dialectic of repetition. Will the circle be unbroken? To some extent this is true of anything that could count as a style: it has to have a set of basic gestures and forms that account for its continuity, and in some cases—such as the blues, Nashville country (neotraditionalism of the late '80s/early '90s, for example), and hip hop ("old school")—this structure of repetition is consciously at the heart of the form. But I don't think there is any style more totally caught up in this sort of loop of return than bluegrass. The closest analogy might be roots reggae music of the 1970s, in which a major theme was the future as repatriation to Africa as the point of origin, in which drum patterns and other features were conceived to be African, and in which the echoes of dub music were a kind of image of repeating diasporas.

Bluegrass, even in its moments of fusion, has always maintained an aesthetic of what we might call genre-centeredness. Monroe told Steve Rathe in 1974 that "you got to be pure in bluegrass. You might come up there and say it's "bluegrass rock," but it should be kept pure, and rock should be kept pure, and jazz should be played . . . where you're born on it."[9] In 1967 he said "the biggest job is to keep out what don't belong in it"[10]: a constant discipline of omission, a constant stripping down to the central gesture, the essence or *sine qua non* of the style, the originary moment. Every excursion was a search for this center, a loop back to the origin. Then every performance, every song, even every innovation would also be a return home and the history of the form a progressive purification. Synthesis is one mode of innovation, but a return is also a change, as Confucius taught. Bill Monroe, as he often said, wanted to be the kind of man his father was, but in an entirely transformed context.

I think one thing we could say about bluegrass is that as a total musical form—in terms of song structures, instrumentation, arrangements, vocal styles, repertoire, and so on—it is a highly rule-governed music. It is more constitutively restricted than most living popular music forms, by which I mean that in order to count as bluegrass, a given band or performance must more strictly adhere to a more restrictive set of rules than most forms, such as country, jazz, electronica, hip hop, or rock 'n' roll. There are other relatively restricted forms: reggae and the blues come to mind, for example. But in some ways even these have proven more flexible; blues survived its electrification in the '50s, and reggae the transition to digital rhythm tracks in the '80s. When people make bluegrass music—something that actually counts as bluegrass—alone in their dorm rooms on Garageband, you'll know the form is over.

Of course, the song structures in bluegrass are varied, or at least fall within a few different groups: waltz, hymns, and blues, for example. But the instrumentation more or less must be acoustic, and must consist basically of the traditional string instruments. The forms of the harmonies have varied somewhat, in particular with the addition of female vocalists, but for the most part they fall into traditional patterns that preceded Monroe. Lyric themes of God, home, family, and nostalgia for rural life dominate the repertoire, though there are also love and party songs, of course, as well a smattering of traditional themes of country music, such as substance abuse and divorce.

Bluegrass, we might say, is disciplined, and one feature of this is that the players are less individuated by distinctive styles than in many other popular styles. A corollary is that the history of bluegrass is more continuous than the histories of other popular music styles. Think about comparing the rock music of 1964 to that of 1984, or think about how different jazz was in 1930 and 1950. The entire sixty-five-year history of bluegrass is more continuous than any twenty-year segment of these other forms, in all dimensions. The instrumental and vocal styles, and again the repertoire, are more stylized or codified. It is important to note the basic performing unit is not usually a solo artist, though a lead vocalist or instrumental virtuoso might be featured; it is more a collective than an individual art; that's what the matching outfits worn by the Blue Grass Boys signified: the band was a team, a unit, with almost military discipline. Collective harmonies are the preferred vocal style. We might almost compare bluegrass to classical or art music in this regard: if you weren't entirely sure just by listening whether it was the Berlin Philharmonic or the London Symphony on that recording of Mozart, no one would be shocked. And it might even be hard to tell at a distance by looking, if the orchestra members were all wearing their little black suits and dresses.

Now let me enter a number of disclaimers: Of course there are distinctive singers in bluegrass; John Duffey, the high tenor of the Seldom Scene, is a fine example, and I do know when it's him. Probably I am pretty reliable picking out Monroe or Lester Flatt or Russell Moore. And there are innovators in bluegrass; the form now is certainly not just what it was in 1950. There are moments of intense individual and collective expression in bluegrass, and so on. But one might also note that many performers over the decades have grown dissatisfied with the constraints and migrated out of bluegrass: Earl Scruggs with his Revue, for example, Bela Fleck, Tony Rice, Marc O'Connor, Dave Grisman, Peter Greene, Alison Krauss.

I grew up in DC, a great bluegrass center in my youth. But listening to the Seldom Scene or the Johnson Mountain Boys made me nostalgic for a childhood I never actually had, and that most of the members of these bands never had either. I would say that these assumed memories made me what I am to some extent, and now I actually live in a little house in the woods: remembering a childhood I never had made me repeat it and try to give it to my own children. I want to be the kind of man Bill Monroe's father was, and what I actually know about that comes from bluegrass music. Bluegrass is not an immediate photographic transcription or mirror image of rural life, but a way of shaping memory and hence the future; an expression of solidarity that tells us who we are by telling us where we came from, and invents who we are by telling us where we are going: namely, back home, to God or to southwestern Virginia. At any rate, my dad used to take me to the Red Fox Inn in Bethesda to see the Seldom Scene. Since then, I've seen hundreds of shows of all sorts, but I still remember these as among the very best: fun, virtuosic, with extraordinary momentum and heart-rending beauty. That's a pretty devastating combination.

The Seldom Scene—John Duffey on mandolin and high tenor vocals, Mike Auldridge on Dobro, Ben Eldridge on banjo, John Starling on guitar and lead vocals, Tom Gray on bass—recorded a double LP of their show from that period called *Live at the Cellar Door.* It's a good representation of their extreme skill and loose stage personae. There's a great piece of byplay as they introduce an extraordinary performance of "Hit Parade of Love": "We're gonna do a little acid grass and then get out of here. This song is from the days of negative stage presence. That's when if you lifted a foot, it was illegal, and everybody just sort of gathered around the microphone and nobody smiled, and everybody all dressed alike, you know, in their little uniforms." Indeed, a couple of the guys in the Seldom Scene had played in bands like that, and the look has continually been revived.

Now, the DC of my youth had a hillbilly underground, part of a migration from the hills and coalfields to the white-trash slums around Washington, Baltimore, and a number. of other cities. Even in my neighborhood in upper Northwest, there was a big family from West Virginia living in a quasi-house in the alley. The Webbs were disapproved of by my parents. They listened to country music. When the dad got drunk, he'd reel down the alley yelling, "I've got a fifth-grade education! Y'all ain't any better than me!"

But the Webbs weren't at that gig at the Red Fox Inn, much less at the Cellar Door down in Georgetown. The audience at those venues was suburban DC: bureaucrats and diplomats, reporters like my dad, secretaries and executives, and some of their kids: hippies and roots music freaks. The Seldom Scene would never have become the sort of attraction they were around DC at that time if they had still dressed in little uniforms. You just were not going to play the DC bar scene like that in 1973. And the members of the Seldom Scene themselves were hardly hillbillies; they featured a physician (Starling), a mathematician (Eldridge), and the son of a soprano at the Metropolitan Opera (Duffey). In retellings of the history of bluegrass, the Seldom Scene are regarded as innovators, largely because on their recordings they (beautifully) covered songs by Bob Dylan, James Taylor, the Grateful Dead, and John Prine. With groups such as the Country Gazette, the New Grass Revival, J.D. Crowe and the New South, the New Shades of Grass and others, they spearheaded "newgrass" or "progressive bluegrass."

Groups such as the Seldom Scene emerged out of the rootsiest side of the early-'60s folk revival, and were intermeshed with the little-uniform-clad folk-grass group the Country Gentlemen. The DC scene obviously sought to expand and update bluegrass music. The Country Gentlemen were a departure from Flatt and Scruggs, and the Seldom Scene a yet further departure, but the Scene went further in a casual and quasi-hippiefied direction. And bluegrass of the '70s went much further than that, as in Jerry Garcia's bluegrass band, Old and in the Way. Full-on hippie or acid grass probably reached its height with Muleskinner, featuring the astonishing lineup of Peter Rowan, Richard Greene, Dave Grisman, Bill Keith, and Clarence White. They looked more hippiefied even than their buddies the Grateful Dead. There is a wonderful television film of them performing in 1973, perhaps a bit underrehearsed as a unit but astonishing in their excellence.

Muleskinner perpetrated many innovations besides the tie-dye and hairstyles; these people contributed fundamentally to their instruments. Grisman could play anything. Bill Keith had introduced fundamental banjo innovations—some of the first since Scruggs—with Bill Monroe's group in the early '60s. I have to say that Richard Greene is the best fiddler I ever saw, reaching for all sorts of wild effects on acoustic and electric violin, and deploying sheer demonic skill. All of them played many different forms of music over the years, variously related to bluegrass; some of them even invented their own: Grisman's dawg jazz, for example, or country rock a la White's Byrds and Rowan and Greene's band Seatrain.

But you can hear that despite the hairstyles, Muleskinner is devoted to the traditions of the form, or even to peeling back beneath Monroe to find the Celtic fiddle structures on which, in part, Monroe based his sound. I think what is remarkable looking back at the Seldom Scene and Muleskinner is how extremely faithful they were to the tradition. Maybe the Seldom Scene's version of "Hit Parade of Love" was acid grass, but in the '50s Jimmy Martin and the Sunny Mountain Boys had also absolutely crushed the thing at ever-faster tempos and in more or less precisely the same arrangement. I bow to no one in my admiration for the Seldom Scene's harmonies, but their quartet style was more or less Bill Monroe's. For me, John Duffey will always be the paradigm of the high tenor in bluegrass, but as he'd be the first to tell you, he inhabited the role in a way traditional since Monroe and Ralph Stanley. The same is true of the way all the instrumentalists played, though Auldridge was an important innovator on the Dobro, and Tom Gray perhaps the best bluegrass bass player of that generation. Their demeanor onstage was entirely different from that of the Stanleys or Jim and Jesse. But their playing, even on the folk and country rock covers, was as bound by the basic structures and traditions of the form as anyone's. Muleskinner may have thrown a lot of hair around, hung out in the Haight, and played somewhat extended arrangements, but their veneration for the bluegrass tradition is palpable in every single moment.

The borders of bluegrass are policed, which is true of many or all popular music traditions. Perhaps you can't have a tradition, or a style with a name, without enforcement mechanisms. There is always a question of what constitutes real hip hop or punk. But I think the police force is particularly potent in bluegrass. *Bluegrass Unlimited* or the IBMA are always of necessity worrying about what is and what is not bluegrass. One thing we might note is that even though a transformation might in part be created to find new audiences, once those audiences are captured, they often demand precisely a return to the tradition: folk fans are always peeling back to earlier ethnic musics in search of the authentic origin. People become aficionados or enthusiasts, and they want the real stuff; probably well-heeled suburbanites and college students are more suspicious of a player from Boston or Denver than are Southern rural audiences. I have actually heard fans at bluegrass festivals hiss when a musician plugged in an electric instrument, a tradition since the late '60s. What is and what is not authentic bluegrass is a central question that informs even the ways the history of the form could possibly be narrated, more thoroughly than in any form I can think of. Now, when I say that there are rules and that they're policed, this doesn't sound too happy, and perhaps you're thinking I'm going to argue for loosening up and letting Richard Greene play electric fiddle. But I want to argue instead that the constraints have been incredibly fertile in creative implications, both within the main line of bluegrass and in the development of the kinds of music and people it has excluded.

There were many forays into electrification among bluegrass players, particularly in the late '60s and early '70s, and some of these produced really gorgeous music, like J.D. Crowe and the New South of the early '70s, featuring a young Ricky Skaggs and Keith Whitley. Even Flatt and Scruggs and the Osborne Brothers adopted electric instruments and drums on some recordings. But I think that the decision was made by the late '70s: it was criterial for bluegrass that it be played on acoustic instruments, though you might get an exemption for a bass guitar—not everyone wants to drag one of those bass fiddles around. Muleskinner is definitely a bluegrass band. On the other hand, the New Grass Revival's music might be an outgrowth of bluegrass, or interestingly related to bluegrass, but it is not bluegrass, which is of course not to say that it isn't good in its own categories. But the music of the Flecktones, for example, is partly defined precisely by its departures from bluegrass; if Bela Fleck were not bent on exploring the use of the banjo beyond precisely bluegrass, the music would be entirely different.

The musicians in the "progressive" groups of the late '60s and '70s took various routes to remake bluegrass as more than a museum; they tried to keep bluegrass alive by making it relevant to contemporary audiences, both in performance and on recordings. A number of these musicians eventually grew completely dissatisfied with the constraints, and the constraints grew dissatisfied with them, and people were exiled or emigrated in all sorts of directions, from Marc O'Connor's classical suites to David Grisman's bluegrass jazz, to Whitley and Skaggs' mutation into mainstream country stars, to Bela Fleck's avant-garde traditionalism. But they also took bluegrass with them by both negation and affirmation, and left behind a transformed bluegrass landscape, a different cultural and performance space, an expanded repertoire and an expanded audience. At this point if a highly traditional bluegrass band such as IIIrd Tyme Out performs John Prine's "Paradise," no one thinks that raises the question of whether they are a bluegrass band.

From Bill Monroe to newgrass was twenty-or-so years. From Muleskinner to us is twice that long. Grisman and Rowan might have played many kinds of music, but they are at this point also really the senior figures, the great ancestors and progenitors for today's young mandolin virtuosi and so on. They are our Don Reno and Lester Flatt. Remarkably, for all their departures, they are also central to the history of the form, repositories of the tradition they pushed against.

For such reasons, bluegrass history is a pretty tight series of loops. "Post-progressive" bluegrass, as we might call it, bluegrass of the last two decades, is eclectic. There are direct reactionaries, like Karl Shifflett and Big Country Show, Dave Evans, or the Dry Branch Fire Squad. The style of artists like Shifflett, who has returned even to the single mike and the "little uniforms," suffers, as Borges would put it, from a certain affectation, where Ralph Stanley handled easily the ordinary bluegrass of his time, which is not to say that Shifflett or Evans doesn't also produce some masterpieces, or that the return they instigate isn't compelling. I suppose my favorite artists of this period are people who effortlessly inhabit the tradition—neither consciously reactionary nor consciously progressive—groups like Hot Rize or IIIrd Tyme Out (who are for my money the greatest bluegrass artists of now). The style is their home, but they're also engaged in craftsmanly home improvement. Indeed, real craftsmanship can be attained only by repetition driven by love: a Nietzschean affirmation of the real.

Now, the fact that bluegrass is so intensely constrained, or more intensely constrained than almost any other living popular form, makes slight deflections intensely meaningful. With regard to any practice, we might develop the provisional thesis that the stricter the rules, the more intense the semantics. Free jazz threatens to become meaningless: where absolutely any gesture is possible, no gesture is significant, or at least any gesture is incredibly hard to interpret. But in bluegrass, a female voice, an electric instrument, a very distinctive solo style—these things have been experienced as throwing into question whether the thing is bluegrass at all. Every departure from the tradition is immediately audible, and hence intensely meaningful.

But one might point out that a set of conventions as strict and static as those of bluegrass would threaten any style of art with death. Bluegrass has produced many, many astonishing and virtuosic players, but even they threaten to merge into a kind of Beatlemania: Monroe and Flatt and Scruggs tribute bands. You know Wynton Marsalis can really play, and is deeply committed to cherishing the history of the music of New Orleans. But if he spent a whole career recapitulating "Dixieland" jazz as faithfully as possible, he and even we might get bored with the same sort of thing over and over again. But somehow, bluegrass with all its apparent rigidity has remained a living style of popular music.

The stricter the institution, the easier it is to rebel against, because almost any place or moment is a place or moment in which the rules can be violated. If you are hedged about with restrictions, it is remarkably easy to express your rejection of them; sometimes you can hardly help it. That is why the deflective or innovative moments in bluegrass are so important to the history of the form, and yet, all things considered, do not constitute very dramatic shifts in the basic style. This cycle of departure and return is more intensive in bluegrass than in other forms. Each departure tests the form; each is an occasion for its reaffirmation; each also leaves behind a change in the mainstream form, by revivifying its original commitments, but also by leaving behind a sense of movement and deposit of new ideas. Bluegrass is like the lives it describes: a cycle of departure and return. It is a cliché that when you return to the old home place, it is changed forever. But your return is nevertheless a return. Bluegrass is itself an old home place.

V

Philosophy of Punk

[2002, early note from 2012]

The first time I saw the power of punk was in 1981 at a show by the seminal hardcore band Minor Threat. The Ontario Theater in Washington, DC, was a plenum of swirling bodies, black-booted, mohawked, tattooed, and in furious motion. People jumped up on the stage and slammed into the band members midsong, which just made them play harder, if less precisely. The line between performers and audience was erased. It was so different from anything I'd ever experienced that I hardly knew whether I was feeling fear or exhilaration as I slam-danced.

More than thirty years later, the power of punk lives on, for better and for worse. In Moscow, members of the punk performance troupe Pussy Riot were sentenced (in 2012) to two years for salutary sacrilege and delightful anti-Putin hooliganism. In contemporary politics, economics, and aesthetics, the levers of power are ever more distant from the average young person. Any given suburban teen might feel extremely alienated and intuit that something is terribly wrong, but be unable to do anything about it. She'll probably have no possibility of expressing herself in mass media, for example. She can't start a super-PAC and start hiring professional videographers. She's unlikely to get elected to the state legislature. But she can participate in punk culture, express herself within it, and find an audience for her expression.

Punk is an aesthetic repertoire available all over the world in music, graphic arts, clothing, body alteration, performance, film, dance, and festival. It revolves around simplicity, roughness, directness, and intensity. To start making punk music, you do not need a great deal of skill; you just need a few chords, a battered amp, a ripped-up T-shirt, some like-minded reprobates, and a hundred Xeroxed flyers. And because punk develops distribution channels outside corporate or state media, you can find your own audience. Indeed, in some ways punk invented the kind of do-it-yourself production and hand-to-hand distribution that now characterize the use of the internet in the arts of many world subcultures. Pussy Riot, justly, is a YouTube sensation. The performance for which Pussy Riot was arrested seems rough or even naive in its comical seriousness. But precisely for that reason, it is intense, sincere, and affecting. You don't wonder what they were trying to say, and neither does Vlad Putin.

The punk vocabulary is suited to the direct expression of extreme or elemental emotions and ideas. In its political dimension, having a punk identity is less a matter of whether you're left or right than of whether you're "far." The persona is oppositional. A punk could be an anarchist, a fascist, or a communist, as long as he's not a Democrat or Republican.

Though punk had a variety of important antecedents, such as the Velvet Underground and Iggy Pop, it's generally agreed that the musical form was invented around 1975 in New York City by such bands as the Ramones, the Dictators, the Heartbreakers (not Tom Petty's band), and the Dead Boys. At the time, punk was received as the acme of primitivism, and the people who made and consumed it were widely regarded as dolts. The Ramones themselves did little to dispel this impression, performing songs such as "Teenage Lobotomy" and "Now I Wanna Sniff Some Glue." What most people seemed to hear at the time was fast and furious noise, dedicated to nihilism as a strategy for personal and societal degradation. The style was dismissed as trivial at best, and deeply stupid and offensive to decency at worst.

But in fact the Ramones were (a) jokers, and (b) rock archivists. The style they and most of these bands played is best considered neoclassical, while the musical context into which they emerged was rank and rococo. The horrors of mid-'70s popular music included "art rock"—the kind of pseudoprofound conceptual claptrap dished up by Yes or Emerson, Lake, and Palmer, in which former conservatory students, or young men who had once aspired to be conservatory students, played real real fast though meaninglessly and inexpressively under lyrics inspired by a superficial reading of Jules Verne.

It was indeed a sad time. The other pole was glossy California rock made by bands such as Fleetwood Mac and the Eagles: utterly slick, though catchy, and dedicated to the idea that cocaine and orgies were the ultimate agents of human liberation. This conceit was exploded some years later as the artists involved declined with awesome rapidity and bounced in and out of rehab, a trend that continues until this very day, as Stevie Nicks declines into an unseemly dotage. Black pop had declined into glossy disco.

Something, as you can deduce, had to be done. The Ramones were a rock band ultimately in the style of the Rolling Stones, interested in finding at the heart of the form its essential gesture, the one thing without which it would lose its soul. They were familiar with every simple and crystalline rock style, from rhythm and blues to girl group to surf and bubblegum, and they recreated them all with an ironic precision that is as close to perfection as rock music has ever come.

The Ramones toured England in 1976, and folks who would soon become the Clash and the Sex Pistols showed up at the shows and were forever changed. But by 1980, the initial momentum had been squandered. Though the Clash pressed on, the Pistols exploded or whatever it may be. The Talking Heads became artistes, and Blondie became a pop act. (The Ramones, believe it or not, continued to deepen and improve, a trend that persisted even after Joey's death in 2001 with the release of his lovely punk solo album.)

In 1979 and '80, the form received a fresh dose of ferocity in LA and DC from bands like the Germs, the Bad Brains, and the Teen Idles, who invented hardcore, characterized by lurching furious rhythm, ditching blues tonality and verse/chorus structure, with bellowed or screamed vocals. Soon there was a blossoming scene of ferocious noise on both coasts, featuring LA bands like the Circle Jerks and Black Flag, and DC types such as Minor Threat and the Faith. The LA bands were more or less dedicated to decadence, but in DC, as befits the town, the bands soon became extremely earnest and political, and merged with activist organizations. The East Coast scene soon developed toward "emo" and "grunge," and gave Dave Grohl to Nirvana and the Foo Fighters, and Fugazi to everyone. By the early '90s, the "alternative" punk revival was in full swing in Seattle, then all over. And by the mid-'90s a revival of straight-up classic punk had emerged, spearheaded on the pop charts by Green Day, and nurtured by a burbling underground of labels and acts who loved the Ramones above all things. Check out some Screeching

Weasel, for example. By then there were probably more punk rock bands than there had ever been, and the dominant pop rock of the early 2000s—Blink 182, Sum 41, even No Doubt—came from and paid homage to punk music. Hardcore is now absolutely global; the form is as Scandinavian and Japanese as American or British.

Now punk is a lot of different things and it supports a lot of different ideas or postures toward the world. American hardcore has included right-wing or neofascist skinhead punk, and bands such as the Dead Boys have played with that image since the mid-'70s. New York City bands like the Cro-Mags and Agnostic Front weren't or aren't necessarily Nazis, but violent thugs undeniably gravitated toward their shows and records. But then of course much punk took on far-left politics, including the Clash, Dead Kennedys, and Millions of Dead Cops.

But I guess the paradigm for me is the DC hardcore scene; I was eighteen in '76, in Northwest DC: Minor Threat, obviously; Rites of Spring; G.I., and so on: the bands that started and the people who continued Dischord Records, especially Ian Mackaye. The basic idea of Dischord Records is that it stays outside the purview of the major corporate record labels: it is fiercely independent. This is also the approach of Jello's label in San Francisco: Alternative Tentacles. Ian Mackaye's band Fugazi was in the Spin top fifty most influential rock bands, as well it should have been; in some ways it invented "emo" and "alternative." But the sales of Fugazi's albums are relatively modest compared to those of, say, Creed, or Stone Temple Pilots, bands that are infinitely less interesting. That's because there's no big promo push, and believe it or not there's no merchandise: no Fugazi T-shirts or bumper stickers, except bootlegged things. Dischord essentially sells disks at cost: maybe 10 bucks for a full-length CD. It costs five or six bucks to get into a Fugazi show, if you can believe that. They cover their expenses, pay themselves a decent salary, but they're not out here getting rich.

Dischord is conceived as a library of DC punk music; they don't have A&R people out trying to recruit hot young talent. And they've managed to hold on to their values for twenty years. Mackaye says things like this: "It's not that I'm out to smash the state. I'm just interested in building my own damn state."[1] He's building his own little system, or his own zone within the system where he can live and create the way he wants to. There are hundreds of bands and dozens of labels operating entirely outside the artistic and spiritual Sahara of major-label music.

I think this exactly the right sort of politics. And now let me do something that may strike y'all as a bit absurd; I'm going to trace some historical antecedents to Mackaye's approach and the approach of what we might think of as the left-anarchist punk world.

We might start out in the early sixteenth century with Martin Luther and the Protestant Reformation. Of course Luther was no anarchist; in fact he was a German nationalist. But his objection to the Catholic Church accused it of insane greed and acquisitiveness, and accused it above all of coming between each person and God. Finally, the scene of religious experience and interpretation for Luther was each individual believer. Early in his rebellion against the Catholic Church, he wrote: "I will tell you straight what I think. I am a Christian theologian; and I am bound, not only to assert, but to defend the truth with my blood and my death. I want to believe freely and be the slave to the authority of no one, whether council, university, or pope."[2] Every believer was, for Luther, a minister of Christ: "All of us who have been baptized are priests without distinction." And the church had to be conceived of as a community of believers, answerable above all to their own consciences, rather than as an authoritarian hierarchy. This a fundamental stroke for what punks call DIY. Make your own fucking records. Set up your own fucking tours. Achieve your own fucking relation to God, if any.

It's a familiar point that the Reformation leads fairly directly to the Enlightenment, where thinkers like Hume and Voltaire became atheists, more or less. That's where their exercise of independent conscience took them. And this whole deal leads to the call for political freedom, for democracy as expressed in the American and French revolutions. Its final flowering is political anarchism: the call for the total elimination of authoritarian structures, religious, political, and economic. And though there are hints of anarchism from ancient philosophy (for example in the *Tao Te Ching* and in Diogenes the Cynic), the invention of modern anarchism must in my view be ascribed fundamentally to the American Josiah Warren and the Frenchman Pierre-Joseph Proudhon. There is a profound antiauthoritarian tradition in America that proceeds from Warren to Emerson and Thoreau, to Emma Goldman and Alexander Berkman, Albert Jay Nock and H. L. Mencken, Abbie Hoffman and Noam Chomsky, Ian Mackaye and Jello Biafra.

Let me discuss Josiah Warren's work in a little more depth, because I think that you'll find there more or less the entire punk thing enunciated starting in the 1820s. Warren was initially a follower of Robert Owen, and participated in Warren's utopian socialist community of New Harmony. But that community was by and large a failure, and Warren attributed that failure to the authoritarian structure that began in the cult of Owen's personality. He dedicated the rest of his life to establishing his own utopian businesses and communities, and the shocking thing (considering that Warren is almost forgotten) is that communities such as Utopia, Ohio, were extremely successful. Eighty quarter-acre lots were sold at fifteen dollars each, and the economy was put on what we would think of as a barter footing: labor-for-labor exchange was the means by which the community was developed. Warren tried intentionally to shield the community from publicity, refusing even to disclose its location. In fact, it was in part publicity that doomed many of the utopian experiments in nineteenth-century America, including Warren's own later attempt: Modern Times, on Long Island, which through no fault of Warren's got processed through the New York press and various PR entrepreneurs into a symbol of free love, spiritualism, and fad diets.

Warren's work, both practical and theoretical, was dedicated to two principles: the sovereignty of the individual and the cost limit of price. On the first he asserted that all people, black and white, male and female—even children—have the right to dispose of their own persons as they see fit, unless they violate the liberty of others to do likewise. And since governmental, religious, and corporate structures invariably proceed by violation of the sovereignty of the individual, they are inherently evil, evil at their very conception. He wrote this: "Experience has proved, that power cannot be delegated to rulers of state and nations, in sufficient quantities for the management of business, without its becoming an indefinite quantity, and in this indefiniteness have mankind been cheated out of their legitimate liberty."[3]

His view was that most of the evil and poverty in the world is caused by the greed for profit and the imposition of interest on the use of funds. Warren held the labor theory of value: what a thing is worth is what labor went into it, and the labor of a lawyer is no more inherently valuable than that of a laborer. As he puts it in *Equitable Commerce*:

> Cost being made the limit of price, would give to a washerwoman a greater income than the importer of foreign goods—that this would upset the whole of the present system of national trade—stop all wars arising out of the profits of trade, and demolish all tariffs, duties, and all systems of policy that give rise to them—would abolish all

> distinctions between rich and poor—would enable every one to consume as much as he produced, and, consequently, prevent any one from living at the cost of another, without his or her consent.[4]

Things should be sold for exactly what they cost to produce and sell: the raw materials and the time that went into their making and marketing. If a community or a business could commit itself to that principle, then it could undersell communities and businesses based on the profit motive, and so in the long run could succeed and spread, slowly replacing an economy based on profit with one based on labor, without violence or constraint.

Warren actually established an extremely successful business along these lines: the Cincinnati Time Store. He sold staple fabrics and foods, and charged according to the time that went into their making. And he accepted "labor notes" as currency: notes that pledged a quantity of labor in exchange for goods purchased. He hoped that a labor currency could eventually replace currency based on gold and silver, so that almost everyone could have sufficient money because everyone has fundamentally the same quantity of time at their disposal. The details of how this would work are of course complex, and I can't really enter into them here; suffice it to say that Warren showed that the practical application of his principles was possible.[5]

This is, it seems to me, a quintessentially American philosophy, and it is totally opposed, for example, to the authoritarian socialism of Marx, Lenin, or Mao. It is exactly the opposite of a command economy. And yet it is also not some laissez-faire, dog-eat-dog corporate capitalism. The economy it envisions is radically decentralized and egalitarian. Perhaps it is also naively idealistic, but it can be tried practically, and essentially Dischord and Alternative Tentacles are attempts to put something like this into practice.

A more recent version of a Warren-type approach is the TAZ, or temporary autonomous zone. The book of that title, written by Hakim Bey and available for free online, or cheaply from the anarchist publishing collective autonomedia, is, I think, an important if problematic political tract. I personally would like to tear down the INS or the IRS or the Sony Corporation, brick by fucking brick, to erase them hard drive by hard drive. But I'm not able to, you see? The systems that we have created or that have been created at us are far too huge, powerful, and unresponsive to be resisted by direct attack. And these systems are getting bigger and more centralized all the time; note the unification of the European currencies, for example, or the way the

United Nations seeks to act as a world government, or the reach of Nike Corporation around the world and its ever growing implication in economic exploitation, or the vicious monopoly of bad software achieved by Bill Gates.[6]

Here's a sample of Bey's book:

> No, listen, what happened was this: they lied to you, sold you ideas of good & evil, gave you distrust of your body & shame for your prophethood of chaos, invented words of disgust for your molecular love, mesmerized you with inattention, bored you with civilization & all its usurious emotions.
>
> There is no becoming, no revolution, no struggle, no path; already you're the monarch of your own skin—your inviolable freedom waits to be completed only by the love of other monarchs: a politics of dream, urgent as the blueness of sky.
>
> To shed all the illusory rights & hesitations of history demands the economy of some legendary Stone Age—shamans not priests, bards not lords, hunters not police, gatherers of paleolithic laziness, gentle as blood, going naked for a sign or painted as birds, poised on the wave of explicit presence, the clockless nowever.
>
> Agents of chaos cast burning glances at anything or anyone capable of bearing witness to their condition, their fever of *lux et voluptas*. I am awake only in what I love & desire to the point of terror—everything else is just shrouded furniture, quotidian anaesthesia, shit-for-brains, sub-reptilian ennui of totalitarian regimes, banal censorship & useless pain.

What you and I might be able to do is find or create little zones outside these systems, pirate utopias that last a few hours or a few years or a few decades, tiny places where you go unnoticed or unconstrained by the bigger systems, like Warren's Utopia, Ohio. There are still gaps in the universal surveillance, still corners where you can hide and hatch your diabolical schemes, places on the internet where you can say whatever you damn please and Google or the Justice Department hasn't figured out quite how to shut you up.[7]

Of course, maybe we'd prefer a real revolution.[8] But that is extremely unlikely, given that corporate capitalism has managed to give most Americans a stake in the status quo. But even if a real revolution were possible, there are a few things wrong with real revolutions, as history makes all too obvious.

You're liable to end up in "the terror." Anarchists helped overthrow the tsar, then were executed en masse by Lenin. The Cultural Revolution and the Killing Fields are examples of what can happen when your basic leftists take over, with their little red books and their automatic weapons. The systematic revolution presupposes a systematic ideology, and the systematic ideology always holds within it the seeds of slaughter.

Well, the TAZ makes a revolution, a tiny revolution, without ideology. The idea is just to carve out a place where people can do what they want. That, I think, is the only revolution worth having, and it was exactly the sort of revolution proposed by Thoreau, say, and put into actual operation by Warren and Mackaye. It's a revolution that's actually being made all the time by punks, freaks, druggies, dissidents, weirdos, and lovers. I do not recognize the right of anyone to control my words or my actions, and I claim the right to resist in any way I deem appropriate. And I am willing to extend the same courtesy to you, to recognize that you are the sovereign of yourself. If I start with that, then I can't also design society according to some ideal structure, because ideal structures are just more or less creative oppressions. I just have to let go and see what happens. That's the only politics that isn't worse than what it seeks to replace.

And that's what I call punk philosophy: DIY; the cost limit of price; the sovereignty of the person over herself; the temporary autonomous zone, not to mention zine; let go and see what happens. We see this in many other of the most vital areas of the culture: for example, in hip hop, particularly in graffiti art. The tag is both an intrasubcultural form of communication and a subversion of public space. You might find similar things if you hit the big bikers convention in Daytona, or start hanging out at skate parks. These are the sorts of places where the culture is not dead; as Deleuze and Guattari would put it, these minor languages and minor threats are the places where the culture becomes; they are at once the flowering and the undermining of American culture. Make your own art, your own love, your own truth, and find a place where you can do that. If you can't find a place like that, start trying to carve one out; make your own island nation of jesters and fools and fops. For God's sake ditch Shakira and make your own music. Get on the web and publish your own fucked-up writing and see whether someone reads it.

VI

Technology and the Future of Beauty

1998

A hundred years ago, George Santayana defined beauty as "objectified pleasure."[1] His idea was that when you experience pleasure in looking at something or listening to it, you attribute the state of pleasure to the thing that causes it rather than to yourself. That is an odd idea because it makes it seem as though sunsets and Leonardos are having a good time as they hang there being beautiful. That's a problem. But another problem comes in associating beauty with pleasure at all.

To give you a sense of what I mean, let's briefly develop a contrast between two painters: Claude Monet and Charles Sheeler. If in your head you can recover one version or another of *Water Lilies* from the McDonalds and the Holiday Inns, you will remember that it's ravishing in its own way. It is above all dedicated to capturing and providing a pleasure in mere seeing: that is what governs the selection of the motif, the technique by which that motif is presented; visual pleasure, much more than lilies, is Monet's theme. That's *why* it's in McDonald's: even now that it's mutated into a kind of wallpaper, been trivialized by sheer repetition, it yields a slight but simple delight. If Monet is quasidespised by folks like me and maybe you, it's not only that we have come to mistrust purely visual effects, or the fuzzy, sentimental, Laura Ashley brand of pleasure he provides; it has something to do with the banality of pleasure itself. Perhaps we're too suspicious now for Monet's sensibility to seem plausible.

Contemplate by way of contrast the industrial images of American painter and photographer Charles Sheeler. His work displays great clarity, both of vision and of mind. It doesn't screw around with little daubs of pink but boldly delineates bold forms. Maybe you're going to disagree with me on this, but I think it is beautiful and macho. His paintings illustrate the reason I want to detach beauty from pleasure. I've got no doubt that most folks get more pleasure from Monet. In some ways Sheeler is weird, disturbing, or even inhuman. His art seems emotionless, for one thing, in a way no one would accuse Monet's of being; one feels the artist almost to be a machine of the sort he is depicting.

And if you don't think Sheeler's *Suspended Power,* for example, is beautiful, I'm betting that one reason is its subject: machinery, here a steam turbine, for example. And I do know what you mean; the things are pretty ugly in a way. I doubt that, had I just walked into the plant where this turbine was located, I would experience it as particularly beautiful. It might even have struck me as hideous. But the turbine—or at any rate its structure, its configuration, its visual aspect—is redeemed after a fashion by Sheeler's painting. Sheeler redeemed all sorts of things this way: giant propellers, power lines, trains and tracks and industrial parks and ducts. He was enraptured in an almost religious way by what I will call the "classical" machine: the mechanical/industrial colossus of the first three quarters of the twentieth century. He systematically reduces the machine to an almost abstract form (as, by an entirely different process and to an entirely different effect, did Monet with water lilies). And of course the sheer fact that he is making paintings is the ultimate abstraction. One does not have to deal with the noise such machines make or the pollution they emit when one is looking at them—miniaturized and squashed flat onto the picture plane—in an art museum.

In the transformations to which art subjects machine in Sheeler's work, his paintings have made me see machines differently and think about them differently. In a way he has helped me reconcile myself to the machine, has made me see the simple and monumental beauty of a steam turbine. What is seductive or sweet about the machine is, precisely, its simplicity, even if, by the standards of previous human creation, the classical machine is pretty complex. But you might notice that in the works of Sheeler, there is hardly a single "natural" thing: not a single plant, animal, cloud, rarely even a person. All of those things, in comparison to the machine, are shaggy, messy, complicated, arbitrary. But the machine can, with some limitations, be encompassed all at once in a single visual act: it is made by people for people and has a degree of complexity apportioned to our understanding. It is precisely that quality that can make the machine landscape seem monstrous or bleak: the machine landscape is a landscape broken by human will: a will that is simplistic, paltry, and morally confused.

I worked for a few years at Penn State Harrisburg, which is just a couple of miles from Three Mile Island. The first time I rolled to work up 441 and passed it, I was intimidated. The gigantic concrete stacks suggest a brutalist engineering project in the old Soviet bloc: the relic of a five-year plan of some two-bit American Stalin. And it feels radically dislocated from its setting. An island rendered over into concrete on a particularly lovely stretch of the Susquehanna, rising over Amish farms and small towns to transform the horizon, it seems to have been built on the wrong scale. But I've begun, under Sheeler's tutelage, to see that it has a certain beauty: the stacks are gigantic hourglasses that embody a bizarre sensuality, and the steam that rises from them is a weather. Sheeler detects and celebrates the disturbing loveliness of classical technology: the cleanness and clarity and simplicity that you don't find in stuff that isn't made by people. TMI is a monochrome, modernist beauty, a reduction of form to function so ruthless that the form itself is perfectly stark, absolutely purified, utterly abstract. TMI's beauty is the opposite of what we might think of as natural beauty. A bird's nest is a mess of twigs and string: a shaggy, chaotic interweaving of things. TMI is a hypersimplified concrete sculpture on a scale beyond the monumental: an expression of almost perfect purity. And it is beautiful in what one might call a satanic way: beautiful as a monstrous expression of pride and desire for power; beautiful, almost, in its hatred of beauty, in its rejection of sweetness, in its insane scale. It is in its inhuman conception a completely human thing, an attempt to transform a whole region into an artifact.

The sort of aesthetic put forward by Sheeler in his art and by me just now with regard to Three Mile Island, is subversive in a number of ways to an aesthetic we might call "romantic": essentially a nineteenth-century aesthetic. It is subversive, first of all, because it dissociates beauty from nature, or perhaps even declares that the further something departs from nature the more beautiful it is. One might see such an aesthetic operating even in the world of human beauty, where makeup, clothing, plastic surgery could be conceived of as ways of transmuting the body into an artifact, making over the flesh into a machine landscape a la Sheeler, simplifying the complexity, the wrinkles, the arbitrary protuberances to make a comprehensible object of desire, humanizing the body in the way that all things are humanized: by concealing, polluting, and breaking.

But when I myself think of "beauty," I usually think of it in a romantic way—the first things that come to mind are "natural" things: trees, skies, birds, butterflies, and perhaps the female nude. That is a standard understanding of beauty at least since the turn of the eighteenth into the nineteenth century, especially in America. So the paradigmatically beautiful objects are natural objects, and then art that reflects such objects: landscape and some still life painting, for example. Well, for Sheeler, a factory is more beautiful than Yosemite. That was a radical notion in 1920, but it's a hell of a lot more interesting than another impressionist landscape even if it's false.

Then, second, Sheeler's art and the cult of the machine are subversive to the idea that art and beauty are useless or above the dirty little world of commerce. Sheeler attempts to demonstrate the beauty of useful objects in a way that would have been congenial, for example, to the Bauhaus architects and the architects of what is sometimes called "high modernism." Sheeler and his aesthetic *pollute* the notion of beauty with use, even as the machines he depicts pollute the beautiful natural landscape. There is the fearsome hint in Sheeler that what we think of as pollution might itself be a kind of monstrously beautiful transformation/humanization of the natural world.

Perhaps the nuclear power plant is the last moment of the classical machine. As I say, it deploys a Stalinist aesthetic of immensity, ideology, and stupidity. It is a machine bigger than, say, a steel mill. But at the heart of the nuclear power plant there is a mystery that is incompatible with its being a machine: the nuclear reaction itself is not "mechanical" in the sense that a steam turbine is mechanical. It is something that people set in motion, but not exactly something they make or accomplish. It has the interesting "natural" property of potentially running out of control and destroying everything, like a typhoon or an earthquake. So TMI gives us a hybrid aesthetic or is a pivot in the relation of technology and beauty: it is a classical machine with something astonishing and incomprehensible at its heart. TMI displays a sort of beauty that is past, but perhaps it also points to something about beauty's future.

Charles Sheeler was born in 1883. So he came of age through the turn of the nineteenth into the twentieth century. He was born only twenty years after the death of Henry David Thoreau, but the world into which he matured was not Thoreau's world. Thoreau felt the onset of industry, and sought to escape it even as it enlivened him. He always found beauty where there were no people, and regarded people themselves, or white people anyway, as a kind of pollution. He tried to hold on to, or rather to invent, a preindustrial aesthetic. Sheeler, on the other hand, moving with a satanic American optimism, tried to make an aesthetic for the twentieth century. He tried to make us feel free in the machine landscape in which many of us seemed trapped; tried to make a beauty for industrial workers rather than farmers. Thoreau was a masochist, letting go into a oneness with nature. Sheeler was a sadist, seeing beauty in what people had seized and transformed. Thoreau dignified the idea of a natural humanity. Sheeler began to conceive and paint our future as cyborgs.

I think it fair to say that we are at a moment similar in some ways to that moment when Sheeler turned seventeen in 1900. Perhaps we are waiting for someone to show us a new beauty or to show us the beauty that is already all around us. The age of the classical machine is over. Those huge industrial landscapes that Sheeler painted are mostly gone now, or are lapsing slowly back toward something we might call nature, in junkyards or dumps, or just standing there rusting. Our machines, if *machine* is still the right word, are much smaller or much bigger. Incomprehensible amounts of energy have been expended in miniaturizing the machine, so that the model device of the turn of this century is not the turbine, but the chip. The machines we tend or work—maybe in our cubicles, or sitting at the airport tapping at a little laptop—are personal computers. We are more and more constantly surrounded by little devices, the use of which quickly becomes indispensable on economic, social, and aesthetic grounds.

But if the devices are tiny, the systems with which they connect us are incomprehensibly vast. If one thinks of the internet as a single machine, that machine is devouring the whole world, or covering it like a system of vines. And it *is* like a system of vines—in comparison to Sheeler's power lines, the internet looks like the bird's nest: what I was calling "shaggy" or what computer programmers sometimes call "fuzzy." There's nothing fuzzy about steam turbines. The more you use a personal computer, the more filled with all sorts of unique or commonplace junk the computer becomes. Really no two PCs are identical once they are in use for a while. The mechanical model of standardized products and processes, while it has not been entirely superseded, is giving way to a kind of mimicry of organic processes in which products simply grow in all sorts of expected and unexpected directions.

That our machines have at once become so much smaller and so much larger has utterly transformed our relation to the artifactual world, the world of human creation. Technology becomes at once infinitely more personal (compare a PC to a steel mill) and also completely out of anyone's control. The incomprehensibility of the internet, however, is due not only to its size, but also to its operation. First of all, each computer wired to the internet harbors a tiny version of the nuclear reaction: the mystery of the chip and the interaction of chips. Maybe you've seen the ads for Intel in which chips are portrayed as little people running around inside your PC. They're all dressed in colorful outfits that cover them from head to toe. I guess such outfits are the kind of things people wear at Intel so as not to dirty the chips, to protect them from organic human messiness. But they're also the sort of things people wear to try to clean up reactor cores after nuclear mishaps. They make a human being over into the image of new technologies: the simplified or mechanical surface harboring a mysterious substance/reaction/intelligence.

Second, the internet is so widely dispersed, so amorphous and constantly shifting, so elusive, that I bet no one has any comprehensive grasp on its configuration; I bet no one has any adequate "picture" of the internet in mind. It is a system or environment with a life of its own, constantly in the process of transformation and growth. Individual human beings like us are more or less bacteria in the body of this thing. In both these ways, technology has transcended and is transcending the classical machine. Most guys who labored in the Pittsburgh steel mills understood perfectly well how the things worked. They had a comprehensive grasp on the entire operation, which was a relatively straightforward mechanical system. Fewer people who work at TMI, I imagine, have got a grip on the whole thing, and they must all resort to metaphor to describe the reaction itself. No one can have a comprehensive grasp on the internet, and in the future technology will assume configurations that perhaps no one understands at all—there will simply be an exponentially exploding accumulation of events. Systems will in some sense be set in motion by people but they will grow on their own.

The elusiveness or even apparent conceptual impossibility of the internet is inscribed in the metaphor of "virtuality." I think the notions of virtual space, virtual reality, and so on will disappear as we get used to living inside the internet. Right now I guess the idea is that there is something false or unreal about the stuff that is on the internet, which is supposed to exist in the nowhere of "cyberspace." We are anxious still about the physical location of things, want the internet to be located in Peoria or something. Our need to find a spatial metaphor, even if we then cut it down or off with the word *virtual,* shows our nostalgia for the classical machine, which certainly was spatially located in a very obvious, circumscribed way. There is nothing really spatially mysterious or ontologically impossible about the internet; it is just that a web "site" is not a site like the site of a factory. Eventually we will stop calling these things sites and conceiving them as some sort of unreal subreality and learn to inhabit them as part of our actual world. The internet or its successors will be "naturalized."

And the art and industry of the computer will stand in a very different relation to "nature" than the art and industry of the classical machine age. As I say, the computerized realm in some ways approaches the condition of nature. The aesthetic of the machines Sheeler celebrated is classical, like the aesthetic of David or Raphael—straight ahead, symmetrical, noble, simplified. The era of the postclassical machine is baroque, a mess of lines and forms and colors too complicated to be readily grasped. But the baroque presupposes the classical: really Rubens cannot be understood unless you understand Raphael. And the era of the postclassical machine directly presupposes Sheeler's machine age—is a direct development out of it that makes use of it in a thousand ways: to generate power, for instance. So if the classical machine is a journey away from nature, as Thoreau would conceive it, the postclassical machine is a continuation of that journey; and as the journey continues we get farther and farther away until we lose nature completely or until the conception of nature actually makes no sense at all. But it also paradoxically approaches the condition of nature, and not just as a *sim.* The sim world, even a sim natural environment, is perhaps the achievement of the maximum distance from nature, the more so as the sim itself approaches perfection. But the processes by which computer systems grow approach very closely to organicity—closer as they become bigger and their components more powerful. The collapse of the virtual and actual will above all occur as a result not of perfect simulation but of ever huger accidents and bizarre turns of events no one expected. No one was expecting nature, either.

Some half-baked, gratuitous predictions: There will be no such thing as nature in a hundred years. We will have radically reconceived the relation of humans to the rest of the world, radically reconceived or annihilated the distinction between the natural and the artificial, between art and life. That should not surprise anyone; nature was an invention of the romantics anyway as they stared into the barrel of the classical machine.

I think you'll find that the other romantic bromide, the distinction between useful and useless, craft and art, commerce and aesthetics, will vanish as well. I really can't tell whether the internet is "useful" or not, and I don't really care. Sometimes I accomplish "practical" things on the internet, like ordering a book from amazon.com, but more likely I just wander around semi-aimlessly checking stuff out. I look at traffic patterns in DC just because I'm already at washingtonpost.com; I trade contentless instant messages with my daughter, who's at her mom's house. The internet is not useful or useless, it's just there, like a forest or a mountain. There is no reason or justification for its existence, but all reasons and justifications, all commerce, will eventually flow through it. The beauty or ugliness of the internet will not be useless or useful; it will be a kind of increate, inchoate fact. This is just an extension of the reality of the computer. Computers seem useful. They "save time" and so on. But in fact no one has any more time now than they did before, and each increase in the speed of computers is compensated for perfectly by the increased demands of the software they run: no gain is a gain and no efficiency is achieved; there is just an ever ascending spiral of signal densities.

Perhaps art in the next century will amount to a kind of terror in which collaborations of unknowable numbers of people and machines will make beautiful things that no one understands. Perhaps in the next century, works of art will start making themselves and interpreting themselves to themselves. Perhaps artists will be growing works of art the way one grows a field of soybeans, hoping for the best. Perhaps the concept of art itself will become otiose or impossible in the face of the self-creating artifact. Perhaps the greatest works of art of the next century will be communicative information viruses which grow by themselves and destroy through communication all communication in diabolically beautiful ways.[2]

The computer virus is a work of art in part because of the intensity and ingenuity of its design. It is a "modernist" work of art because it attacks and interrupts our comfortable assumptions and activities. Maybe you've heard about the sculpture designed by Richard Serra and erected in the Federal Plaza in New York. It was called "Tilted Arc" and consisted of a huge, curved, rusted steel wall. The point of the thing, or one point of the thing, was to make it harder for people to move from building to building. And the folks who worked there hated it and finally succeeded in having it removed. It was in their way. If you are a federal official idiotic enough to hire Richard Serra to make a work of art for your plaza, that's what you get. Serra wants to make it a little harder for the government to function; he thinks that's a legitimate function of art. So do I, come to think of it. The computer virus is like that: in a sense it's a nostalgic victory of romantic individual creativity over the nonfinite silicon/electronic/organic machine. The dude who made the Melissa virus is a contemporary Toulouse-Lautrec: he named the thing after a stripper he admired, and sat in his little room all night every night working out how to transform the visible and intelligible world. But on the other hand the virus itself consists of code—it is part of the silicon/electronic/organic machine it targets. The possibility of making it or introducing it exists only in the "virtual" world it seeks to interrupt or destroy. The perfect computer virus, like the viruses that kill people, would destroy the system it fed on, thus destroying itself. The perfect work of art for the twenty-first century is the self-consuming artifact.

Some even more gratuitous, impossible predictions: The beauty of the next century will be a shaggy, pseudo-organic beauty that is silicon rather than carbon-based. The forward-thinking artist of the next century will make works too complicated to be grasped in a visual or auditory act. Already we see something like that in Gehry's Bilbao Guggenheim, for example. The machine will grow ever smaller and ever larger until we are hooked into huge communication systems all the time through tiny devices on or in our person. Institutions and governments will seek to control the net and us through processes of simplification, screening, monitoring, etc., but will find that surveillance is impossible in the beautiful mess; the whole concept of power will have to be radically reconceived as communicative and pseudo-organic rather than ideological. The classical machine will play for the twenty-first century the role that nature played for the nineteenth: it will be the object of longing and nostalgia. Already we have imitations of classic phones and blenders and cars (Beetle, Viper). We will wish for industrial production in the way that Thoreau wished for oneness with nature. The industrial worker will take on the iconographic status of the cowboy. Paintings by Charles Sheeler will appear on posters in hotel rooms. People will design useless pseudoclassical machines, or they will make postclassical processors that look like classical machines. Self-perpetuating and self-annihilating technologies will make art a branch of horticulture. New and inconceivable hatreds will spring up and yield beautiful things. Sex will get even stranger than it is right now. Beauty will be viral: impossibly profuse and self-replicating and arbitrary and infectious and lethal. And finally, beauty will once and for all detach itself from pleasure, so that there is no reason for anything to be beautiful or not: no goal, no justification, only an inconceivably huge communication system awash in an arbitrary syntax of electronic impulses imploding into a beautiful death, as when you look at the remanufactured corpse in the funeral home, and all you can say is: "Don't he look natural?"

VII

I Speak for My People

A Racial Manifesto

2013

To the real question, How does it feel to be a problem? I answer seldom a word.
—W. E. B. Du Bois, "Of Our Spiritual Strivings"

I am a middle-aged, middle-class, rural, white, male heterosexual. I will refer to this constellation of identities—particularly the last three—as my "race." If you don't think that being a member of my race is a problem, you haven't been reading, for example, the *New York Times* op-ed page, where we are continuously excoriated—with, let me admit, some justice—as the most reactionary and bigoted portion of the population, bent on maintaining our privileges against the tide of justice and demography. Here are some of our racial characteristics: We are opposed to science and are in general congenitally or perhaps willfully ignorant. We are what's the matter with Kansas. We are hoarding ammunition as we grow ever more disgruntled. We despise the poor and blame them for their poverty, which is actually, of course, due to their exploitation by us. We think people ought to be allowed to starve so that we can save a few dollars on our taxes. We're the only reservoir of homophobia: bullies almost in virtue of our very identity. That may well be because we're actually closeted gay people, who must insulate our pseudomasculinity in imagination from the awful drag queen within. We are bent on maintaining our control of the bodies of women by a thousand anachronistic mechanisms, from laws concerning abortion and contraception to our very glance, which carries with it the preternatural destructive power of the evil eye.

All of this is at least approximately true, and I think it is time we admitted it straight out: the history of my race is one of unremitting evil relieved only by spasms of hypocrisy. My people have visited every sort of disaster upon yours, from colonialism and the slave trade to capitalism, housewifery, and atomic weaponry.

My race lives at a deranged distance from nature, for we are the agents of technology and climate change. No doubt we hate our mother the earth just as we resent our real mothers, or any woman who seems to have any power over us, such as Hillary Clinton. We don't think Barack Obama is an American, because we are certainly Americans and he is certainly not us, whoever in fact he may be. Deep inside, despite our huge flimsy compensatory egos and infinite capacity for self-deception, we know that we are over, and our every reflexive paroxysm comes from fear and resentment of this situation. We are always fighting a rearguard action against the forces of the future. We want time to run backward, against the great tide of freedom carrying you on.

In short, we are the inventors and perpetrators of all oppressions. Amazingly, we convinced ourselves at various times and in various ways that you wanted us to oppress you; you needed us to oppress you; we were oppressing you for your own good. I admit that was insane. We white male heterosexuals are a gutter race, irremediably flawed. When the Nation of Islam referred to white people as "devils," quite possibly it had a point. One might speculate as to the respective roles of genetics, environment, and blood guilt, but there is no denying that something has gone terribly wrong somewhere. My race has a streak of moral degeneracy, a counter-evolutionary tendency.

Some of my people once conceived of "the negro" as a problem or worried about "the woman problem," but everyone is now agreed on who the problem actually always was: me. Du Bois explored how it felt to be *regarded* as a problem; I am exploring what it means actually to be a problem, in fact to be *the* problem. Think about what sort of dilemmas this imposes on my people, or what it's like to be colorless me. For example, most folks can vote in good conscience for their own self-interests, broadly construed. You can't blame black people for voting for black people in the interests of black people, or women for voting for women in the interests of women; people have become heroes by making that possible. But if white male heterosexuals vote for white male heterosexuals because they are white male heterosexuals and will defend the interests of white male heterosexuals—for example, gender hierarchy, heteronormativity, and white privilege—we are doing wrong. When you pursue your interests, your voice is a cry for justice. When we pursue our interests, we are doing real harm and real evil. Harm and evil *are* our interests.

Admittedly, my race has to its credit some achievements as well. It is hard to tell, historically, who really counts as a white heterosexual male. But perhaps you could give us William Shakespeare, Isaac Newton, Ben Franklin, Napoleon, Vincent Van Gogh? (Wait, maybe Shakespeare was gay?) We could make some T-shirts. But it will be a long time before my race gets its history month. Expressions of white or male or heterosexual pride are unbelievably problematic; no one articulates such things publicly except insane supremacists and hate criminals. We dare not, and indeed perhaps we should not, speak frankly as ourselves, or for ourselves. That is why so many of the machinations by which we have retained power have been hidden, even from ourselves.

I suspect that to take real pride in our identity, history, and customs—and for us to rise to real racial consciousness and knowledge of self—the members of my race will have to pass through a subaltern or abject phase, a time of trial in which we shall be humbled and brought low. We have been begging for it for centuries. For our own good, we need you to impose extremely aggressive affirmative action programs by which we could be systematically excluded from even a vestigial grip on power. We are in any case ill-suited to mainstream education. We may need to live apart in ghettoes or on reservations, where possibly we could be accessed for breeding purposes. All the time we could be transforming our suffering into art, which would certainly be an improvement.

After that, we will need to undergo a Booker T/Mao stage of our racial destiny, in which we learn the dignity of hard manual labor in the fields or sweatshops. We must slowly establish that we are an industrious, sincere, and above all a nondangerous race, which may take some generations. At that point we can generate a "talented tenth" or a racial intelligentsia, the white male heterosexuals who are most like people of color, women, and gay people. This cohort, I prophesy, could lead us toward integration into the culture at large, and possibly even toward a measure of pride in some of the achievements of the great white male heterosexuals of the past, if any. A movement of dignity and identity might then emerge that wouldn't carry the full taint of our genocides. We might reappropriate *cracker, breeder,* and *jerk* as honorifics, but we must stop short of outright white male heterosexual nationalism. Nevertheless, our blood too, pooling or coagulating here and there, might have a lesson to teach the world, or at least a cautionary tale to warn it with.

It is far too early, then, to emphasize with a pure conscience the contributions of my race to humankind. Nevertheless, I would like to describe some of them for future public service announcements. We are, I think, in a modest way naturally musical, and even though Jimmie Rogers and Hank Williams are inconceivable without African-American music, my people might someday take pride in their achievements. Some elusive quality of whitemalestraightness, a font of ancestral creativity, emerges in their work. To take another example, I'm not sure that the colored, female, and gay races have produced cynics as magnificently destructive as H. L. Mencken or Ambrose Bierce. Admittedly, their sheer assholery is characteristic of the whole debased history of my people; nevertheless, there is art in their prose, art that could be recovered as their actual political positions sink into historical oblivion. Ours is not the most athletic of races, but figures such as Lance Armstrong have carried forward the banner of my race with distinction, if also with our characteristic cheating. A certain rudimentary mechanical ability is native to my race, I believe, and for every semi-sane Tesla we have produced an eminently practical Edison. Admittedly, this racial tic has given rise to the weaponry by which we have dominated and infuriated the world. But it could in principle be turned to peaceful purposes.

It sometimes seems that being a straight guy like me is nothing but a set of exclusions and dominations. What, I often ask myself, is my straightness without my homophobia, my misogyny, and many other vicious prepossessions of which I may only dimly be aware? Also, it is certainly plausible to hold that the mating of a man with a woman is unnatural, a monstrous copulation between members of different species. But anyone should try to love anyone they want to try to love, and if heterosexuality could be relieved of its immense burden of normativity, it might be more fun. In other words, if I were just having sex with you and not also thereby oppressing you, we might both enjoy ourselves more, or at any rate be less angry at one another. That might be legitimate within a certain significant sexual subculture of the distant future, because there is something to be said for heterosexuality. Men and women are not the only sorts of people who fit together, but when we do fit together, we really fit together, if you know what I'm talking about, and this idea I feel could someday constitute (partly) a contribution of my race to mainstream culture.

Admittedly, my race has developed the narrow and idiotic normative standards of beauty that have become the mechanisms of your self-oppression. We made you conk your hair, starve yourself, bleach your skin, dress all fem or not fem at all. We made you try to produce yourself as the body we wanted to see. Partly, I would speculate, that is because members of my own race are not notably attractive. We are gross, actually, though occasionally we do throw out a Brad Pitt or other genetic outlier. We can distract you from that if we can make you focus instead on your own alleged ugliness. But even our bizarre standards of beauty might be incorporated into the mainstream if they were just part of the vast diverse tapestry of human aesthetic preferences. We could eventually reach a situation in which it was as permissible to prefer skinny or lingerie-model-type women as to prefer any other sort of otherwise weighted or gendered person. Some folks just have a type.

The political traditions and rhetorics of my race focus on autonomy, individualism, self-reliance, pulling yourself up by your own bootstraps, competition, and whatnot. We like to talk about individual rights rather than interpersonal connections. Now admittedly this ideology is a tissue of privileges, falsifications, and contradictions. No human being ever accomplishes anything by himself, but each of my people is trying to make himself an invulnerable autonomous being; we want to armor ourselves all in Kevlar™. Putting it mildly, we need therapy. It must always be borne in mind that Emerson's composition of "Self-Reliance" was made possible by his wife and a small domestic staff; perhaps its composition didn't require Emerson at all. That Jefferson was a great defender of individual rights and was also engaged so multidimensionally in slavery shows the problem; his status as an autonomous gentleman required the constant labor of others and the erasure of the subjectivity of the people who performed it. He could at least have apologized. In industrial capitalism, the doctrine of individual rights becomes an ideology of oppression. The idea that a worker in a capitalist system is free because he can sell his labor on a contractual basis is just a rationalization of the most pervasive forms of economic exploitation, precisely those which benefit us and affront you.

Nevertheless, I think that there are elements of individualism that you might pluck from the flotsam after the wreck of my race's swagger. You might contemplate what happens when the human individual is actually regarded as in some sense unreal or not ontologically primary. One devastating effect is essays like this one, or the persona of the racial spokesman. Also, it is a very short trip from unrealing individuals to liquidating them for the collective good, as many collectivist regimes have actually done. I would suggest that a version of Jeffersonian or Thoreauvian suspicion of centralized power might be worth retaining in a library somewhere just in case. Our elders have set it down as part of our traditional lore that a government that provides your food tells you what and whether to eat. Well, you can take or leave that, but you might end up finding it useful.

And so as we recede from history, we bid you a semifond adieu. We certainly created many psychological and practical difficulties for you, but I'd be lying if I said we didn't enjoy our time atop the pinnacle. With tremendous gratitude for all the collusion you gave us, we now step aside to spend more time with our families. As we exit the stage, we acknowledge that we got pretty much everything wrong. We leave you with our sincerest apologies, but not a dime in reparations.

VIII

I Was a Teenage Terrorist

2005

The classic Molotov cocktail is an open wine bottle with a gas-soaked rag sticking out of the neck. But I figured only an idiot would hold something like that in his hand and light it. So I sealed the bottles, scrubbed them off, and tied rags around their midsections.

I stayed up until 3:30, dressed myself in black including a ski mask and gloves, and snuck out the back door. Maneuvering up the block, I emerged in the woods. Shaking in an adrenaline rush for the centuries, I lit the rag and lobbed the first cocktail onto the backhoe. A sheet of flame spread instantaneously over the area, singed me a bit. Then the thing exploded. I tossed the second cocktail on, just for the hell of it, and ran. I had been lying in bed for a few minutes when I heard the sirens.

My friends and I had played every day in the woods at Livingston Street and Broad Branch Avenue in DC. In the late '60s, when we were ten or eleven, we played chase. By thirteen we'd moved on to guerrilla warfare. I was pretty damned serious about it. I bought a copy of Che Guevara's classic book on the subject, memorized most of it, and used that as a guide. Under Che's guidance, I'd sneak up silently on William O'Brien and plug him before he knew what was happening.

One day when I was fifteen we went up to mess around in those woods. There was a big yellow tractor parked up in there. A bunch of old trees had been removed and there was already a gash in the ground and a stack of cinder blocks. I poured sugar into the gas tank of the earthmover. They towed it off and brought another. I poured sand in that one. The third arrived with a locking gas cap. I went to the auto parts store and bought a gas can, then to the station and pumped a gallon. I fished out of the trash a couple of Ocean Spray cranberry juice bottles, selected for their thin walls and large capacity. In the bottles I mixed gasoline and Sterno.

Twenty-five years later, a week or two after the shootings at Columbine High School, I was on C-SPAN talking to Brian Lamb about Eric Harris and Dylan Klebold when it occurred to me that maybe I understood these kids better than I thought, certainly better than the people quoted everywhere proclaiming the boys' actions "incomprehensible." And then I heard myself confessing to the backhoe immolation. People started calling in to berate me or to demand I make restitution to my victims. My life for a week or two was a shitstorm of controversy and of memory; I tried for the first time in many years to make sense out of my descent into violence and rage and of my fitful, incomplete recovery: the process by which I reached the point at which I was blowing stuff up and the process by which I became an irritation rather than a danger to myself and others.

My kids' school in rural Pennsylvania has implemented an antiviolence campaign called "Be Cool," which seems to consist entirely of posters hung here and there which say "act cool." Like most indoctrination aimed at children, the campaign is notable only for its emptiness. But the right way into this problem is empathy: you need to think about what it would be like to be Kip Kinkel, the Oregon kid who was convicted of killing his parents and two students at his high school while wounding 25 others. A solution won't come from the comfortable and self-congratulatory thought that future Harrises and Klebolds and Kinkels will be ameliorated by slogans, or, on the other hand, that they are incomprehensible monsters.

Kinkel wrote in his journal: "I know everyone thinks this way sometimes, but I am so full of rage that I feel I could snap at any moment. I think about it every day. Blowing the school up or just taking the easy way out, and walk into a pep assembly with guns. In either case, people who are breathing will stop breathing."[1] All right. You're Kip and you're walking down the hall of your school and you can't stop thinking about guns and bombs and their effects. Now you run across a poster that says "act cool." Better now? In fact, seeing that poster just makes you a bit angrier; it's an institutional expression that isn't aimed at anyone in particular, and it's a demonstration of what you realized a long time ago: that these people are so out of touch with your life or indeed with reality in general that they seem barely human. Seriously, there they are, muttering phrases in unison.

Eric Harris, after a series of petty crimes, was sent to "anger management" class. This doesn't appear to have been particularly effective. Just before the Columbine shootings, Harris said "More rage. More rage. Keep building it on." Harris and Klebold were consumed by rage and they identified themselves with it. They brought it to the point where, in all seriousness, they wanted to kill everyone. But if you think that they cultivated rage because they found it pleasurable or amusing, consider that they also killed the rage inside themselves by committing suicide. They sought the state of mind that killed them and a dozen others. They committed themselves to the obsession that broke them. They committed themselves to it *because* it broke them. Most of the shooters, such as T. J. Solomon, the Conyers, Georgia, teen who wounded six of his classmates, have been suicidal as well as homicidal. They wanted to kill the sources of rage outside themselves, but above all they wanted to kill the rage in their own heads.

Perhaps that seems incomprehensible to you. But it needn't. Many people have such experiences. It's like an addiction, for example, where you are so absorbed by and identified with your compulsion that you learn to want it to kill you. Addiction is associated with self-loathing, and so is rage. As Kinkel wrote in his journal, "I don't want to see, hear, speak or feel evil, but I can't help it. I am evil. . . . If there was a God, he wouldn't let me feel the way I do. Love isn't real, only hate remains. Only hate."

If you're wondering what made me so mad, the answer is that I'm finally not sure. Any explanation I have assayed feels like a just-so story I manufactured for a therapist or a newspaper, and also a way to remove the cause from myself, to give someone else (my parents, say) the responsibility. I still want my rage, want to insist that it is mine. Sometimes it's been almost the only thing I had left.

Maybe you can be born enraged. Look at the babies crying in a hospital nursery. While some of them are expressing a discomfort that is for the moment almost tolerable, others seem wracked by a despair so deep that it and the child's body are identical. I imagine myself in DC General in 1958 crying that way, knowing without cognition that the world is wrong and that I want to die tearing it apart.

I imagine it that way because I have no memory earlier than the rage: I don't remember a rageless pleasure. And the most real and in some way satisfying moments I do remember from early childhood were moments of perfect expression of rage; my mother called them "tantrums." I probably didn't look much like I was having fun as I was screaming and tearing things apart, but those were the only moments when my body matched my mind. At all other times I was holding myself in, holding myself back, and even as a small child I was aware of this as dishonesty, as hypocrisy: as a hiding of my self in fear from the world.

From the start, then, expressing rage outwardly was a moral imperative. I always thought, though I may have been deluded, that I could have kept my rage from leaking into external enactment, that I could have appeared to be just another friendly kid. But I always experienced that as a temptation, as cowardice and self-betrayal. I believed that what's good is what's true—I still in some sense believe that—and what was true for me was that I wanted to destroy authority. If I didn't enact that externally, I was just another peon chump like everyone else.

So I demand responsibility for my own rage. But there's no doubt that the people around me shaped it. My father, Frank, was a writer and an alcoholic. He could be fun as hell but he was wildly inconsistent. One day he'd play with my brother and me for hours, the next he'd be so wrapped up in his own head that there was no reaching him, or so out-of-control angry that it was a punishment just to be near him. I got angry back, or I was always already angry, as maybe he was too, and I'd fight him like hell all the way down the line until I simply physically could not fight any longer. We had intellectual arguments, we had screaming battles, we had physical contests, but whatever we were doing he always beat me and I never fucking gave up.

My baby brother, Adam, two years younger, backed off, buckled. From the time he was small, Adam was passive and sad and withdrawn. When he got high, he'd barely speak, and by the time he was fourteen he was getting high all the time. He had a girlfriend named Martha, and after she left him he was hardly there at all; he liked to sit alone with a huge mug of neat gin and study chess books. By thirty he was dead of a heroin overdose. But even when I was little, I knew without thinking that whatever it was that kept me fighting was keeping me alive, and I always fought like my life was at stake.

Frank died in 1980. And I guess he gave me a picture of what authority is: arbitrary, irrational, worse than useless, something that must be destroyed. And he also taught me to destroy it and to claim it precisely in and as the act of destroying it.

My mother, Joyce, is fundamentally a moralist; she expected something like moral perfection from herself and from my father and from us. Her rules were enforced not just by punishments, though of course by those too, but above all by her ethical disappointment, her judgment. Somehow she taught me not to compromise, even with her, and it was her authority and her morality that I was, finally, dedicated both to destroying and to enacting. I thought of her the way I came to think of institutions: implacable and wrong. I came to be even more morally implacable than she was. And I was implacable first with her; to me the small child it seemed heroic not to give in to her rationality.

She also taught me to hold the world and the people in it to a standard. And I did, though it was to mine and not hers, and I trained my rage on it and them when they didn't live up to it. And I learned to turn my rage on myself too at any moment when I was out of control, or false to myself. The true moralist is motivated by rage, and the true moralist had better start with himself. My inner life, in exactly the same way as my outer life, was marred and adorned by my violence.

When I was eleven and twelve, my parents split and my mother remarried. My stepfather shared my mother's moral intensity, but he was a gentle man in a wheelchair who had been a conscientious objector in World War II. And he brought with him my two stepbrothers: Jim, who was five years older than I was, and Bob, two years younger than Jim. Jim had hardly moved in with us when he was busted for armed robbery and stuck in the Maryland State Pen. But Bob settled right on in. He was a party boy extraordinaire: it was wall-to-wall drugs and girls.

I idolized the guy and loathed him. When I brought Beth home after a date, she ended up in his room. Bob had the car, the pot, the cachet, a wicked grin, and an insatiable set of appetites. I wanted to be Bob in a pretty bad way, wanted to be a mannish boy the way he was. Bob and I had a secret: he spent years trying to make me have sex with him. One of the first things he said when he moved in was did I know what a blowjob was and did I want to try it? I didn't and I didn't. But for all the years of my adolescence he badgered me: followed me around trying to catch me masturbating, tried to blackmail me into having sex by every possible means. Once he found a couple of copies of Penthouse under my bed and said he'd tell the parents I had them unless I jerked him off.

I never gave in to these advances (though I've always wondered what happened to my brother Adam), but I did let them infest my head. And one thing I wondered about was whether I was gay. I was extraordinarily anxious about masculinity, especially since Bob wasn't the only problem. By the time I was fourteen, I was continually being chicken-hawked. A man on the bus would sit next to me and put his hand on my crotch. I'd be hitchhiking and the guy who picked me up would start with "So, have a girlfriend?" To which the only answer has to be "I'll get out right here."

In 1983, when he was 28 and I was 25, a guy he knew shot him when they were both smoking PCP a quarter-mile from the driveway of my parents' house. I was there, heard the shot, ran out onto the road. Bob was crumpled up on the shoulder on his knees, like he was kissing the ground. I could see he was dead because his body was perfectly relaxed. I lifted him up and saw the blood coming out of his mouth. His chest was collapsed inward, a red mess.

Masculinity, rage, and violence are so closely connected as to seem synonymous. To "assert one's masculinity" is to kick ass. And I deeply admired and still deeply admire masculinity in this sense. Indeed, it is deeply admirable: rather than trembling in the corner feeling his little feelings, a man turns all feelings into anger and violently transforms the conditions that oppress him. That is one of the most admirable human impulses and a condition for any great creation. That's the way I thought of it at the time: that's who I wanted to be. I wanted to show the world I was a man and Lord knows I could find the rage inside to do it.

So I had the rage and I had the target. I wanted to fight against power in all its forms. I wanted violence as a rite of passage to manhood. I was an anarchist, and at the tail end of the '60s I was an eleven-year-old leftist revolutionary motherfucker. Revolution was the perfect place for me to put my shit. My first target was my school.

For an extreme antiauthoritarian, a large public school is a hard place to be but a beautiful target. It's hard to miss when you're shooting at the whole environment. The institution is essentially carceral: it's a crime not to attend. And my school in the early '70s, Alice Deal Junior High in upper Northwest DC, was a particularly extreme case. No one was doing much teaching or learning. The administration had reduced its goals to keeping people in the building. All the doors were locked, and the administration hired bouncers ("community aides" at 250–300 pounds a pop) who prowled the halls with two-by-fours. I remember my English class gathering at windows to watch a kid running away from the school with an "aide" at his heels. The bruiser tackled him and then started wailing away with the board. One kid was so severely beaten by a French teacher that he disappeared for a couple of weeks and came back in casts.

But it wasn't even primarily the violence against students that hooked onto my rage; it was the lack of connection between the administration and the reality of adolescent life. I regarded the administrators as idiots who were completely out of touch. At every assembly, the principal, A. Lyman Warner, would get up and mutter the same empty catch phrases and clichés, telling us to pull together and, say, reject drugs and violence without having the vaguest notion of where the violence was coming from or why we needed the drugs. It was almost as bad as watching Al Gore run for president: someone had replaced his brain with a collage of idiotic clichés. What I felt most vividly is that these fools with their groupthink and empty theories wanted control over my body. They wanted it to move from place to place according to the bells, wanted to control what I ingested, what I said, what I read, what I thought, and who I was. I simply refused to be treated that way.

My holy text in eighth grade was a book called *The Student as Nigger*, by Jerry Farber, which describes the oppression of students by analogy to the oppression of African-Americans. This seemed doubly appropriate to me because the school was mostly black, and because DC was one of the most racially polarized cities in the world; it seemed to consist exclusively of rich, powerful white folks and dispossessed black folks.

The Student as Nigger is out of print, but I found it on the net. Here's a bit: "You may only study geometry for a semester—or French for two years. But doing what you're told, whether or not it makes sense, is a lesson you get every blessed school day for twelve years or more. You know how malleable we humans are. And you know what good learners we are—how little time it takes us to learn to drive a car or a plane or to play passable guitar. So imagine what the effect must be upon our apt and impressionable minds of a twelve-year course in servility. Think about it."

I thought about it. And I decided that servility was effeminate and the people who tried to reduce you to it deserved destruction. So I dedicated myself to that.

I read *Steal This Book* and *The Anarchist Cookbook*. I seized the mike at numerous assemblies to deliver antiadministration screeds, ran for class president on the "No More Bullshit" platform as the assistant principal ripped down my signs, started the *Alice Deal Free Press* for which I was twice suspended, led a student walkout and strike.

Finally, my friends and I were cutting letters out of the newspaper and threatening the principal "and his school" with destruction if he did not capitulate to our demands to end compulsory attendance and grading. My friends and I broke into the school and spread a stink solution all over the administrative office. Five years later, the place still stank. I organized a group to do the same thing to the US Capitol. We scouted the building and made a floor plan, but somehow it never happened. I tried to bomb some construction trailers at Livingston and Connecticut Ave., but the explosives fizzled. And so on.

And then I took that stroll up Livingston and saw what that backhoe was doing to the woods. I figured I'd strike a blow for the environment against the depredations of man. So I blew it the fuck up.

The moment I sent that sucker to heavy-equipment heaven was one of the most ecstatic moments of my life, because I was released from my rage utterly. Violence is both an expression of and, more importantly, a treatment for rage. At the point where your violent fantasies become real, you don't need those fantasies anymore. That's why a kid who is obsessed by violent thoughts may act on them knowing full well the cost he may pay: because the action is a release from the obsession that devours him. That release can easily be more important to you than your life, especially when, like most of the school shooters and like me, you are consumed also by self-loathing. Bad things, and perhaps good things as well, happen when you really, genuinely don't care whether you live or die.

I was infected by extreme moral seriousness. With all the diagnoses I am offering of myself and the school shooters, I do not want to dismiss as irrelevant or a mere rationalization the extreme revolutionary commitment that my act expressed. It was not a casual set of beliefs, but, for a teenager, a pretty coherent and informed critique of power. My mother and stepfather were leftists and peace activists. By the time I was twelve I'd read a bunch of Marx, and by thirteen I'd converted to anarchism, reading Emma Goldman and Peter Kropotkin. I believed then and I believe now that my hostility to authority is not only a pathology but also a profound truth. We speak of freedom and democracy; we practice war and subordination. The destruction of structures of authority is—and I am saying this as seriously as I can say anything—the only hope there is for equality, decency, and survival.

Perhaps even more significant than the content of the terrorist's political, religious, or moral beliefs is the sheer fact of being willing to kill and die for them. That is a quality of heroes. It was a quality of the people I most admired in both fact and fiction: Malcolm X, for example, or Joan of Arc, or Frodo Baggins. (I spent much of my teenage years immersed in *The Lord of the Rings*, a tale of the epic confrontation between good and evil, truth and lie, and a bloodbath that ends an age of the world.) I wanted to destroy authority, but I wanted to be the sort of person who had the guts or heroism to do something about the state of the world. I wanted to view myself as an extraordinary person.

Now that I'm a middle-aged, middle-class teacher and daddy, I am a better person—less violent and dangerous. I'm also a more cowardly, more mediocre person, a person who's made a thousand safe, self-serving compromises. But this impulse—almost a desperation to achieve moral heroism or martyrdom, to be extraordinary—is what connects Dylan Klebold to Mohammed Atta. A generation or two ago, a hard and fascinating question for historians and biographers was this: what were things like in the soul of Hitler? They were asking after the source and nature of profound evil in human personality. For us, the hard and fascinating question is, what are things like in the soul of a terrorist?

The soul of a terrorist is the soul of a saint. A suicide bomber is an idealist with an absolute commitment to the ideal, a holy person with an absolute commitment to God, a moralist with an absolute courage of conviction. In short, the suicide bomber is a most extraordinary person. In any era, and particularly in ours, truly selfless action is rare, and many thinkers have hinted that it is not possible at all. But in every era, people—especially the young—yearn for selflesssness, yearn to transcend or overcome the self and merge into something greater. They long to show by a heroic act that they are not merely self-interested and that they are dedicated in the most serious way to helping their people, or all people, or the world. It is a romantic yearning, and though selflessness is at its heart it also acts as a claim to be recognized as an extraordinary individual; it is a claim to be recognized as extraordinary precisely in virtue of one's overcoming of the self.

No more convincing proof of that sort of moral heroism is possible than being willing to die for one's fellows and one's values or the God in whom one believes. Many of the early Christian saints were willing martyrs, and many secular heroes possess a mystique in virtue of the same qualities: Martin Luther King, Jr., for example, or Abraham Lincoln. I believe that some of the causes championed by terrorists—for example, the preservation of a culture or of a religious tradition or the autonomy of a people (Kurds, Chechens, Basques, Palestinians)—are worthy causes which demand and justify selfless action. I also believe that blowing people up who are not directly involved in the conflict one is prosecuting is counterproductive and utterly wrong.

But I believe that the impulse of the suicide bomber is fundamentally heroic, though the actions in which it eventuates are monstrous. In many ways it is quite the reverse of the soul of a Hitler: power-mad, ready for murder as a direct aggrandizement of the self. In the terrorist, the greatest good and the greatest evil of which people are capable live in proximity: merge almost into identity. Terrorism results from the application of moral heroism to a situation in which constructive action seems impossible or real targets inaccessible, though I believe terrorism would be utterly wrong even if that were true, and I also don't think it is true; that is, I believe that in a situation in which armed resistance is called for, the military and political machine—the direct instruments of oppression, the people bulldozing or bombing your homes—are vulnerable, and that there is all the difference in the world between attacking it and attacking people on a bus or at a party.

But one has to understand how the terrorist arrives at the place where suicide bombing becomes possible. There is a reason that terrorists are often presented as and thought of as martyrs and heroes. The terrorist, like Hitler, shows how horrendously wrong people can be. But the terrorist, as well, shows how extraordinary people can be. In both directions, in other words, he shows that we mediocre people do not really know our own limits, don't know what we're capable of. The suicide bomber is a monstrous saint.

As late as my early twenties I was capable of getting pissed off enough to try to destroy things. But I also started to learn how to express my rage without destroying myself. For one thing, I medicated it: it's possible to stay high on pot all the time and still be violently angry, but you are unlikely to do much about it. And I learned to write instead of mixing Molotovs: I was a freelance rock critic, and I took it out on the Police rather than on the police. I wrote some very nasty reviews.

I still despise authority. Rage still washes over me from time to time. So I've been asking myself, hard, why I and the people I've despised over the decades are still alive. First, and of most immediate practical impact, was that I managed to get out of authoritarian institutions. My expulsion from the DC public school system was a very good thing. I wound up at a storefront "free" school in Adams-Morgan, where the only ongoing academic program was group therapy, but where the first priority was respecting the autonomy of the students—a positive educational program right out of *The Student as Nigger*. (The school ended at the end of my senior year, when the entire staff was busted for "contributing to the delinquency of a minor.") College seemed pretty voluntary to me, and though the bureaucracies in which I've worked have deeply irritated me, I haven't so far in my adult life had the sort of profound experience of powerlessness I had in public school. I do avoid such experiences to whatever extent that is possible.

And in the ordinary human fashion, I've had to compromise my dreams: I'm no Malcolm X or Joan of Arc; I'm lucky just to make it through a day without a major fuck-up. My rage and my commitment to freedom are still under there, and the rage can still screw up my jobs and my relationships. I am capable of being so angry at people I love that I find a way to get them out of my life just to stop the anger in my head. I often thank God that people in positions of power over me can't read my mind, and I often wish that I could simply stop thinking altogether so I could stop thinking the way I do.

But I want to tell you something: I would not, even now, like to be rid of my anger or my condescension toward authority. Someone who is impressed by authority will never do anything very interesting or original; they're going to be happy to make themselves over into whatever the institutional structure demands. In a certain sense their existence is redundant. People who hate authority, including the school shooters, have done a lot of evil in this world. But by far the greater evils have been perpetrated by authority's enthusiasts and slavish minions: under the Nazis, the Khmer Rouge, the Chinese Communist Party. The thing most to be feared in this world is that people will cease to resist power that is exercised over them.

Of course I do not have a solution to the problem of school violence. But I do know what I would say to Dylan Klebold if I had the chance: The goal is for you and the people around you to survive your rage; it really does not have to kill you. Bad as it sucks, your rage is interesting and useful. And the fact that you're not like everyone else at Columbine High School is nothing but excellent. Try to laugh at those people. Go ahead and ridicule their slavishness, their conformism, their nasty little enforcement of mindless cultural norms. Ridicule them, but don't kill them. Believe it or not, they're in more or less the same sort of predicament, figuring out what to do, muddling through. And then realize that this violent, destructive impulse that you have is actually a saintly and artistic, a potentially heroic, impulse, that you can destroy by creating. Learn to survive the impulse and then learn to use it; we need all the iconoclasts we can get. Do something with what you've got, and praise God that you're no peon.

IX

Detritus

2008

Hating inanimate objects seems entirely senseless. Mere things have no intentions, make no decisions, commit no crimes. They aren't responsible. Why or how would you hate elements of the periodic table, clouds, liquids, rocks?

Nevertheless, far more than I hate any person, I hate alcohol, marijuana, cocaine, tobacco, methamphetamine, heroin. These stuffs or substances, these chemicals and vegetables and the fumes they emit when immolated, take away everything I have and everyone I love, every time. They are mindless, worthless, without value. They are empty. Meaningless. But they are the theme of my life. I came here to think, to study, to write. I came here to make love, to make babies, raise children, make a home, a garden, find some quiet joy. And my life has been dedicated to alcohol, tobacco, marijuana, and annihilation.

Addiction, I tell you, isn't an epic tale of redemption, material for your amazing memoir and appearance on Oprah. It isn't a James Dean movie, a Hemingway story, or a Jimi Hendrix/Kurt Cobain song of suffering, hyper-intense genius. It's dying by choking on your own vomit. It's common as excrement and as profound: reeking, valueless, purposeless, pointless, meaningless.

There's no little essence of wisdom suspended in the whiskey, no sparkling geode inside the rock, no signal in the smoke. There just is nothing there.

My father was an alcoholic, which broke our family when I was ten or so. He died of his addictions at fifty-two, which I believe is longer than his own father lasted. I lost a brother in 1983 to an incomprehensible murder fueled by PCP; I found him crumpled up by the side of a country road, his chest imploded by a .357 projectile. I lost a brother in 1991 to suicide by heroin overdose, after watching him turn from a hopeful little kid to an utterly despairing addict, a liar, and a thief. My third and last brother spent five years in the state pen for armed robbery. He was a junkie, crackhead, and so on, and then a recovering junkie, crackhead, and so on for many years. He expired two years ago in his sleep, his body ravaged by hepatitis, diabetes, and heart disease. In our family, that's success.

I loved all these people, and at many times in their lives they were lovable: smart, funny, real people; loving people; creative, interesting people. They and I lost all that about themselves to piles of stones, lakes of polluted liquid, to chemical processes of purification and adulteration. They and I lost everything we had that we cared about, about ourselves and each other, to inanimate trash, detritus, an ugly little slag heap of rubbish.

I've just come through a marriage that, starting in ecstasy, descended into hell for the sake of drinking, hers and mine. I couldn't stop, and I couldn't make her stop, to hold our family together, to save our home or my sanity. In order to stay alive, I had to leave, full to the brim with love and with loathing. Now I live alone, sober for some six months, in the woods, chain-smoking Lucky Strikes. The woods is the safest place for me. You wouldn't want me in your circle of friends.

My every act of love, every home place, every hint of peace or happiness, is the premonition of another recapitulation of the endlessly repeated loss that has no point or purpose, and has no end but in death.

I've got four children and stepchildren in their teens and early twenties. Daily I expect to hear the worst: the car crash, the overdose, the end. I've already premourned their substance-abuse-related deaths. I expect that my eight-year-old daughter, the most beautiful, joyous little sprite in the world, will grow up and marry an addict, or be an addict, or both.

I've been involved in family interventions, begged people to stop, poured out my soul, shared my experience, driven people to meetings. Tried persuasion by love, or laying the smack down. I've seen people in and out of rehab. My brother Adam was in residential treatment when he overdosed; they'd let him out for a court date. He went down to 14th Street and scored, then died at my grandmother's apartment. She was in the hospital at the time. She herself died a week later, having lost a husband, a son, and a grandson to addiction.

Everyone finds their own road, and their own abyss. Some survive and some don't, for no discernible reason, with no regard for what they deserve. There's nothing I can do.

In my own case, once I start drinking, I don't know when or whether I'll stop. I've had periods from months to many years without alcohol, and I've found my way through various circuitous routes back to drinking. Then I become an evil idiot. I have no self-control or self-respect. I lie. I hide bottles around the house and drink the clock around. I puke my guts out. I'm alternately maudlin or consumed by rage. And I do all this in the service of nothing at all, of an illusion, of something that has never given me any enduring pleasure, only idiotic pain. I've devoted my life to it; it's my theme; my greatest love; my most intense relationship. And it's nothing.

Putting it mildly, I'm not alone in these sorts of experiences, and a lot of people have been through even worse. What it's like being a meth addict or actually dying of alcohol poisoning, I don't literally know, yet. But if you think people are doing things like that in order to feel good, I say you're crazy. In my experience, in certain circumstances, booze makes you feel kind of giddy and loose for a little while. It makes you feel close to people. It makes you feel bold. That lasts about an hour, which is followed by years of just feeling physically sick, acting badly, feeling guilty, lying, pretending to be the person you used to be, breaking promises: in short, suffering, and making people suffer.

Marijuana may be a youth cult, a medicine, a sacrament, a symbol. But really it just makes you feel kind of fuzzy and dazed; it amounts to a kind of apparently enthusiastic self-lobotomy. I've smoked every day all day for years at times in my life, and never gotten back anything worthwhile or even pleasurable.

There are various ways to try to make addiction make sense, but I think that in the end it shows us nothing but the void, a kind of yawning maw of meaninglessness. Addicts often turn to God, and Lord knows our only hope may well be omnipotence. But addiction, in my view, stands as a refutation of the existence of a benevolent deity. Any God that created these materials, and who created addicts, and then placed us all in the same world is, at best, morally blank.

For that matter, addiction refutes the theory of evolution, at least the version on which we're adapting ever more successfully to our environment. Folks like me aren't adapting to our environment, we're using it to drive ourselves and everyone around us into despair, then using it to commit suicide. But amazingly, generation after generation, we're passing forward our calamitous genes. The drugs, they tell us in the current neurobiological metaphors, light up the pleasure centers of the brain. Then they dull these centers, leading to the need for ever higher doses. But the pleasure, in my experience, is fleeting and valueless, the dullness interminable, eventuating in excruciating pain and unredeemed death.

I've been in hundreds of twelve-step meetings, and one thing you often hear is people affirming even their own addictions. There was something they needed to learn, and they came out better people. In the end, they found a kind of peace. This is sort of true in some cases, and I have tried to think it through that way myself. But fundamentally, we wouldn't need this particular redemption if we hadn't subjected ourselves and everyone else to this particular degradation. And if addicts and addiction can be redeemed, we just as or more often simply descend by endless pain into meaningless annihilation.

If you think that addicts are hedonists, or that we suffer from lack of willpower, I tell you that you are wrong. Addiction is an incredible discipline of pain. It takes will to keep drinking in the face of a crumbling world and a crumbling personality, to keep giving yourself over to the nothingness when there are real people, things, and values all around you. It takes incredible dedication.

During our marriage, Marion took heroic measures to keep drinking, every day. I was sober thirteen years when I married her. A daily heavy drinker for many years, she said the fact that I was a recovering alcoholic was one of the things that drew her to me. She declared herself to be an alcoholic (a declaration long since totally repudiated) and swore off. Once she started again, two years into our marriage, nothing I could do stopped her for a moment, could give her pause: no argument, no effusions or withdrawal of love. Not staying; not leaving. Not my binge drinking, or attempts to recover. No suffering, endured or inflicted. No lies, heard or spoken. No betrayals, of her or by her.

She had her reasons. There were drawbacks to my husbandry from the get-go. I have trouble trusting people; I have "control issues," perhaps familiar to people raised by or partnered to alcoholics, or both or several. I also, I must say, gave a lot of love; I was a fiercely monogamous husband and devoted to our home and children. At any rate, drinking became a symbol, the symbol, of her autonomy, freedom, and integrity. That's a lot of weight to put on a glass, far more than it or I or our marriage could possibly sustain. Indeed, the image of substance abuse as freedom is, in my world, too fatal to be ironic. She loved me totally and forever, didn't want me to leave. And when I asked her to quit for a month, for what I conceived to be, for me, a matter of life and death, she simply refused. I don't have a problem, she said, over and over. It's your problem (well, no denying that). Then: I won't change my whole life. Can't you love me for who I am?

The nadir in our relationship came last December 26th, when after yet another of my struggles toward sobriety, and after yet another week during which she was out drinking every day, I started swallowing the contents of and then smashed her bottle of pinot noir on a counter. Smashing that bottle was a threat, a cry of despair, an expression of desire and of hatred, an act and an end of communication. It exploded the brittle form of our marriage and splattered the black-red stuff of our very blood all over the kitchen.

Then I was driving randomly around Pennsylvania with a liter of vodka in my passenger seat, or passed out in twenty-dollar hotels, learning nothing. Trying not to think about who I was or what I'd done. I thought about driving north for a couple of days, becoming someone else. But I am a coward, and I came back to that same damn house. And after that? In a house back in the woods, no longer living with my kids or my garden or my lover, gone from what had been my life for a decade. Among other things, doing to my children what my father did to me.

No matter that these things we drink or smoke or shoot up are small simple materials of limited usefulness; they always become an astounding symbol, until people are using the words synonymously with freedom, love, integrity, truth, art, self-esteem: synonymously with their own proper names. In their essential relation to us, they are lies; and the spawn and origin of lies, our selves as lies. *In vino veritas*, or maybe just fucking alcohol, a sign only of nihilism, of the journey we make—together, and each in our isolation—into oblivion.

The stuff is the void not only around us but inside us. We swallow it, and it in turn swallows us. Finally, it's all that's left: "who I am," "my whole life." From a recreation, it becomes our origin and our destiny.

I'm sorry to show you only the rage and emptiness. But the emptiness is my true home, the darkness where no one can hear me raging or sobbing; giggling maniacally at the fatal ironies; reciting the mindless, mechanical repetitions; telling over the losses; where no one can find me where I'm hidden. The loss is infinite, and infinitely repeated, and utterly unredeemed by time, God, or meaning.

It may be that addiction is genetic; or that, as they like to put it, it has "a genetic component." My family seems to confirm that. Maybe it is a biochemical problem. Perhaps addicts have no control over our ingestion. One thing that believing this might do for me: relieve myself and people I love of some of the overwhelming, the unbearable responsibility for the terrible things we've done to ourselves and each other. It gives us the gift of fate. And though having a dark fate is depressing, it's also of course comforting in comparison with retrospectively examining the decision to shape the disastrous future we now inhabit.

I find myself confused about this. Every time I have raised a bottle to my lips, I have felt free, and I have felt compelled. I made a decision, and the decision felt inevitable. I could have done otherwise, and I did what I had to do, what my identity and history demanded. Indeed, every time I raised a bottle to my lips, I kept faith with my father and brothers and my wife, my love; I shared their life and death. I kept faith with what we are, and I betrayed us.

Finally, I don't forgive, and I don't want to be forgiven. I don't forgive my father, who left and never could be counted on to be where he'd said he'd be, or be what he said he was. I don't forgive my brothers, and my love for them is mixed with hatred and the most bitter disappointment. I don't forgive Marion, who, like all these other people, chose blank stuff instead of me, over love. And I don't forgive myself. I want responsibility for every act, and I can't bear it. I swing back and forth day by day, and on a bad day like today, minute by minute. Maybe it's our genes, our upbringing, our disease. But I don't forgive.

If it comes to us as fate, addiction makes us into inanimate objects. We are the sheer substances we abuse. But I can't even stop blaming mere things: the crap we imbibe. That too, might offload some responsibility, might be a lie that gives comfort. On the other hand, maybe alcohol can't support hatred any more than it can love; perhaps it's no more an adequate symbol of stupidity and degradation and lies than it is an image of God and beauty and truth. But I can't achieve any real neutrality, and if it were up to me, I would simply erase abusable substances and substance abusers from the universe, and believe that the universe had become a better place.

I'd like to leave you with a positive little moment, a warming hint of redemption. I have not entirely forsworn that possibility, even in a world of pointless self-inflicted suffering. Despite all the rock-solid evidence to the contrary, I still have hope for myself, and for any of us who have survived thus far. I'm still looking for a map of the void.

If there is redemption for me in addiction, it is in being made to see, by force, the darkest of truths; being forced to see, through the destruction of illusion after illusion, the emptiness at the heart of everything. Finally, what I hate most about addiction is its lies, our lies, layer after layer of jive. In my darkest moments, I conclude from rich experience that there is always a lie even at the center of love. Truth sucks, but lies are murder.

But though addiction makes us lie, feeds on lies, it also finally—or at least this is what I hope—makes the falsity of these lies undeniable. Peel back the lies and you find, at the heart, nothing. And arriving at nothing is finding the truth. I worry that in finding what we need to recover and to forgive, finding God or identifying our actions as a disease, we just find more illusions, that we're still, after all the awful confrontation with the truth, lying to ourselves. I want any illusion that will keep me alive. And I want out of all illusions, to see plainly the awful heart of reality.

I turned fifty yesterday, itself something of an achievement in my world, and I keep wanting to be alive, to believe love can be real, to grow tomatoes, to take care of children. My little woods are beautiful and alive with birds this time of year. There's something that so far keeps me quitting, which is why I've outlasted most of the people and things I've loved. I still want it all to make sense, and still suspect that every way of making it make sense is another layer of falsehood. But at this moment the only account that's true to my experience is one that keeps faith with the senselessness, the sheer loss, and leaves it at that.[1]

Postscript on my great love: nicotine gum. I have been addicted to it for years. It has its drawbacks, especially that it's kind of expensive. But I'll tell you this: it shows addiction in its pristine form, and in my life the distractions and layers of jive have slowly been pared away through the administration of pain, and I realize that there's nothing left but an addict in his pristine form.

There are all kinds of reasons people engage in substance abuse, or that they say they do. They are medicating their depression/anxiety/psychosis. They love the social dimensions down at the bar or the crack house: it's the fellowship, baby. They love the ritual: filling the bong, fumbling with the cigarette, cooking the h. Every and any reason besides that they are actually addicted to the active ingredient. Now I suppose nicotine is some sort of mild stimulant; even if so, no dose at this point actually has any discernible psychotropic effects on me. The stuff makes no change in my consciousness that I am aware of.

Of course, sadly, people can reach this point with vodka or crack too. But I don't think anyone would say they chew nic gum for the way it makes them feel, much less for the social aspect, or to treat their depression. Indeed, I can keep drinking or smoking pot even though I actually hate the way it makes me feel. I've had moments where I liked the way booze or pot made me feel, but whole long periods where I didn't at all, where I just felt stupid and sick and profoundly inactive. That just isn't the reason I did them; indeed it might be closer to true to say that I did them because I wanted to feel bad. (Maybe that sounds bizarre, but let me ask you this: Have you ever wanted to be sick? Ever feigned sickness or convinced yourself you were sicker than you were? Ever wallowed in sickness, lingered over it, delectated it?) But after a bit, it hardly mattered either way.

No, the only thing addiction to nicotine gum has going for it is that you chew it, then you spit it out, then you jones for another piece. Believe it or not, you start to think it's beautiful; you start to love the nonflavor, the funky caulklike texture. But that's just your mind, addicted: actually these things just can't be lovable; without nicotine they palpably would have no allure. I've heard people after they smoked like mad for years saying that they're as addicted to the ritual as to the nicotine, or even that nicotine has nothing to do with it. Um, horseshit. You'll tell yourself any damn thing to keep going; you'll actually feel the amazing allure of the ritual or whatever even though you actually don't feel it at all, believe it or not. This shows you with extreme clarity the human capacity for self-delusion.

It would surprise me if alcohol or heroin were used as a treatment for depression: it makes depression worse in a dozen ways at once. That doesn't matter, because you're addicted. Then you try to work it out in therapy. Good luck.

Addiction to nicotine gum won't destroy your life, or put you in the cancer ward (I hope!). So it's a good addiction in that sense. On the other hand, it won't alter your consciousness, which might be unfortunate. But it is addiction—real disease and real commitment—in its crystalline form: the very essence. It is me, purified.

X

Tangled

What If Aesthetic Properties Were Real?

2009

So here's how to think about the universe. It's sort of a fabric; or, better, a skein, or perhaps a tangle, snag, snarl, mesh, mess of rough twine, tied back on itself in many knots of many kinds. It is a network of knots, we might say, but the arrangement is not fully comprehensibly ordered; it is not a very convincing grid, especially as interpreted or construed from within.

I am going to use *skein* as a quasitechnical term expressing the midpoint between a sheer mess or pile of tangled, knotted string and a Cartesian grid. The world consists of many strings or ultimately a single string tied together or back on itself, forming something that looks like a fabric at a distance, consisting of myriads of knots closer up. Each knot is "an individual"—a person, tree, appliance, county. Each knot has a distinct form and location and physical composition (that is, the portion of material of which it consists is different from that of any other); but it is itself absolutely nothing but a set of relations to other portions of the skein: it consists without remainder of string in connection. Different points of view on the skein produce different impressions, so that at a wider angle larger structures emerge: clusters of knots etc. But the skein itself does not depend on any point of view, cultural practice, interpretation, description, though groups of people operating in a practice are themselves knots of knots in connection or conversation.

Emerson says: "A man is a bundle of relations, a knot of roots, whose flower and fruitage is the world. His faculties refer to natures out of him."[1] It's true that "the fabric of reality" is an old saw or the merest cliché; you keep running into it in everything from Confucius to the Greeks to the latest popularization of string theory or what I am calling knot theory: the theory of entanglements, universe as macramé or crochet. From one point of view, the fact that I am harping on a cliché is a drawback. From another, of course, it suggests that I have latched on to some fundamental insight.

With regard to the science or everyday experience of the knotscape, we might say that you could pick out indefinitely many structures or introduce various ontological ordering principles for various purposes: taxonomies of knots, identifications of subknot elements to show the structure of particular knots (precisely the function of skein analysis in knot theory). But for a given claim to be true—for us to say something true about the universe—entails that the skein actually has the structure attributed to it. In some sense what counts as a knot has to be fixed and poses a question—Is that tangle a single knot or a stack of knots or not a knot at all?—the answer to which always depends on the standpoint taken up, or the rough ontology.

The way we order the array into individuals, however, is not whimsical or merely conventional. Indeed, if we did not order our experience of the world more or less the way the world actually is, we would long ago have been extinguished. We order the world from within the world, as part of the world. If we didn't distinguish lions from various portions of their environment, we'd merely be prey for something in turn able to distinguish us. Nevertheless, of course, the body of the lion or the human being is not fully distinct from its surround, and as the lion is breathing, seeing, smelling, eating, excreting, growing, aging, it is in interchange. We are actual creatures functioning in an actual environment; we are of necessity continuously responsive to actual features of it in their emergence through us. We have to "mirror" reality, we might say, but I see attention and perception as much more intimate than that, as an actual taking-in of external objects: perception is ingestion.

Like many people, I at once use or even glorify the term *nature* and suspect it of harboring the entire environmental problem, wrapped up like a seed. But if *nature* means anything, then it means the whole of the skein, whatever in turn that might mean: the skein as it really is under all dimensions of experience and analysis, in all its relations. So what are these dimensions? If I were trying to issue a description of the skein, where would I begin? If I were trying to issue an ideally replete or full description, what would I have to include? And I am of course again speaking from within the world—I am included in what I am describing—and my speaking in it of it is itself a deformation of or a tug on it, a material event.

If I said, for example, that this skein or tangle displayed aesthetic properties such as (for example) beauty, what would I be saying? Or I might point or mark out certain passages, knotscapes as it were. Maybe I like it when they fall into a regular or predictable repeating pattern; or maybe I like fantastic concatenations of string. Maybe I reach up and make adjustments, in illustration of some point, or just as a matter of more or less arbitrary preference. So if I were trying to give a description of the skein, I might resort to aesthetic qualities as holistic sensible qualities of particulars, of regions, or of the skein as a whole. As significantly, aesthetic values may be guides for interventions in the knotscape: ways of tying etc.

If I said of any such thing or array that it was "beautiful," you could take this to denote approval, but typically there is also more that I could say, and there is certainly more that I can say if I'm a professional: about what qualities it is beautiful in virtue of, about what makes the pebble or the painting or interstellar space beautiful. Well, essentially we are in this position with regard to all qualities; they are qualities, as it were, of the ontological object that consists of a culturally embedded perceiver/speaker/body in juxtaposition with the thing or situation being experienced or described, suspended in juxtaposition in an atmosphere or tangle of air and light and language.

There are—let us say: provisionally or apparently—four salient moments or zones or aspects of the act of asserting of something that it is beautiful: (1) the object or array as it exists outside the interpreter (let us suppose) in space (let us suppose); (2) the perceiver of whatever sort; (3) the set of vocabularies and, more widely, social practices that have to do with beauty, and (4) the environing conditions, as light or weather, or the objectual surround and so on. Now I start by distinguishing these dimensions or aspects—the objective, the subjective, the social, and the environmental—but the idea that "physical reality," "social practices," and "subjectivities" can actually be distinguished in a principled way is the very notion I want to destroy.

Twentieth-century philosophy took it upon itself to collapse the distinction between the individual and the social: you see this in the work, for example, of Mead, Wittgenstein, or Foucault. And you saw it in Rousseau, Hegel, German nationalism, and Marx. Now I think that this collapse often took a distorted form; it just reduced the individual to the social, whereas the collapse should have been mutual and simultaneous. But at any rate, having collapsed the social/individual distinction, we should proceed to destroy the distinctions between the material surround—that is, nature, the objective—and the social, and between nature and the individual. Bruno Latour's work should be exemplary here, and his view that each object that sociologists could study is a "lash-up" of (what have been considered) social, individual, and material factors finally motivates a desire to completely forgo/destroy all the concepts involved, particularly "nature" and "the social."[2] "The social" is a version of what is also called "the artificial," the fabricated or man-made, and of course "the artificial" is the proper complement to nature, so that finally the term *nature* only registers our own apartness from the world; nature is itself an artifact of this artifice, "nature." This is why I say the whole environmental problem is wrapped up in the concept. Whether nature is the garden from which we have fallen, or the mere material over which we as spirits have dominion, the human and the rest of the material world are bifurcated in a false but potentially conceptually fatal way. In particular, the social is opposed to the merely or the rawly material; "social" explanations of race, gender, and so on, resist precisely the naturalization of various socially determined vocabularies or taxonomies.

At any rate, if I use the term *nature*,—and I may—I intend to pick out absolutely everything, including everything we are as human beings and everything we've made and every intervention we have performed in reality. Really we have no idea what the universe would be without us in it or with only us in it. Of course, this idea of talking about the whole or the one without the other may be nonsense, and is itself apparently outside the set of which it is a member. But on the other hand I don't think we are going to be able to stop talking about the whole: we are so adept at the encompassing abstraction that the ultimate encompassing abstraction beckons irresistibly. And among other things when we talk about the whole, or when we order things, including individuals, into wholes, we are entering aesthetic territory.

Latour argues that we ought to replace the social in the surround of the physical: there are no people, practices, institutions, conventions, truths without nonhuman things. The social is entirely embedded in "the material," "nature," the non- or less than or more than human. Without physical objects, he points out, "the social" is an entirely inert mysterious powerless essence that doesn't do or explain anything.

Now when we think of the aesthetic properties of an object, we may think of its form, or qualities of its form. If form were to be understood, or could be thought, apart from matter, then this would indicate that in some sense the aesthetic properties of a thing are not, as it were, real properties of it; not, for example, "objective" or scientifically ascertainable or studyable properties. But on the contrary, the form of something is precisely its material arrangement. (Here I think we are close in some ways to the dispute between Plato and Aristotle on "form.") The Parthenon, we might say, is that very material under that very configuration. At each actual site, form and material are identical. Every actual object is a site at which matter and form coincide: they coincide at that site, and neither ever appears independently at any site, that is, in any object. Skein analysis describes possible knot configurations in an "abstract" way, but the description is a concrete set of inscriptions or image-tokens, and every real knot is made of string.

If we believe that, at a minimum, to describe the form of something is to describe that very thing, which is a material object, then insofar as the aesthetic aspects are the formal aspects, the aesthetic aspects are germane, and material. So for example, of the skein, the question whether it is as a whole well or comprehensibly ordered: is that a scientific question or an aesthetic question? Well, I think that is precisely the sort of thing you hope to find out, detect, or even adore in the practice of science. What would it mean for a system to be well ordered? Various dimensions of fact-value suggest themselves; one is surely aesthetic. We might say that the epistemic standards of science are aesthetic through and through, that the practice demands a standard of rationality that we might call an aspiration to or a reflection of an experience of beauty, its trace.

For example, we might think of an ordering principle like Ockham's razor: a nice way to cut cognitive costs, or maybe not, but above all a standard of beauty in explanation. Indeed the standard is identical to Hutcheson's: the compound ratio of uniformity to variety; individuals comprehended under the single category in taxonomy.[3] Ockham's razor gave us both materialism and idealism, opposed to the death, *aufhebunged* in Hegel and so on, but both committed to the ultimate singleness of the universe, the assembly of all on a single ontological plane; that is, though the materialists and idealists of the modern period disagreed about ontology, they agreed about aesthetics, and that is precisely why even Berkeley at times threw up his hands and said the dispute was verbal: as long as you give me these things—this world, ordered under this aesthetic—I don't really care whether you call them material or mental. He certainly believed that once one no longer believed in the material world, one would just keep doing science the same way as always—an extraordinary idea considering the usual association of science with materialism through the nineteenth century.

Consider a shadow as an object. It is best conceived as a situation, or an aspect, feature, portion of a situation. We might say that the shadow is caused by the light source, object, etc., but in truth it is a mercurial chunk of that situation. The shadow is not called into being by the light etc.; it is the light in its flow, implicating an environment and certain sorts of sensory apparatus. The "modern" account of human consciousness as a *sensorium* or an arena of "ideas" conceived primarily as mental images—the basic notion underlying both "rationalism" and "empiricism"—reifies the shadow, isolates it, severs its connections, or actually deletes the situation that makes it possible and the material of which it consists.

We ought to think of human perception as a penetration of the body by the world: a strand going in and helping to compose the knot, and then emerging again and on to the next. When I see something, light literally enters my body and works its way through it in a series of transformations: my act of perception encompasses an external-world situation, or is itself an external/internal-world situation. My body/my consciousness is composed of stuff appropriated from the environment; it is not distinct from the environment in any sense. My consciousness is a trace or shadow in, or better, a knot of, a physical reality.

The same is true of the social both ways round. So first of all, all these individual events/situations of perception are parts of the social. My consciousness is a portion of the social as a knot is part of a larger section of skein, or indefinitely many larger sections. But social vocabularies, narratives, descriptions, and so on, are massively constrained by a physical universe. That social systems in some sense emerge from physical environments is a commonplace idea, though no doubt controversial in the sense that a linguistic idealist such as Rorty would not even give me the term *physical environment* or would regard it as an artifact of social practices, language games, and the like. Well, it is an artifact of social practice, but no more than social practices are artifacts of it. Again Latour's work is exemplary here, and he shows minute by minute, detail by detail, how social practices are continuously embedded and re-embedded in physical objects, as they transform those objects according to their recalcitrances, are transformed by those objects according to our own recalcitrances, and so on.

Truth, we might say provisionally, is a snarl of such portions or aspects, their mutual compromise or annihilation into each other. So "The tree is beautiful" implicates the social in, for example, a romantic celebration of nature. (Behind it lurks Muir or Thoreau or Wordsworth etc.: a whole history and vocabulary of appreciation characteristic of big swaths of culture.) It implicates the social for that matter in that *beautiful* is a word and there are no private languages. *Tree* is a word too, believe it or not. That it picks out what it does and fails to pick out what it doesn't isn't any individual's decision. Perhaps it implicates the social in that in emitting the utterance I am trying to do something with you or to you: impress you, agree with you, attack you, distract you. Of course "The tree is beautiful" notoriously implicates the individual in her subjectivity; in fact some thinkers make it merely a trace or expression of a supposedly purely subjective experience, a variety of pleasure, for example. This, as even its advocates such as Santayana have seen, appears to make sentences like "The tree is beautiful" sheer mistakes, since it is on this account not about a tree at all. But at any rate, entirely delete the "individual" or "subjective" dimension of the experience and it is senseless to talk about beauty. But I also insist on this—and here I call on the shades of Muir, Thoreau, and Wordsworth to testify—when I say "The tree is beautiful," I am talking about the tree, not about myself. "The tree is beautiful" does not mean "I feel funny."

Meaning is neither only out there among things themselves nor only in the head or the language but is an interaction of persons and environments, physical or virtual, stone or televised image. The attribution of an aesthetic feature to a thing involves a language and a culture and an experiencer, but if it's true, it picks out a real feature of that thing in its context. Attributions of aesthetic properties to things are not merely objective, not merely subjective, and not merely culturally fixed: the aesthetic features of a thing are features of it in a situation that implicates all of these, in every case. We might allow this to show us that the distinctions between the personal, the social, and the material simply cannot be maintained. It's skein all the way across.

Again, in my view, aesthetic features of an object—its shape, let's say, and the ways that shape has meaning within a culture—are no more subjective than any other qualities of an object, for example its weight; indeed it is not hard to imagine cases where weight itself is an aesthetic feature of an object. People can be simply wrong about the aesthetic features of an object: aesthetic features become evident in interpretations of an object, but these interpretations are called forth and constrained massively by the character of the object, its origin, its material, as well as by real and recalcitrant features of the culture from which they emerge and the discourses in which they appear.

That is, attributions of beauty are true only under conditions that implicate "the natural," "the linguistic," and "the subjective" in every case. What makes truth possible in this sense is that these aspects are not insular, but strands of the skein all snarled up together. If we said beauty is in the eye of the beholder as opposed to being in the objective world, we would be entirely confused. The eye of the beholder is itself in the objective world. If you don't believe me, pluck out your left eye and look at it. There it is! This is true of your "mental images," true of every aspect of human consciousness. In fact the characteristic derangements of human consciousness derive from losing or severing some of these strands: someone tried to cut off the psychotic's knot.

Now I'm not sure what to do with properties in general in ontology, but allowing them in and to function nonproblematically for a moment, we could also try to treat them according to the skein or snarl idea. So for example, I suggested that under certain circumstances weight is an aesthetic property. That's one of the reasons building in stone is interesting or important, or that the fact that a structure is made of stone is an aesthetic aspect of it. The weight of the pyramids, or the sheer fact that relative to the human body they are immensely heavy, is at once a physical/external, a political, and an aesthetic feature of the pyramids. (Politically, we might say, the weight is an expression of the immense strength of the pharaoh, or his immense ability to annex the strength of others; cf. the Pentagon.) Well, every physical object has weight (I think!), so it follows that every thing that exists has an aesthetic property, or has properties that in the right circumstances/juxtapositions/connections can be considered aesthetic. Weight is chosen almost at random here, and in this way of thinking about it, in connection to certain lash-ups, every object has myriad aesthetic properties. These properties are as objective and as nonobjective as any other real properties: they are as objective and as nonobjective as weight, for example. The aesthetic is lashed to the weight properties, color properties, size properties, and shape properties and with the ways all of these interact with each other and with an entire physical/social/individual world.

Now you might think that, for example, aesthetic features like beauty have no actual physical effects, or have such effects only in relation to perceivers.

Of course when I see Lauren Bacall or her image on the screen and think she's beautiful, this does have physical effects: I reorient my body, stare, blood rushes here and there, neurons fire, etc. But that is because of my experience of the image; these things are happening in a conscious experiencer experiencing this image. But if weight is an aesthetic property, then subjectivity is not required for an object to display an aesthetic property. If you dropped a pyramid on me, it would smash me flat as a pancake, and not because I was interpreting it in a certain way. Yet it would not crush me if I did not exist as a body of a certain kind. If another kind, maybe I could catch it and toss it back, or brush it off like a fly: different "subjects" have different responses.

So let us entertain this idea: aesthetic properties are exactly as objective as any other properties, which is to say that they are features of a situation implicating many levels of "being": again, a physical object in a physical context, a set of social practices, a set of personal experiences. Delete the personal experience and you have deleted the beauty, not because beauty is subjective, but because subjectivity is one strand in this knot; it ceases to be the particular knot it is when this strand is disentangled.

The approach I'm suggesting means that environmental aesthetics ought to be considered epistemically legitimate: it is engaged in discerning the real qualities of real things. Indeed, the reality of things is at the heart of one's respect for them; to say they are real is to acknowledge them; that is, to exist is to count one way and another: ontologically, epistemically, morally, aesthetically. And then the question is, in any particular case, how and how much? So values are in play in ontology from the outset, and I'm pushing the idea, of course, that you cannot fail to broach questions of aesthetic value in particular.

But I'm also going to issue some cautions: We are not some outside force pouring artificial materials into a natural atmosphere, hence damaging it; we are creatures doing what we do with and as the materials we find around us. I'm not sure we could even make sense of the idea of "damage" without having at least two agencies, or an agency in juxtaposition with an object. But if we are hurting nature, of course this is nature hurting itself. Our "destruction of nature" is its own self-destruction, though I don't think that "destruction" is ultimately going to make sense here. And then a question might be: how if at all would such an insight—if it is an insight—change our practice with regard to particular environments or environmental issues?

That might be the question that would most interest you. I cannot really try to deal with it in any full-fledged way here or perhaps anywhere.

But I do want to suggest that a complete acknowledgment of our complete inherence in the natural world would indeed change some of our practices. We have to start with an insistence on acceptance or affirmation—this world, exactly as it is with us in it, is the world. We have to try actually to experience our connections, in detail, an experience that has withdrawn under the pressure of a bad metaphysics or a wrong self-image—self-congratulatory or self-loathing—of the social, artificial, human, as a different order or position within the whole. And one thing I am saying is that withdrawing our grandiosity about ourselves as either masters or stewards of nature, as its users, destroyers, preservers, does not require us to stop deploying values or trying to act in accordance with them.

On any reasonably naturalistic conception of human beings—any conception even vaguely compatible with science, for example—we are natural creatures, one variety of mammal. And on any even slightly empirical account of natural history, ecosystems are volatile. Most environmentalists, surely, would accept these assertions. And yet almost every sentence out of their mouths contradicts them.

On certain construals, the environmental movement rests on a picture of human actions as encroachments on the order of nature: according to this picture we are distorting, manipulating, and destroying the earth. We have lost our connection with it. But if you believe that we are part and parcel of nature, that we emerged as an animal species by natural selection, then the picture of us as attacking it is an impossible picture. We are it. Everything we do—from hiking the Appalachian Trail to spewing toxins—is completely natural.

Environmentalists often seem to want to return ecosystems to a pristine condition, a natural balance or harmony that we have disturbed. But ecosystems are not static, not even strictly cyclical, and they are in continuous interaction with one another: no ecosystem, not even the entire earth, is a biosphere sealed off from elsewhere. Species have been appearing and disappearing and traveling the globe since life emerged, colonizing this environment, abandoning that one. Some ecosystems display some elements of balance or harmony for significant periods of time. But such harmonies are always provisional and always in the process of being compromised, whether we're the ones doing the compromising or not.

I live in rural Pennsylvania, more or less in the woods, though there is a strip mall about three miles away, with a Walmart and a Wendy's. (The video store, of course, is defunct, thus destroying the balance of strip mall.)

People have lived around here for centuries, and their traces are everywhere: in the fields cleared for farming, the old stone fences and ancient structures slowly crumbling into the earth. There are little middens here and there, where folks in the good old country tradition have dumped their broken bottles and kitchen scraps.

I haven't actually done a census, but it's hard not to see that there are "invasive" or human-introduced species everywhere. The English ivy grows luxuriantly along the ground and is ascending the trees. Gangs of starlings waft hither and yon. Chinese chestnuts feed the gray squirrels. Invasive European-Americans appear in abundance, though they are fewer here than in some spots. This year we were invaded by stink bugs.

But the place is deliriously alive. I think of the poison ivy out here as a single entity taking over whole regions with its lustrous green leaves and its nasty toxin, perhaps enhanced by climate change that has made the place just a bit more lush and tropical. There are layers of birds, from the hummers and finches and chickadees, through the doves and pigeons, to the several species of woodpeckers overseen by the big pileateds, to the kestrels, sharp-shinned and red-shouldered hawks, to the turkey buzzards floating at altitude. There are voles, chipmunks, colonies of feral cats, foxes, bobcats, coyotes, deer (along with tree stands for those who enjoy shooting them). The other day a raccoon toddled into my house when I let in my cat; I'm not sure which of the three of us freaked out most.

That, I must say, is a good enough ecosystem for me, and I think that perhaps we should think of any such system in terms of its vitality and volatility rather than its stability. We should note and we can value its imbalances and disharmonies as well its balances and harmonies. And I participate, not only by a feeling of oneness or something, but with my chainsaw, the old mops I toss into the old dumps, my herbicide. I grow roses and butterfly bushes and hybridized tomatoes. My house is as much a part of this ecosystem as the boulders, and I as much as the raccoons.

Plants and animals, as I say, have been moving around and expunging one another since they existed at all. We are one way they do that, and we are animals who do that ourselves. The globe has been cooling and warming since there was a globe, and we are one way it does that too.

The picture of us as disturbing or destroying nature is exactly as supernatural as the religious orientations according to which it was all put here by God for us to do with whatever we please. The environmental movement is still locked into a picture of us as immaterial souls—or at any rate things well beyond nature—who are invaders or visitors on this earthly plane. And it is just as devoted to controlling or altering this order as the rankest industrialist. We are still trying to transform the world according to our little conceptions, only now our conceptions are slightly different: we'll control it to return it to a pristine balance that emerges only out of our imaginations and has the status of a deity that prescribes moral standards.

We had better think about what the aesthetic properties of this . . . eco-system, network, skein, web, fabric, really are. For one thing, as I say, it's not a steady-state or really even a cyclical system, though it displays all kinds of epicycles or loops; it's a volatile system. It's explosive: more like a Caravaggio than a Raphael. This is true of global temperatures, of course, and we are just one of many factors that have cooled or heated the atmosphere of this earth. This is, I'm afraid, a reality to which we are going to have to reconcile ourselves, but it is an aesthetic reality among its other dimensions. We can no more produce a steady ("sustainable") condition than we can detect one already out there, or detect an equilibrium or balance that we are disturbing. There is in nature exactly as much equilibrium as there actually is, with us in it. We are not dealing with an invariant or cyclical nature but a tangle in time, tangled time. We are in a situation/juxtaposition/collection of ourselves and everything that isn't us. It/us is in the process of shifting: growing or shrinking, heating up or cooling down, bringing up the volume or turning it down.

We have to understand the human effect of nature, in other words, as nature's effect on itself: of course, what else could it be if you have any tendency toward naturalism? The idea that we are called upon to save or redeem the earth is exactly as committed to an ontology of supernatural beings (namely, the people who endorse the idea) as is the idea that we are the masters of the world and can legitimately, for example, use members of other species however we see fit.

Even within the wacky pluralism and mere metaphor of which I've availed myself so far, I want to say that I remain committed to some sort of basic materialism. We have got to try to hold on to the materiality of an aesthetic experience in a forest or in a museum; we need to hold on to particular bodies and objects: that's part of what it would mean to love the world or for the world to be beautiful. Materiality is what makes the world funky, what makes it external to ourselves, but also what makes ourselves part of it.

Thoreau writes: "What is it to be admitted to a museum, to see a myriad of particular things, compared with being shown some star's surface, some hard matter in its home! I stand in awe of my body, this matter to which I am bound has become so strange to me. . . . Think of our life in nature,—daily to be shown matter, to come in contact with it,—rocks, trees, wind on our cheeks! the solid earth! the actual world! Contact! Contact! Who are we? where are we?"[4] I think matter is mysterious and more or less adorable. Or it's a bitch, really, but I wouldn't do aesthetics without it, not when every artistic process is a transformation of materials by person and person by materials.

In other words, to begin with, art has to be conceived in terms of human/nonhuman assemblages: conceptual art is all very nice, but there really is no private art any more than there is a private language, and the work of art is a development in materials, an array of "facts": human/nonhuman material assemblages or skein regions; acts of communication among people and things. All art is environmental art in the sense that it all consists of processes within ecosystems, as well as reflecting objects, expressing emotions, and so on: art is above all a material intervention. This is rather a precious thing to say about a Brancusi sculpture, perhaps (but perhaps not), but it is not at all precious with regard to the design of a city or an approach to land use. Both of these, of course, are of necessity engagements in aesthetic value as well as other values; they are sites at which dimensions or arrays of values converge or are actualized materially. Even to make land-use policies or to design buildings in the complete absence of a desire for beauty or a rejection of it—as in the architecture of Marxist dictatorships—is to manifest aesthetic commitments and to have real aesthetic-material results: really to change the shape of things.

Well then, we need to think about the values we deploy in transforming the world, and here the approach I'm suggesting is compatible in many ways with the tradition of environmentalism. But even acts of imagination and government policies are material transformations. Many values are in play, or they all are, and they themselves have to be conceived as inherent in the world. For example: Do we want to live in an entirely humanized or technological environment? Or maybe out in the woods with Thoreau? Well, neither of these is more natural or more material or more socially articulated than the other. And among other things we ought to think about the dimensions of beauty that open up to experience in each such context. Then we may choose. But the transformations are not merely personal; they are always a participation in, an alteration of, the whole.

So I'm giving a plea for the materialization of art, and hence for the continuity of art with reality, the understanding of human making as an upwelling within nature, a series of natural transformations, tantamount to erosion or vegetation. On the other hand, the aesthetic dimension of nature—perhaps opened up within nature by human making, perhaps not—is factual: something we detect, a series of juxtapositions within the reality in which we and our artifacts and our world are, in our entirety and theirs and its, entangled.

XI

Holding on for Dear Life

The Value of Realism in Art

2012

Let me try to say, first of all, how I intend to use the term *realism*. It's used in a variety of senses, both within and outside the arts. For example, to say of someone that she is a realist might be to say that she has her feet firmly planted on the ground; she's practical. "Realism" might be thought of as the opposite of "philosophy" in this regard, which traffics in abstractions of dubious usefulness, as illustrated by the fact that a realist in metaphysics is someone who believes in a real world external to human consciousness, or alternatively in the actual existence of apparently abstract things such as numbers.

"Realism" can also denote a Machiavellian political orientation or approach to political analysis, cutting through high-sounding rhetoric to the fundamental truths of raw power and self-seeking.

Approaching nearer to our target, "realism" picks out a nineteenth-century literary movement, associated with figures such a Balzac and Flaubert, which often focused on the quotidian lives of what we might term ordinary people. A connected movement in the arts, now associated above all with the name Courbet, criticized academic history painting, for example, by exhibiting rough-hewn depictions of peasants painted on a heroic scale. Among other things, realism in this sense is highly political, and it turns to human reality—the truth of impoverished or stunted lives—in part as a motivation for a democratic or communist transformation.

Courbet's realism is related to the sort of realism I want to talk about, but they aren't identical. I mean to pick out a recurring tendency in the history of Western visual arts, and in the arts of some other cultures, toward accuracy or verisimilitude, a devotion to the way things really look and, since the way things really look is a feature or aspect of the way they really are, a devotion to the way things are. Names I might mention as falling roughly into this history: Van Eyck, Dürer, Brueghel, Ruisdael, Chardin, Eakins, Harnett, Bechtel. Now I admit that the distinction between realism and all its opposites and relatives—idealism, impressionism, abstraction—is an extremely elusive one. Whether Ingres or Manet or Velázquez is a realist, or to what extent or in what dimensions their work is realistic: these are difficult questions. Certainly it's a matter of context and degree, and every intermediate point is occupied; a painting is relatively or extremely or sort of realistic, but it's never perfectly realistic, I believe, or else it would be an indistinguishable replica of what it depicts, a painting of an apple that was actually an apple.

Now the very idea that a painting can look more or less like what it's a painting of, or be more or less accurate, has been called into question by a number of philosophers and art theorists. All in all, no painting is much like a bowl of fruit. I have had a stab at some of the definitional questions elsewhere. Here, I am gesturing at certain works as realistic and others as unrealistic, or defining "realism" by ostension: paintings *like that* are realistic. I will leave it open right now whether "realism" marks out a family of conventions or practices, or whether in some direct sense realistic pictures are more like their motifs than are unrealistic pictures.

One of the traditional opposites of realism in all its manifestations is idealism, a concept at least as multivalent and ambiguous as its antagonist. But at any rate realism and idealism are not only styles of art; they are theories of representation. We might term these accounts of representation *mimetic* and *eidetic*. On a mimetic theory of representation, a picture is a picture of what it is a picture of in virtue of "imitating" it or reproducing certain aspects of it. This is a very ancient theory of representation and, more or less, of art, in both Plato and Aristotle, for example. But developing in the Greeks at the same time is the idea that a picture might generalize from the particular, or might present something better or less contingent than everyday physical reality. Aristotle asserts that poetry is more philosophical than history, on the grounds that poetry shows general truths, history, particulars. From this point of view the great artist occupies a hallowed station as giving us a vision of a better or truer or more beautiful world.

The most ancient theory of art is the mimetic theory: that art is an imitation of reality. Plato, in *Republic,* Book 10, compares a painting or a poem to a mirror that shows the appearance of the world, and he condemns the representational arts on that ground: they are deceptive, leading us only into ignorance. Leon Battista Alberti, in perhaps the most important treatise on art theory in the Early Renaissance, says that painters and sculptors "strive, though by different skills, at the same goal, namely that as nearly as possible the work they have undertaken shall appear to be similar to the real objects of nature."[1] "That painting is most praiseworthy which conforms most to the object portrayed," Leonardo insisted, though one may wonder how well this account applies to Leonardo's own paintings.[2] Vasari, in his life of Masaccio, says that "painting is simply the imitation of all the living things of nature with their colors and designs just as they are in nature."[3] The mimetic view was the common wisdom from around 1400 until at least 1700—the Renaissance and baroque periods—both in Southern and Northern Europe.

The mimetic tradition runs in parallel with what I'm calling eidetic or idealistic views, which hold that the artist does not merely imitate real objects, but improves things, idealizes them, makes them more beautiful, or reveals their essences. In the *Symposium,* Socrates describes the allure of beauty as a seduction into the realm of the Forms: loving a particular beautiful person draws you into trying to understand what beauty itself is. He does not explicitly tie this thought to the representational arts, but many followers for a couple of thousand years did just that. This is "neo-Platonism" as applied to the arts: they are a route from the particular to the general, from the physical to the spiritual, and they accomplish this by an idealization of everyday reality made possible by the imagination. Cicero, in a typical formulation, says this of the sculptor Pheidias: "When he produced his Zeus or Athena, [he] did not look at a human being whom he could imitate, but in his own mind there lived a sublime notion of beauty; this he beheld, on this he fixed his attention, and according to its likeness he directed his art and his hand."[4] I term the underlying view of representation "eidetic" after the Platonic Ideas.

The great neo-Platonist Plotinus argued that the most beautiful things are the most abstract things, the least material things: the Forms, and in particular the Form of beauty itself, which was also identical to goodness, truth, and God. He and like-minded figures in the Renaissance such as Marsilio Ficino conceived art as a transformation of sheer ugly matter by spirit into a semblance or image of what is unsullied by the material realm. Within this tradition a kind of realism could be incorporated: art is a bridge between the real and ideal, and so the real is indeed represented, but as idealized; for example, in painting an ideal of female beauty, one was to study many beautiful women and assemble, as it were, the best bits of each into a semblance of the very Idea of Woman. This is one of the most ancient conceptions of the artist's task; Shaftesbury held a version of this view, as did Hegel. The initial activity is mimetic, but the final product approaches the ideal of womanhood. Then the sexuality of the nude itself was supposed to have a spiritual dimension, and the relation to the ideal that transcends the mundane is an erotic relation that is first called forth by particular bodies.

I think this neo-Platonic orientation, which was cultivated by many humanist philosophers, literary figures, architects, and visual artists from let us say 1420 to 1600, particularly in Italy, accounts for the basic way that works of art tend to look in particular in the Italian High Renaissance. Raphael provides perhaps the very clearest examples. Looking at his paintings, you are in no doubt about their representational content and disposition of the elements in space: the perspective rendering is perfect, and the people and things more or less familiar. That is, there are obviously many mimetic elements. But they are arranged with consummate consciousness into a geometrical or almost abstract array; they are extremely composed. Each person and each thing is a sort of emblem, more or less a perfect example of its kind. One does not dwell on wrinkles or imperfections or idiosyncrasies. And we might remark that this approach relentlessly emphasizes the divinity of Jesus: his transcendence of embodiment into a realm of celestial light.

Idealism of this sort, if I may be so bold, is perhaps an inspiring vision, but as regards the visual arts it is something of a dead end. I do not think that it's a coincidence that Raphael's Madonnas are, as has often been remarked, rather emotionally blank: in her sort-of divinity they transcend any particular personality. Beautiful as they are, they are just a little inhuman, a little too perfect for viewers as flawed as we are; they are disconnected from reality, quite intentionally. We still narrate the High Renaissance as embodied by Leonardo, Raphael, and Michelangelo as a culmination, and though there could be and have been other eidetic arts, I'm not sure there have been or can be better eidetic arts. Idealism is designed to be teleological; when art comes as close as possible to realizing the ideal in reality, then it has performed its task and, as Hegel hinted, it might end. Indeed, the High Renaissance is often represented in sketches of art history as an almost instantaneous or infinitesimal moment of perfect equipoise. The stretch between Leonardo's emergence from the Early Renaissance and Michelangelo's falling off into mannerism is pretty short, and shrinks up shorter the harder you look. Have you ever jumped off a swing? First you rise, then you fall and land or crash. But there's that instant in the air when you at least have the illusion that you are quite still and weightless: that's the High Renaissance. Well, it's been a long fall since that momentary culmination. Hardly had art reached perfection before people grew weary of perfection and started pulling it apart or distorting it quite intentionally: a mannerist and baroque distortion and excess and whimsicality break out in your pristine ideal universe, almost at the moment you've finally got it cleaned up.

We have lost a sense of what is valuable about realism in the arts. This has to do with the turn in romanticism and modernism to the genius of the artist and the intensity of his expression as distinguishing features of art. And in complement, we now actually have devices that are capable of producing images instantaneously that might make Kalf or Chardin gasp or give up: mere mimesis is now something that can be done mechanically or digitally. My idea here is that in recovering the tensions and connections between mimetic and eidetic representations, we can recover some of our sense of the value of realism, and hence reconnect more fully to important aspects of our visual traditions.

It is worth saying that before a series of disciplinary reconfigurations that took place in the late seventeenth and early eighteenth centuries, art was not necessarily clearly distinguished from science: both could be accounted for in part as ways of showing us how things really are, including the conditions under which they are perceived. In Renaissance humanism, the visual arts and the texts of antiquity are equally treated as sources of empirical knowledge, and careful observation in the sciences has always been reflected in careful illustration. Alberti and Dürer, indeed, argued that art is what we would term an empirical science, and they and other Renaissance figures pursued it as such, accompanying it with scientific accounts of light, color, and vision that relied heavily on the theory of perspective. Many, of course, dissected corpses in order to accurately depict the human body, and brought various sorts of items into the studio to render them as accurately as possible. Svetlana Alpers has documented the persistence of this vision of the arts in the use of lenses and instruments such as the camera obscura in seventeenth-century Dutch art and science, and in the connections between the artists and the scientists of the period. Paintings and drawings by great masters could serve, in an era before photography, as both historical documentation and instruments for the development and dissemination of empirical or scientific knowledge. Of course pictures in general, and graphic representations of many sorts, have been central in the development of the sciences, which is usually recovered historically as a series of textually expressed theories, but which is also a history of depiction.

I want to emphasize one other feature of the post-Renaissance reconfiguration of disciplines: the emergence of the fine arts as a sphere of activity in distinction from craft skills. The paintings of someone like Gysbrechts or even Zurbarán are virtuoso displays of skill, something like conjuring tricks. When you go to see a stage magician, you know very well that you are not seeing a display of supernatural powers, but that the illusion is, finally, due to the skill and ingenuity of the performer. This skill is itself necessarily hidden or concealed, which is itself a display of skill. At least some realist paintings are extremely impressive displays of hand skills in this sense, and they conceal the skill from the audience, which makes it all the more evident; you don't see the brushstrokes at all, and yet you know it's a painted surface and yet you can't not see it as a letter rack. Now in romanticism, and certainly by the time of high modernism, art is associated with intense emotional expression or the expression of genius. Van Gogh is certainly not as good a craftsman as Gysbrechts, but that's not the point, and there was a moment—say 1955—where one might have asserted, without great fear of disagreement, that van Gogh was an artist and Gysbrechts not. But let me say this: skill is intrinsically admirable, and it is fundamentally connected to our appreciation of the arts. Indeed the ancient Greek term that is usually translated as "art," *technē,* means, roughly, skill. Even now when we are seemingly well beyond modernism, hand skill is undervalued in what are termed the fine arts, though it is also perhaps coming back into style.

It is traditional that the Renaissance in Northern Europe hewed closely to the mimetic program, whereas the Italian Renaissance always proceeded with a greater admixture of idealism, though of course the matter is immensely complex. Roughly, however, I accept the traditional way of formulating the distinction. As we gaze astonished at the unimaginable skill of a Van Eyck, devoted to getting every detail of the world as exactly right as possible, we see, I believe, the development, which lasted centuries, of a very conscious refusal of the ideal. Taking it the other way round, Northern European realism is a pointed affirmation of the actual. It is above all a this-worldly art. Among other things, this has theological implications; especially as applied to religious paintings, it suggests that God is found in the ordinary as well as the extraordinary. It emphasizes the embodiment, rather than the divinity, of Jesus. Raphael paints Mary as a Platonic Form. In Rembrandt's view, Mary is a perfectly ordinary young Dutch woman raising a baby in an artisan's household, though she is visited by bird babies. (It's hard to tell if her illumination reflects the manifestation of God or of Caravaggio.) In the north, they located transcendence precisely in immanence.

As an artistic orientation, realism has one considerable advantage over idealism: the world is visually and in many other aspects inexhaustible. In the service of this program, artists, we might say, concentrated intently on certain sorts of objects or zoomed in on the details. They invented pure landscape and pure still-life painting, for example, and also the genre scene. These became artistic specialties, and a Ruisdael or Heda or Saenredam could never have emerged in an eidetic tradition. They reached the point of specialization at which an artist could spend a whole career on flowers, or food, or dogs. And I believe that seventeenth-century Dutch artists, and many of their northern predecessors, consciously, pointedly rejected the Italian idealizing style (though of course many also emulated it). In particular, they rejected its grandiosity, even as Italian idealism was being criticized from within by artists such as Caravaggio. Well, imagine what the history of Western art would be without still life or landscape; there are other things out there besides the idealized nude, and even the human body is more or less an ordinary physical object. As far as the visual resources that the world affords, there is no need to stop there, and one might focus a career on a single kind of flower—the rose, say—or even on painting with perfect truth a single flower. One could look ever more deeply into the world—more and more deeply, apparently without limit—by microscope or telescope; the seventeenth-century Dutch saw a world of inexhaustible visual riches opening before them.

Alpers argues that seventeenth-century Dutch artists and scientific illustrators turned to the camera obscura and all sorts of other visual devices in part because these things yielded an event in which "it is as if visual phenomena are captured and made present without the intervention of a human maker."[5] We might think of one sort of tradition in the arts and in philosophy, for example, as turning inward or as trying to explicate the world by means of explicating the human. Even the greatest realist moments in Italian art, for example, center on the human figure. On the other hand, we might first of all represent the thrust of Baconian experimental, empirical science as trying to understand nature on its own terms, or "objectively," which might mean so far as possible taking ourselves out of the equation or trying to erase our own subjectivity in certain respects, in order to allow what is before us to reveal itself. Its proponents thought of this at times as an attitude of self-deflation or humility. "All depends," wrote Francis Bacon, "on keeping the eye steadily fixed upon the facts of nature and so receiving their images simply as they are. For God forbid that we should give out a dream of our own for a pattern of the world."[6]

The realism in seventeenth-century Dutch art arises in part from a scientific orientation. But the way that the sciences themselves were understood and the way they were pursued in the Netherlands and other parts of Northern Europe (notably England) also drew on a history of realistic depiction that was already centuries old; it extends back beyond van Eyck. There are many names one might give this and many connections one might make in the economics, politics, and religion of the region and era: by the seventeenth century the art is intertwined with capitalism, Protestantism, colonialism, and republicanism, for example. Articulating the opposition at its broadest swath, we might narrate Western art history and intellectual history beginning in the Renaissance as a competition and dialogue between transcendence and immanence, or Ficino and Bacon, or humanism and experimental science, or even God and the material world.

So I provisionally want to identify a sensibility of love for this world that pervaded the seventeenth-century culture of Northern Europe. This shows itself in many ways: in a delectation of luxury merchandise and exotic stuffs, in observations of the natural and artifactual environment of unprecedented exactitude, in masterful craft in dialogue with materials, in what might be termed a cult of the ordinary. If Plato condemned the idea of getting to the truth by mirroring reality or picturing it accurately, for Bacon and others who articulated the empirical method the mirror and the lens were metaphors for truth and also practical instruments for developing or investigating it. In the Netherlands, for example, the father and son pair of Constantijn and Christiaan

Huygens systematically prosecuted the Baconian scientific program, using optical instruments including the telescope, microscope, and camera obscura, all of them recent innovations in the intensification and broadening of the faculty of vision, for seeing more and seeing more accurately, precisely the project of northern art. Christiaan Huygens, in the preface of his *Treatise on Light*, expressing his hopes for the book, wrote that "I would believe then that those who love to know the Causes of things and who are able to admire the marvels of Light, will find some satisfaction in these various speculations regarding it. . . . [The properties of light are] the main foundation of the construction of our eyes and of those great inventions which extend so vastly the use of them."[7] One interesting feature of this formulation is that it attributes the structure of the eye and of the microscope and telescope to the properties of light itself; or, generalizing, that the structure of our artifacts and even our biology are reflections or results of the qualities of the external world. Obviously, light is a, or even the, great theme of seventeenth-century Dutch art: famously in Vermeer, of course, but also in many different ways in many different painters: no less in Rembrandt than in Vermeer, though to almost opposite effect.

The notorious pantheist/"materialist"/"atheist" Baruch Spinoza was connected to the Huygens circle; he certainly knew the illustrious Christiaan, the inventor of the pendulum clock and discoverer of the rings of Saturn. Spinoza "polished lenses" for a living, and one would think it likely that he prepared lenses for Christiaan's telescopes and microscopes; Christiaan expressed his admiration for Spinoza's lenses in letters. The right lens in the right condition was absolutely essential for the new sciences being developed and for the new general conception of science—its abandonment of its humanistic origins, which one can see happening very vividly in the writings of Constantijn and Christiaan Huygens. The right lens made it possible to see what was really there, and the creation and use of lenses was connected to the theory of optics under development in philosophy, science, and the arts since the discovery of perspective. The great innovator of the microscope van Leeuwenhoek, who also knew the Huygenses, possibly supplied a camera obscura to Vermeer, who possibly depicted him in *The Astronomer*. Well, that's a lot of possiblies, but what I think should be beyond dispute is that the empirical and realist orientation in the art is connected to the realist or "posthumanist" orientation of the science and of the philosophy.

It would be usual to oppose the empirical, this-worldly orientation of the Northern Renaissance and baroque to various more spiritual or profound or poetic styles of thinking and rendering. But I would like to consider the northern empirical orientation as itself a deep and perhaps even spiritual commitment that underlies together the science and the art (as well as much of the theology and philosophy). I would not explain the pictorial style by the science, nor the science by the pictorial style, but speculate that they arise together from something that runs even deeper. The northern tradition turns away from transcendence and even from subjectivity toward an immersion in and celebration of the things of this world. This actually is perfectly evident from the writings of scientists, which often rapturously and poetically pay tribute to the beauty of real things: the stars, for example. But it is certainly, certainly evident from the art. The still lifes of Kalf, the landscapes of Brueghel or Patinir, the portraits of Hals or Rembrandt: these are just enraptured by the things of this world: celebrations of its amazing stuffs and our amazing artifacts. And in realist portraiture—in which we might provisionally range Holbein, Hals, and Rembrandt—there is a reintegration of the human with the material world; Holbein loves stuff as much as countenances; Hals and Rembrandt try to reproduce through the external appearance the whole range of human experience, a la Shakespeare, for example. I think in Vermeer this orientation produces objects of an intense, almost devotional beauty. You don't get that by coincidence; you find it in love.

Spinoza was obsessed with collapsing the dualisms between mind and body, spirit and matter, freedom and necessity. But despite his overweeningly rationalist method, Spinoza was at heart both a mystic and a materialist: a fascinating and apparently transgressive combination. He wanted to identify God with nature because he wanted to *adore* nature or to find in the real world a worthy object of his love and his inquiry. Schelling says of Spinoza:

> Instead of descending into the depths of his self-consciousness and from there attending to the creation of two worlds in us—the ideal and the real—he surpassed himself: instead of explaining out of our nature how the finite and the infinite, originally united in us, arise out of one another, he at once abandoned himself to the idea of an infinite outside us.[8]

Schelling thought that this was Spinoza's great mistake, but I am suggesting that it arises from an adorational stance toward the real, a love of the world that rises into mystical identity. The notion that Spinoza both "surpassed" himself and "abandoned" himself seems exactly right to me, and what Schelling doesn't quite see is that Spinoza recovers himself into identity with God and nature. But Spinoza wants to start with "an infinite outside us" and not from within himself. Like his realist contemporaries in the arts and sciences, Spinoza wants to know what the world would be like without himself in it. Spinoza defines "God or nature" as "a being with infinite attributes": God is all that is, and the world-God is an inexhaustible, infinitely infinite object of inquiry from which we ourselves are not, in the end, distinct.

So I am arguing that in seventeenth-century Dutch realism a hard-nosed dedication to accurate empirical observation coexists with, and beautifully comports with, a sort of religion of reality. These painters consciously turn away from Christian themes to dwell in fastidious detail on the qualities of glass or the appearance of a particular insect, but perhaps they are religious painters in their own way nevertheless, and not only because one can often find religious symbols in them. One way to understand Dutch realism is as a pantheist prayer: in landscape, still life, portraiture, you get a celebration of the natural and artifactual environment, an attempt to release oneself from consciousness or subjectivity and to see clearly what really is.

In the centuries that followed, I would say that in many ways this tradition was left behind in the arts; its value became harder and harder to discern, despite outbreaks such as the one around Philadelphia in the late nineteenth century associated with Eakins and Harnett. In philosophy, various forms of idealism emerged which sought to lodge reality in consciousness. And in the arts, romanticism and modernism turned ever more intensely to subjectivity, and perhaps finally lost the world. The arts and sciences go their separate ways at latest by the late eighteenth century.

I don't know how much there is left to explore about the inner terrain, particularly when it is separated in imagination from the external world. Actually, I might say that I'm bored with my consciousness: sick of my four little emotions or whatever; tired of my own little stories. But I think we're still only beginning to explore and understand the external world and show how it also creates and shapes consciousness. Perhaps even if the goal is the exploration of our own consciousnesses (and I don't see why it should be), we can do it through an exploration of the world in which they emerge and with which they are engaged. By itself, consciousness is not much of anything. But whether or not moving outward is the best way to move inward, the world itself is a helluva deal: in the world, we have constant access to an inexhaustible source of beauty and ugliness and sublimity, as well as knowledge and craft and wonder, a being with infinite attributes.

We live now in a world in which realist images appear everywhere all the time: as I say, anyone with an iPhone can make images that would be wonderful to a seventeenth-century Dutch artist or lens polisher. The introduction of photography indeed contributed to the decline of realism in painting: the reproduction of reality was not a worthy project for a genius when it could be performed mechanically. But I do want to remark that realist painting continues, both among weekend hobbyists and avant-garde artists: the project has never been fully abandoned. And in a situation in which you can just snap a shot, to spend weeks carefully crafting a realistic image is a more intense expression of devotion to the real world even than it was four hundred years ago. To apply great craft to the production of a realistic image today is to express a love of the actual that is perverse, but needed. The real is always disappearing behind a screen of images, as many modern and postmodern theorists have insisted. But the character of devotion in some of those images continues to express the eruption of the more-than-human into the human world.

XII

Presence and Resistance

Process in Graffiti Art and Crime

2002

At this point, graffiti is a traditional art, like country music, or like Shaker-style furniture. Generations of writers have moved through the style, rediscovering traditional elements and pushing them ahead. It's possible to have a retro style, or a retrofuturistic style. And at this point too, graffiti has been absorbed and eliminated by the high art world many times: displayed in galleries and museums, then pushed back onto the train. And it has also been appropriated by the advertising world and absorbed into legal urban mural-painting. Surprisingly, though, it retains the power to offend and it continues to be defined in part by its antiauthoritarianism.

I wrote about graffiti once for the *Los Angeles Times*. I defended it in this way. Think about the appearance of advertising in public places. It's everywhere, and though sometimes it's clever or subtle or artistic, more often it's puerile and stupid and it hurts the eye. If you have money, you can put up your tag everywhere, all the time, in all media, from the billboard to the vehicle to the pop-up ad, from buses and buildings to television screens and magazines, from public parks to huge skyscrapers shaped like your logo. Money brings with it an absolute right to convey your message and your name and your image to everyone, to completely dominate space of all kinds. This is an effect, we might say, of capitalism: cash rules everything in this motherfucker;

it brings with it an effective control of public discourse. Speech is free in the sense that it is more or less protected by the Constitution; it is not free in the sense that it costs money.

So graffiti is a medium of public expression for people who don't have the money or the proclivity to advertise. It's an equalization of expression in public contexts, a seizure of space for noncorporate, nongovernmental messages. It's free speech in every sense of the term. It's also a demonstration as clear as any could be that "public" space—parks, highways, public transportation vehicles, etc., etc.—are in fact state-owned spaces. You can't use them without permission of the authorities, though they are often enough peddled to advertisers.

You would not believe the reaction I got to this piece. People actually dug up my phone number and called me at home. I got dozens of emails. And every single one of them went like this: Tell me where you live and I'll come paint all over your house. You don't understand basic property rights. Graffiti is gang-related, sheer vandalism and defacement. It brings a city down to the primal tribal level. It's unhygienic. The people who do it are animals, said one correspondent, while others implied much the same. Don't I understand that I'm condoning criminal activity? That makes me a criminal too. I ought to be arrested, etc. Now I wouldn't have thought that graffiti still had this kind of power to rouse people who identify with the authorities. But it's good that it does.

Really, think for a moment about who are the vandals, the taggers, the lovers of ugliness. Out where I live in rural PA, they've recently added a McDonald's, an Arby's, a Walmart Supercenter, etc. The corporate logos appear on signs along I-83. There are huge signs everywhere. The buildings themselves—cheap, depressing, gigantic architecture—started with the removal of trees, proceeded to the digging of huge pits, eventuated in rectangular concrete bunkers set in seas of asphalt. The idea that the people who do this sort of thing, or even people who tolerate it, would turn around and call real art defacement and vandalism of these same structures is not even ironic. It's sick. All over America, police are protecting concrete abutments, shattered warehouses, and filthy freight trains, not to mention advertising itself, from the original, personal, at times brilliant expression and perfect craft of real artists.

Actually, I hope we're beyond having an argument about whether graffiti is art. That was a reasonable question twenty years ago or more, when people, including writers themselves, were trying to make a case. But now graffiti is art history as well as a living medium. Obviously art of various kinds has been illegal. Modernism was essentially banned by the Nazis as "decadent" and "Jewish." You could lose your life for it. And there are plenty of examples along those lines from all over the world; various regimes ban various forms of art, and set something official in their place. One might think of socialist realism, for example, and the banning of constructivism in revolutionary Russia. It's always legal, however, to erect huge statues of the dictator of the moment.

It's worth thinking about how much the art history that we have is the history of the art sanctioned and funded by the authorities. Much of it in the West, for example, is the history of the arts of the Catholic Church: art paid for and pre-approved by a priesthood. That, of course, is why if you take an art history survey course you end up with an endless procession of crucifixions and Virgins. Many of these are works of genius, from Giotto's Arena Chapel to the Sistine ceiling to the sculptures of Bernini, and so on. But it is also true that the strictures that gave rise to these images—the money available for their production and the punishments inflicted on those who made other sorts of things—had an obviously impoverishing effect on the art that emerged out of them. You've got to be satisfied with formal solutions to a set of problems that were produced by dogmas and bureaucracies. As the graff writer Dmitri Wright says, "Many art forms, which are sanctioned, forget their roots. When you go to the museum and look at the masterpieces you have to realize that a lot of people were oppressed in order for that form to take place."

I'm certain that through all this history there ran a little note of subversion. The paintings of Caravaggio are an example; he was always working on the very edge of what the Church could tolerate. But I'm betting that people throughout this history were also producing illegal art. They were defacing the approved forms, or scrawling subversive messages, or secretly in the black of night doing blasphemous easel paintings and selling them illegally. I don't know how much of this history of illegal art can be recovered. Not much, perhaps, and that is itself a tribute to the power of authoritarian structures to shape not only the visual environment but the understanding of themselves by later historians. The history of the arts brought into being by Imperial Rome, the French court, the Vatican have been written over and over; it is now time to try to write the history of the arts that have been painted over, the history of art crimes, though obviously piecing it together will be difficult.

It seems obvious that criminal art has always been less finished, less beautifully composed and wrought than official art. But no doubt it has been bolder and more sincere. I don't know whether we can write that history or not. But at least we are writing the history of the arts that are being painted over right now, the arts that aren't funded by state grants, or that end you up in jail.

The term *artistic freedom* is, I think, widely misused these days. There was outrage in the late '80s when a bunch of avant-garde artists got their NEA grants rescinded or got kicked out of megamuseums because of political pressure applied by conservative senator Jesse Helms and others. But first of all, that sort of thing is just what you ought to expect in the realm of state patronage and the realm of large art institutions. In fact, I think it's actually wrong for taxpayers to be made to pay for art that offends them, and Helms's political pressure was not only something that should be expected, it was right. Why is a North Carolina farmer paying to display images of Robert Mapplethorpe with a whip up his ass? The artist and a lot of the arts community cried censorship. Let's have the argument. But there's all the difference in the world between being disappointed in your expectation of state funding and actually being expunged by state programs. Withholding your grant is one thing; allocating resources to eradicate your art is something else. And indeed, being part of the basic avant-garde art world—even on its cutting or subversive edge—is one thing, and actually doing art crimes is another. The one is a subversion approved by the authorities; the other is a subversion the authorities still obviously find dangerous.

Let me tell you what art is. Art is process. Or, to give you a more official definition, a work of art is the product of a process engaged in for its own sake, and not merely for the sake of the product. Art is immersion in making; a work of art is the product of an immersion in making. The various forms of art are defined by the processes they involve. Painting is the process of applying pigment to a surface, for example, and if you engage in the process with devotion to the process itself, if you are absorbed in the process of applying pigment to a surface, then what you're painting is art. If you want to know whether something is art, and, if so, what sort of art it is, then you have to focus on the process that leads up to what you see.

So if we want to understand graffiti, we have to understand the processes that lead to it. Here are a few of the fundamental features: Graffiti is made largely by people without a whole lot of money for supplies. Spray paint is the medium because it's fairly cheap or shopliftable (though getting it free of charge gets harder and harder and hence presents more and more of a challenge all the time). And spray paint is the medium also because you can create large and visible forms quickly, which is obviously desirable when your point is to be seen and when the cops might be coming. Really, if you want to understand the medium of graffiti, you have to start with its illegality. It's not too much to say that crime is the medium of graffiti. Now of course some "graffiti art" is legal, and people hire graffiti artists to do murals or vehicles. Many of the best graffiti artists do legal walls, and get paid for doing them. And I personally don't begrudge them this at all. For one thing, kids grow up, and sometimes they get married and have children, and they have to make some money. Legal walls are better for preserving the styles since they won't be expunged by antivandalism squads. Furthermore, you can spend as much time as you want and really do something amazing. Fine. But every good writer started by tagging neighborhoods, trains, or walking bus routes in the middle of the night with a backpack full of cans. That's how writers learn their trade, and that's how a great majority of writers work today as well.

The process of making art illegally has got to be particularly absorbing. It involves concealment, sneaking around in the dark while avoiding the authorities: in short, the medium entails the artist actually risking his safety, whereas so much art involves no real risk. Graffiti is of necessity an adventure. It involves running, infiltration, escape. To say that such things provide the opportunity for immersion in process is an understatement. They fill your art with shots of adrenaline, and even people calmly looking at your art get a reflection of the rush that must have happened when it was made. There's precious little art being made today, after a hundred and fifty years of the relentless avant-garde, that still yields any frisson. Go masturbate in a gallery and people will just yawn. But put up a huge piece over a billboard or in an apparently inaccessible spot on a bridge, and they will react with anger or wonder or amusement or admiration. Street art still retains something like innocence: it's not quite riddled with the decadence and overwhelming self-consciousness of the legit art world.

If the medium is crime enacted with spray paint, the basic motif is the name or the signature: usually a name one gave oneself, a persona invented specifically for graffiti. So one names oneself and then repeats this name to infinity, everywhere, all the time. It's first of all an act of self-invention through making: you create yourself as the legend that did all these tags and has this name. Then you express and assert that self in the art; the art is the signature of that self, often taken to an almost unbelievable pitch of sophistication and elaboration, the letters turned and twisted and run onto each other and inverted and rendered over into pictoricity and so riddled with symbology that they are at once incredibly dense semiotic artifacts and well nigh impossible to read. Graffiti has taken the personal signature and made it into a whole series of traditions and innovations, of self-effacements and self-assertions. And, we might add, collaborations, as crews and collectives cover surfaces, or as the living keep alive the tags of the dead, as Smith with his brother Sane, for example. It's hard maybe for someone who has lived a privileged life to understand the centrality of self-assertion that you find in hip hop MCs and in taggers. I include myself in this. I am actually looking for ways to divest myself of authority, not to sink into egomania, to act like a nice low-key guy. But self-assertion of various kinds is obviously one of the wellsprings of the arts, and painting your signature all over everything is a kind of primordial act of expression: basic, fundamental, but also capable of taking on the character of consummate craft.

Because of course what the best of these folks learn to do with spray paint is really astounding, comparable to the most skilled imaginable work in any of the arts or crafts. So that graffiti, along with its illegality, has the absorbing qualities of any medium: there is no upper limit to the skill that can be cultivated; the medium, like all mediums, keeps beckoning one on toward mastery, and past it. Graffiti first of all shows that there's something fundamental about the artistic impulse: you may be too broke to go to art school, but you can't really be too broke to make art until you have actually starved to death. You may not really be able, or you may not want, to make art that is approved by the authorities, displayed in galleries, worth money, etc. But you can still make art, and some people are really driven to. And furthermore, you can still make great art. ESPO says, "Anything that reflects somebody trying to solve a problem with very limited means at their disposal, but they're making it happen . . . that's graffiti in a nutshell. That's the kid with three cans of spray paint trying to make something beautiful happen. That's somebody with no money and a few supplies going out and making art happen."[1]

Graffiti, furthermore, is temporal in a way that is basically contradicted by the practices of preservation in the fine art world. You've got to expect your work to be removed by the authorities or overpainted by other artists, or simply to weather away. The art of Navajo sand painting is a similar case:

the painting is destroyed in the ceremony for which it is made. Such practices have the effect of a relentless emphasis on process; you can't be aiming at an eternally available work that can be displayed and absorbed through the generations. The work is a work of and for this moment, a work whose point is that it was made, and how it was made, and why it was made rather than in the arrangement of lines itself. Graffiti, we might say, is its own reward, and that in germ is the ideal condition of all the arts.

And the medium of graffiti, we might point out, does not stand outside the cultures that produce and eradicate it. It is related to all the popular arts of the twentieth century in myriad ways. Obviously, for example, it is influenced by the lettering and lettering effects (KA-BLAM) of comic books, which many graff writers cite as their fundamental influence. As the graffiti writer EZO says, "At the beginning, I looked at art in comic books. I mean everybody from 1950 on. . . . That's how we learned, from comic books and television. That's our art school in this country, because we don't have a formal art school to go to. You've got to be a rich kid from somewhere to have that. If you're not, your art teacher will be Jack Kirby or Hanna-Barbera."[2] Stephen Powers writes: "Blade drew extensively from the pop culture that surrounded him. First and foremost the music, from Motown to Black Sabbath. . . . TV shows like *Welcome Back, Kotter* and *The Gong Show,* kitschy artifacts like the 'Pete Pisstolini' doll, or corporate logos like Burger King and Ronald McDonald all came to the party Blade was hosting. . . . The trains Blade painted told the story of the 70s through the eyes of a Black youth."[3]

The relation of text and image—image as text and text as image—is close to the comics, and close also to many developments in the fine arts in the twentieth century. And of course it has also been absorbed back into these worlds. Fine art lives on popular art as it were vampirically: the blood of the marginal keeps the art world half alive. You can see this with comics in Lichtenstein's art, for example. But this appropriation, though it may be a bit dangerous for the spirits of all concerned, is also understandable and even laudable: the fine arts are plundering living visual culture for everything that has power, and of course their images gain real power by doing so. The last straw of such activity, I guess, is graffiti artists who've migrated into the corporate world and designed logos etc., but even this is both a tribute to the power of their art and also a way to make a really good logo.

Modern graffiti arose with hip hop, or as an "element" of hip hop, in New York and Philadelphia in the '70s. It represents many of the same impulses and techniques visually that hip hop represents in sound. The idea of using prerecorded tracks and rapping over them (a technique that originated in Jamaica) is a cheap and relatively simple way to make music: analogous to spray paint. And the rapper repeating his name, bragging on his abilities, and threatening his enemies in crews: all of that is parallel to graffiti. They both grew out of regional or even neighborhood styles, but as hip hop was disseminated in tapes and vinyl, graffiti has been disseminated through painting trains and now, especially, through the internet. And so both hip hop and graffiti have become truly international styles, and you can see Bronx- or Queens-style graffiti in Barcelona, Amsterdam, Sao Paolo, Mexico City, Tokyo, Ulan Bator, and Johannesburg. Indeed, it is one of the few truly vital aspects of international visual style, as hip hop is of audible style. Both are now multiracial, multicultural, appearing continuously in a million hybrids of localism and internationalism, and also as still connected to their origins.

You can still make art that has a real effect on people and that they find relevant to their lives, and just as important, you can make art that pisses people off or that they will repress. Of course the very same works can have both effects with regard to different audiences. Art can still, thank God, be subversive, or unapproved. The squalor of some graffiti is itself a commentary on the squalor of the sites where it appears, though it invariably adds visual interest to its sites. Even a disorganized wall showing the traces of many writers over a period of many years has a certain effect of profusion and the display of the history of styles. Sites that have been painted over or scrubbed and then rewritten can also have such an effect, as a display of persistence and a capturing of the illegality and boldness central to the form. The quick though stylized scrawl shows the determination of the artist to "get up," and is often suited to particularly dangerous, vulnerable, or observable sites. Such tags are perhaps the basis of the classical styles of graffiti: the bubble letters, the style of lettering with markers, and so on. And these styles are in turn used in more serious pieces or revived in a neoclassical quest for purity or the essence of the form.

And then of course there are the real masterpieces: walls on which a crew has lavished all its time and creativity and its best paint. These often combine the image and the signature in ingenious ways, and often display characters, drawn or signed, inhabiting a shattered urban environment. They are always commentaries on the site as well as commentaries on the relation of the writers to the site and to the urban environment they inhabit.

There are a lot of ways to make revolution, to attack authority. The arts are not, perhaps, the most efficacious in terms of their actual effects on hierarchies: no tag, no matter how good, is really going to disturb Dick Cheney's grip on political and economic power. But the arts are the most joyful, flowing, and creative sites of revolutionary activity. Graffiti is real; graffiti is enjoyable to make and to see; graffiti is persistent and it literally changes the world.

XIII

Beauty, Sex, and the Banality of Pleasure

2000

Probably you remember that Jeremy Bentham had a riff he called the "hedonic calculus." The idea was that you could figure out what the right thing to do was by calculating "units of pleasure." So for example, going out and getting drunk and dancing tonight would give you seven units of pleasure but cost you four pains tomorrow morning. Obviously you're coming out ahead of the game, and I guess we should conclude that you are morally obligated to get drunk and dance tonight. Bentham put a lot of intellect into making this apparently ridiculous approach plausible, and you've got to say that he did a surprisingly good job considering how hard it really is to calculate even one's own pleasures and pains. Is the blast worth the hangover and perhaps the regret etc.? Well, it's hard to say, isn't it? And the answer's likely to be different last night and this morning.

You probably also remember the early attack on utilitarianism, or at least the attacks that Bentham and Mill themselves canvassed on the way to the argument. There was the "pushpin" objection, where the question that arose was whether a children's game called pushpin was as good as reading Milton if it yielded the same number of pleasure units. And then I remember Mill considering the objection that hedonistic utilitarianism was a philosophy for pigs because it would seem that the best life was just grubbing for slop and enjoying the pleasures that accompany such activity. Bentham and Mill disagreed about how to deal with this, if I remember rightly: Bentham bit the bullet and said that if the quantity of pleasure really was the same, then pushpin really was just as good as poetry. Mill, on the other hand, tried to formulate a hierarchy of pleasures and say that some pleasures were better than others. And he appointed experts to judge about this: people who had experienced both the supposed pleasures of the mind and the alleged pleasures of the body were to return from their safaris into ecstasy and tell us what to do. This is the same way Hume tried to sort out matters of aesthetic taste: well, if you want a reasonable opinion, go to the man who knows.

A couple of hundred years of attacks on utilitarianism is plenty, but I want to focus here on the meaning of the word *pleasure.* Let's think about some experiences: taking a hot bath; having sex; reading *War and Peace;* smoking crack. Now is there some one sensation that all these experiences have in common? Really think seriously about that for a minute. Well, there's not. But all these experiences can be positively valued in the sense that they could be experiences we seek. Maybe that's all we mean by pleasure, in which case I guess various forms of hedonism would be trivial.

The thing is that *pleasure* is an ordinary-language term and not, or not only, a philosopher's term of art. And it seems to me that it indicates a sort of fuzzy generalized enjoyment into which you can lapse or relax; I think *pleasure* is the perfect word to describe the warm bath experience, for example. Now on the other hand to say that sex is pleasurable is not exactly wrong, but it's also not exactly right. I want you to think about your most intense sexual experiences, and I think you'll see that *pleasure* is the wrong word. It's not that you "enjoyed" such experiences; it's that they were extreme experiences, what Bataille calls "limit experiences," or experiences "at the extreme limits of the possible." If you roll over in bed and say "I enjoyed that," it's almost a critique.

Very intense sexual experiences often experiment with taboos and their transgression. There is of course a rush in doing something one is not supposed to do. But the feeling that one gets as one lapses or is seduced or attacks one's way into the transgression is not pleasure, though perhaps pleasure is involved at some point at some level. Often sexuality plays with and in pain, for one thing. But my point really is the inadequacy of the terms *pleasure* and *pain* in the face of very intense experience.

Or let's try food. The experience of eating a good meal is more or less a model of pleasure; even Mill and Bentham were on to that. And if you and

I go to Baskin-Robbins for sundaes, we'll be having a pleasurable experience. On the other hand, good food or serious food is what we might call difficult. If you go to a Thai restaurant and order hot, I wonder if you are doing it because eating extremely hot food is pleasurable. Well not exactly, if you follow me. I remember how long it took me to cultivate a taste for beer: I didn't keep drinking it because I enjoyed its bitterness. Or we might even think of the effects of beer (which is what I was actually seeking). There is a pleasure in being drunk, at least under certain circumstances, but just as often it is a complicated experience of self-medication in which your consciousness is dulled and you are seeking that. And it's not quite right to say that you're just seeking escape from pain either. What you're seeking is a kind of extreme experience that is really not about pleasure or pain at all.

My wife, who's a former heroin user, recently told me the story of the first time she shot up. She was with her friend Lowell and they got utterly sick; she says that they were lying on her front lawn puking their guts out. After that, she went back after that experience over and over again. If you think she was motivated by pleasure, then I think you don't really understand what substance abuse is like or why people do it.

Let's consider my friend Karmen MacKendrick, the philosopher. Perhaps you know that she has wings scarred into her back. She had them made by cutting with razor blades, and they have to be recut every year or two. Now I wonder if you think that would be fun. And yet there's no doubt that she consciously decided to undergo that experience. In fact, trying to get an experience like that onto some little schedule of pleasures and pains, trying to slap the hedonic calculus on it, is just utterly the wrong approach. You've got to *get past* the talk of pleasures and pains if you're going to get any decent view of this thing or of most things.

So one thing that is wrong—utterly and obviously wrong, it seems to me—is that hedonism is descriptive of human actions, that people are always or even usually motivated in their actions by pleasure and the avoidance of pain. Descriptive hedonism is radically inaccurate in two ways. First it lumps experiences into the category of pleasures that are so varied and incompatible with one another that using one term to cover them all just makes a hash of them. And second, it's just flat-out wrong: people often or perhaps characteristically seek pain, or pursue experiences that are not clearly either pleasures or pains, or are both, or to which the vocabulary of pleasure and pain is radically inadequate.

Pleasure, let's face it, is banal. The simple pleasure of the sundae is banal in comparison to the complicated experience of the beautifully prepared meal. The pleasure of the sundae is sweet, childish. I'm not against pleasure because I'm not against banality: you can't live without it. But what I am saying is that the concept of pleasure doesn't help us to understand our most interesting or intense experiences. That is a truth that has been known to all the great ascetics; they knew that in turning away from pleasure they were turning toward a whole range of intense experiences in which pleasure was not even in question. In the religious ecstasy that may be the ascetic's goal, or in the continual experience of self-overcoming that moves him toward that goal, pleasure is repudiated until it is simply no longer in question. One reaches precisely toward experiences of which pleasure is not even a dimension, and one values them in part precisely because it's not.

The ascetic's basic truth is that the experience of pleasure is mundane; that the intensity and reality of life in the body begin at the moment in which pleasure is repudiated. The ascetic regards pleasure in its banality as a distraction and a temptation, tries to reach the point at which pleasure does not even need to be repudiated because it is not in play at all, tries to make himself over into a creature for whom questions of pain and pleasure do not arise. It is often thought that pain itself is the goal of an ascetic, which seems strange and perverse enough. In fact, according to the hedonist, such a person is impossible or thoroughly self-deluded. But the ascetic in the best case or the most ascetic case is not seeking the experience of pain even as he flagellates himself or whatever; he's seeking to reach a state of elevation in which pleasures and pains don't count at all, don't motivate, don't even finally enter into consciousness. The ascetic seeks to transcend pleasure precisely on the grounds that pleasure is banal, seeks a state from which all banality, all easy answers, all fluffy sweet concepts, all cotton candy, have been eradicated. God is not about pleasure. In fact God is about self-mutilation, stigmata: about the human condition and its elevation or vaporization into a state in which the banal or mundane has been annihilated.

But the goal of the ascetic is also to return to the mundane, purged of his own banality. The world is the arena of asceticism: its labor, its test, its combat. Asceticism continually brings you back into the world by expunging the escape into pleasure and pain. One responds to the world initially as primarily the source of pleasures and pains: nipple, anus: sucking, shitting: full and empty; need, satiation. But that is first of all too generalized a taxonomy of the world and of the self: so generalized indeed that it loses the world and the self and declines into a kind of phantasmic arena of experience in which all that is real about the world is its effect on consciousness, and all that's real about consciousness is its bifurcation into seeking and evading. Asceticism seeks to reimagine or revive the world, seeks to discover and explore experience's complexity and multivalence, seeks to affirm it in its complexity and externality to will.

To be sure, this experience of the world as a profusion can itself motivate a flight, and it is not coincidental that asceticism is conceived fundamentally as a technology for the repudiation of the world or as a yearning to overcome the body. But it devotes itself to achieving that precisely by an intense experience of the body in the world and a rendering up of the human into a chaos to which the bifurcation of experience into pleasure and pain is irrelevant or insufficient.

It seems to me, as I guess it seemed to Plato (judging by the *Symposium* [which I speculate is a slice of a much larger Socratic apocrypha: an eroto-philosophical gospel]) that the fundamental erotic experience, the fundamental experience of desire or ravishment or being swept away, is the experience of beauty. And beauty has always been associated with pleasure. Santayana, for instance, defined beauty as "objectified pleasure."[1] Well, let us think about that, now that we've taken on board the idea that pleasure is banal. Beauty, insofar as it gives pleasure, is also banal, as we should certainly see, for instance, in the history of twentieth-century visual arts and art music. The artists of the twentieth century, or the important ones, repudiated beauty as a seduction, as something too easy or even trivial.

I think I read someplace that people are regarded as beautiful to the extent that their features are typical or average. That is, if you find out how wide the average person's eyes are apart, or how long an average person's nose is, it turns out that people who are regarded as beautiful are close to that. So Brad Pitt and Christy Turlington are beautiful in that way: their noses aren't too long or whatever. Now *that's* banal. What Brad Pitt and Christy Turlington engage, of course, is sexual desire. And all our experience of beauty is parasitic on the fundamental experience of desire.

But we have already seen that sex plays in and around pleasure in complicated and unpredictable ways. And the white-bread fantasy where you're doing it with Brad is only the most predictable fantasy imaginable. Really, I hope your fantasy life is a little more fucked up than that. But what we might say about beauty, to return it from the realm of the banal into our complicated experience, is this: that what is beautiful is an object of desire and what is an object of desire is beautiful. In that case, banal beauties would comport with banal desires. But complicated, conflicted, or self-overcoming desires might correspond to more messed-up and interesting beauties.

Some beauties are fearsome or noisome or destructive or painful or bewildering. Some beauties are wrong or hateful or terrible or impossible. Really the world as a system is beautiful in all those ways. The world as a whole can be the object of desire, indeed is the paradigmatic object of desire and of dread toward which and away from which we are living our lives.

So anyway, this is how we can set beauty and art free from banality and philosophy: detach desire from pleasure. Desire is multiple, contradictory, patinated, and distressed. You can desire pleasures, you can desire pains, and most often you desire sensations that are neither pleasures nor pains and you desire things that are not sensations. We've still got to decouple desire from Aristotelian practical rationality, in which we organize our life for ends construed as constituting happiness. You know and I know that desire is impractical and irrational and that its objects use us as much as we use its objects; its objects seek us.

Now if we start rethinking beauty along these lines, funny things happen. For one thing, much of the art of the twentieth century might turn out to be beautiful. A famous example of unbeautiful art is Picasso's *Guernica:* all those bodies being blown into distorted smithereens. It's a postcubist rendering of a postcubist scene: its horrifying distortion creates an objective correlative of the distortion it seeks to capture and convey. But you know what? Someone wanted those people to be torn to bits. And Picasso wanted to paint it. And we want to experience *Guernica* maybe because we too want to see people torn to bits and here we get to do it at a safe distance in representation. And we want the Picasso too: imagine what would happen if the thing came up for auction.

You know beauty is about as sick and perverse as we are, because beauty is articulated in our desires. Look in the back of the *Village Voice* or the *NYPress* and see what it is that people want sexually: they want to copulate with monsters, maybe. The hermaphrodite body or "she-male" is a favorite style of pornography and prostitution: we want to enter the interstice and have it enter us; that is our desire and hence that is the beautiful.

And now I want to think about what happens to art when we release desire and hence beauty from banality. Picasso's beauty is a disturbed beauty or a distressed beauty and a complicated or disgusting beauty. But whatever kind of beauty it is, it is the beauty of a master. Picasso, as is well known, had a dictatorial streak: he was a "master" in the various twentieth-century acceptations of that term. Power is at the center of his aesthetic; he imposes on us, as well as on his subjects and on his medium, his mastery of form. As we look at his work, he is *our* master. I think one might say the same of many of the figures of high modernism in all the arts, whether it's Wallace Stevens or Arnold Schoenberg. The beauty these figures achieve is correlated precisely with the scope of their will: they create beauty out of and as power. They are virtuosos of their media, and though a gesture may be apparently random, it is always recovered into an overweening intentionality.

But along with the evolution of mastery in twentieth-century art we had the sly development of art that was an easing or an abandonment or a destruction of constraint. These two strands correspond to two conceptions of freedom: Picasso is free in the sense that his external reality assumes exactly the form he desires and dictates. The other sort of freedom involves conforming your will to what is, or rather, letting go of will into the world. The first is a kind of ascetic discipline, the second is an asceticism of ecstatic self-abandonment. I have in mind, for example, surrealist poets who engaged in "automatic writing"; or Andy Warhol, who simply drew our attention in a slightly altered way to objects already in our homes or in our popular culture; or John Cage, who tried to make music out of random sound, tried to let music occur rather than "compose" it.

I suggest that conceptions of beauty and desire float with changes in the technologies that articulate our environment, that distribute it into objects and collect it into living space. And I suggest that the decisive detachment of beauty and desire from pleasure will occur under the auspices of what are now called "information technologies." My model here is the computer virus. Think about the relation of the "I Love You" virus to its maker: he designs it, makes it live, writes its code. But once he sets it free, it simply grows exponentially in what are entirely unpredictable or massively chaotic accumulations of events. I think that is what will happen to art and to the artist: art will eventually be something we make and then set free to occur rather than something we master. It will be something no one knows or controls: a massive gathering and distribution of events that expands explosively or contracts and disappears.

Already this is happening. I used to be a master of the "mix tape." I had all the albums and I would take all the best songs or I would find a theme and then I would put the songs together in a highly intentional order. But I don't do that anymore. Now what I do is load 101 CDs into the player and hit "random." (Or I hit "random" on twenty-four thousand songs in MP3 format.) A computer generates a running order out of the materials I assembled. Maybe the juxtapositions are felicitous, maybe they're not, but either way they cannot be anticipated. It's the technology that creates the possibility of such a work of beauty.

It's like if you loaded a set of words into a computer, perhaps with a grammar program or perhaps not, and then made the first hundred juxtapositions your next book. See, maybe that would look boring or stupid or repetitive. Well then, you've got to go in and write a bunch of new code. And when it starts coming up with shit you love, then you're done. You're still making something, but it's also making you. You make and release and read and then make. You interrupt the structure of practical rationality or the pursuit of pleasure and find a viral beauty, a beauty that is its own thing and that exists both within and outside the pleasure/pain continuum.

So that's where I want us to go; that is a final release from the oppressions encoded in Western art and ethics: we make that release by allowing things to become. At that point, our arts resemble and merge with natural systems, which grow or consolidate or collapse by chaotic and systematic uncontrolled interactions. Then our arts are themselves living things, themselves organic systems. And at that point our arts are like ourselves; as perverse and fucked up and cool as people are: beautiful as the perfect hermaphrodite.[2]

XIV

Guns, Dub, Technique

2008

Questions about technology are, of course, bound up with questions of power. And if our posthuman present and future are defined in part by technological environments and technological enhancements of or interventions in the body, then a central question will be whether these will amount among other things to strategies of subordination. Here we can see continuities between the human and the posthuman; in the will to power, and the use of every new dimension of technology as a way to turn people to account within ever more pervasive power structures.

We might think, for example, of the gun. Like many technologies, the gun is designed in relation to the human body, as, we might say, a prosthesis: the pistol-as-hand or rifle-as-arm. And of course the gun as an enhancement of the body's capacity to kill has been central to power in modernity: a key to the slave trade, colonialism, genocide, and just the everyday policing that represents the small-scale or pedestrian saturation of our lives by the state.

On the other hand, the gun has provided a mode of resistance, and one can't conceive of an "unarmed" insurgency or guerrilla band. The gun, as it were, exceeds its intended application as prosthesis of power and is also the instrument or even the very body of the resistance. It introduces and enhances forms of order, but it simultaneously and in complement induces chaos. That chaos in turn drives the technology of the gun and its ammunition, the projection of the body into other bodies, the penetrative purpose which is the real power of the gun, its trajectory from my body into yours that expresses the gun's actual power. I fuck you at a distance, and then you're fucked. We introduce ever new generations of the gun to enforce order on the ever spiraling chaos. The gun locks down Virginia Tech, or secures its students, but then also erupts in the insane or unaccountable explosion of violence. It's the principle of order and the whirlwind of alien, suicidal strangeness, the essence of both rationality and insanity at one and the same moment at one and the same place.

If we think of technology in its conceptual structure or, as Heidegger might put it, its essence, as purposiveness, we can begin to conceive our problem and our hope. The idea of technology is the idea of controlling our environment and each other in accordance with some *telos,* of bending the world and each other, or including each other, to our will. This of course divides the world into subject and object, animate will and the inanimate reality over which it wants dominion. This is in one sense the origin of the human individual, of the phenomenological detachment of the body from the environment and from other human bodies. But it is of course also the continual compromise of the individual, now nested in a power structure that proceeds through it or that manifests itself within it as it environs it in instruments. The gun is an assertion of integrity or even invulnerability, a defense of the body that increases the space it occupies in potential, the carving out of a defended space that asserts and preserves the body as an individuated object. That is, the gun individuates the body by asserting its identity with the space around it, by increasing its scope beyond the skin and into the space beyond, or even into the bodies of those that might co-occupy this space. The gun is an instrument of self-assertion or defense, but also in both directions a demonstration that the body does not end at the skin, that the skin can be penetrated and the body can be projected into surrounding space.

Technology typically has this multivalent or contradictory effect. It increases the integrity of bodies or expands that integrity: of the human body, of the state or corporation, of the specific inanimate thing. So, for example, the cell phone, surrounding each of us in a haze or aura of wavicles, projecting that haze or aura to others, right through their ears and into their heads, creating a new layer of the atmosphere that unites our bodies and separates them from one another. The history of cellular technologies has been and will be at once a making-public, an increased pervasion of waves over the earth, and an intensification of the private, an ever more intimate incorporation of these waves into each nervous system: an internalization that is also at the same time a connection. And of course the cell phone will at once serve power—make money, enhance surveillance, and so on—and create uncontrollable chaos, a storm of signals inside which to make drug deals or to detonate improvised explosive devices.

The IED or improvised explosive device is a pretty good emblem of technology gone mad or awry, turned from the concerted, systematic technologies of bureaucracy into the semi-sane suicidal outbreak of unaccountable intervention in that very bureaucracy. Indeed the idea of improvisation itself is interesting in this regard. To move from violence into art, the technologies of control, of systematic generation of and pursuit of purpose, always also enhance the possibilities of improvisation. Improvisation is one way to "turn" or deflect technologies, one way of showing their excess to their own essences, or to mount a demonstration that they have no essence, that each instrument packs within it indefinitely many potentialities in excess to its conceived purposes. Each assertion of control is also an atmosphere of improvisation or makes possible improvisations heretofore unimaginable.

Here I'd like to consider Jamaican dub music. In its origin, for example in the work of basic dub originator King Tubby, dub is a technological music in the sense that though its materials originate in the music-making of guitarists, drummers, etc., what makes the music dub is the technological intervention in the song by the "engineer." The engineer proceeds, first, by subtraction: removing vocals and dropping instruments out, then bringing them back in. And by enhancement, adding echo effects or reverberations that create a sense of vast space and then close it down, that project the sound into an imaginary world and then collapse that world back in on itself. And by addition: of beeps or snatches of other songs, often in a different key, an explicitly foreign element disrupting or fragmenting the riddim, creating a fractured surface.

One effect of dub is to break down the integrity of "the song," and dub's expansion and destruction of the song is now common coin in the world's popular music. Like American pop, Jamaican music of the 1960s presented the listener with integral songs suitable for radio play, three-minute temporal organisms characterized by internal "narrative" order: verse/chorus verse/chorus bridge chorus. The basic way these songs were presented was on the

Sound System at outdoor parties or dancehalls, where the system operator would set up a speaker system and a DJ would spin records. These began by playing American jazz and R&B records in the 1950s. By the early '60s, when Jamaica achieved political independence from the UK, the sound systems were spinning Jamaican ska records, which, like subsequent Jamaican waves such as rock steady, reggae, and ragga, in turn colonized England, Canada, and much of the rest of the world.

In emulation of American radio DJs, the Jamaican sound system DJ would chatter into and out of the records, and soon DJs such as Lee Perry, King Stitt, and U-Roy were stars as important as the top Jamaican recording artists. Jamaican producers began making versions of their records especially for DJ/sound system performance, first removing the vocals from records (usually recorded on four tracks), often issuing the instrumental versions as the B-side of the vocal single. By 1970, early in what is known as the roots reggae period, the DJs themselves became recording artists, rapping over pre-existing instrumental tracks. Now producers realized that they could sell a series of singles from a single song: the vocal, the instrumental, and the DJ version.

King Tubby, a stereo builder/repairman/sound system operator in Kingston, began improvising "dub" versions of tracks brought to him by various producers. He used improvised effects to create shattered soundscapes that would be comprehensible to people already familiar with the song. He would throw or drop a reverb unit, for example, to create crashing echo effects. He would pull pieces of the vocal and DJ versions into and out of the mix, or delete the bass, suddenly pushing it back in in a way designed to create a different atmosphere for sound system dancing. Now a single song could support an indefinite number of versions, at once an economical strategy for reducing overhead and a profound compromise of the very idea of a song. Some songs have sustained dozens of versions from the rock steady period to the present, been extended to whole sides of LPs or provided the vaguely recognizable underpinnings of entirely new generations of vocal, DJ, and dub recordings.

In the '70s, dub became a Jamaican industry that came to be emulated in many ways all over the world. In the United States, disco producers made "extended mixes" so that people could dance for ten or fifteen minutes at a time to, say, Le Freak. Hip hop masters such as Kool Herc (from the Bronx, but raised in Jamaica) started versioning or "sampling" previously recorded funk and disco records and putting rappers over them, first at parties, and then on separate singles. These various uses of sound technologies (the turntable, the mixing board) had never been conceived by the people who invented them, but they have been absolutely central to world popular musics since the '70s.

One aspect of these practices is that they introduced new dimensions of improvisation, both in the sense of using technologies in unintended and unpredictable ways, and playing with them as a jazz player plays with his horn: by feel, as it were. Improvisation is in some sense opposed to the conceptual framework of technology, which relies on systematic administering of means toward a predetermined end. Both the ends and means were put at stake by dub producers: songs undermined, combined, indefinitely extended or suddenly cut off in midstream. Michael Veal, in his amazing book *Dub: Soundscapes and Shattered Songs in Jamaican Reggae,* writes as follows:

> Given the heavy demand for dub mixes from sound systems preparing for weekend dances, it is important to realize that these mixes were improvised on the spot. . . . Most dub mixing was done on Friday evenings, when producers deposited their master tapes with engineers, and sound system operators gathered at the studio so that each could be given a unique mix of a currently popular tune. Under these circumstances, an engineer might create dozens of mixes of a given tune in one remix session. . . . [E]ngineers had no way of preparing a mix beforehand; they usually improvised their way through dozens of mixes of the same track. King Jammy's approach was typical of most engineers: "I don't plan it before I get into the mix, it just comes creatively. I don't plan like, Okay, I'm going to take out the bass at two minutes or whatever. It's just instant creativity." . . . Using the mixing board as an instrument of spontaneous composition and improvisation, the effectiveness of the dub mix results from the engineer's ability to de- and reconstruct a song's original architecture while increasing the overall power of the performance through a dynamic of surprise and delayed gratification.[1]

Every new dimension of technology brings with it the possibility of creative misuse; you can throw it at the wall and see what happens. As the world becomes more subject to control, it exceeds or undermines the mechanisms of that control, or pulls them into a subversion of themselves.

One way to frame this would be in terms of Deleuze and Guattari's idea of territorialization, deterritorialization, and reterritorialization. Technology territorializes the world, maps it, surveils it, brings more and more of it into the scope of comprehension. But people appropriate technologies in all sorts of bizarre ways, often with transformative effects, as dub music transformed world popular music. Then of course such developments are themselves colonized, comprehended, exploited, driving a new series of technological innovations (for example, in this case, digital sampling). Dub and digital sampling undermined such ideas as intellectual property or the integrity of the work, its authorship, its origin, which in many cases became untraceable or impossibly complex. These ideas then have to be reconstructed or elaborated at different levels, with different effects, which are in turn encoded in new technological means of definition and elaboration. Then of course these are in turn subject to misuse: they will be torn apart and turned to use and beyond use in sequence.

Technological innovation produces new ontologies, new levels or planes of reality, conceived as ersatz, virtual, each level a simulation and subversion of the one underlying it. At the same time, each level authenticates the level beneath it, leaves it feeling organic, anarchic, a people's technology. Or put it this way: each posthuman layer of reality humanizes the level beneath it, or shows forth its authenticity or humanity by contrast, makes it an instrument of truth and resistance. The weaponry of the state is the weaponry of the next generation's resistance or of terrorists. This is in part because of the technology's very dissemination: what is exotic, expensive, or cutting edge becomes common as dirt, cheap, and correspondingly useful and subject to improvisation. The art of the cutting edge looks finished, clean, perfect, like glossy computer design. The art welling up from beneath looks pointedly human, imperfect, rough-hewn, improvised, even when it serially appropriates last year's dominant methods. Punk bands advertise by screwed-up hand-scrawled posters, reproduced by Xeroxing. But the Xerox itself begins to look authentic or truthful, it gains the aura of the original, it comes to be understood as a trace of the hand, where it was once precisely the opposite.

It's worth saying that Jamaican recording and remix studios, which created many of the most radical technological innovations of modern popular musics, were primitive by the standards of cutting edge Los Angeles, London, or Nashville recording facilities. No one is going to take a beautiful expensive new piece of technology and see what happens when you drop it. In superseding the technologies available to King Tubby or Scientist, the advances in recording technology suggested that the previous versions were trash, which opened up a space of freedom for their exploration. As it were, the technologies are made into pretechnological authentic equipment, hand tools or acoustic instruments; they are disinterpreted, we might say, underdetermined and hence enriched. Or we might say their determination and interpretation had lapsed, so there were no longer right or wrong ways to utilize them. They were rendered over into improvisational environments. Lee Perry famously buried unprotected tapes around his studio and then used the weathered, degraded material as masters. He treated his tapes with rum, smoke, and urine, among other things.

What circulated from the studio to the island, from the island to the world, were snatches of a torn-up revolutionary consciousness, a black nation in disintegration and recohesion. Veal speculates that the reverberations and echoes of dub mixes were a symbol of the yearning for and disintegration of the African origin thematized in the original Rastafarian-oriented lyrics and Nyabinghi drum styles. Echo is a sonic representation of multiple repeated diasporas where the music circulated—Africa/Kingston/London/Toronto—where at each point the origin is lost and recovered, reconstrued, reasserted, mis- and displaced.

Technological innovation itself relies on this process of the reinterpretation of its own history; you don't know how the posthuman moment should be articulated except by the human purposes welling up from below; we rely wholly on the primitive, and the primitive is as volatile and as progressive as the cutting edge of technologies. The cutting edge is arid, yanked out of the human context, but is continually being recontextualized in the human from below. The first world provides its last-generation technologies to the third world or the internal third-world pockets within itself, then skims off its artistic improvisations; controls the third world and depends on it to live; takes its resources and reexports them as trash; then reimports them as art and reinterprets the art in technologies. And so on.

This process, the acme of injustice and the heart of the cry for justice, a killing and a resurrection, a meaningful destruction and a constructive meaninglessness.

XV

Cynicism

The Characteristically American Philosophy

2013

My late brother Jim had a slogan: "No matter how cynical I get, I can't keep up." A cynic never lacks material: material for his disaffection, his skepticism of power and prestige, his individualism, his realism, and above all for his comic monologues, of which Jim was a highly honed master. This has been true since Diogenes, who ridiculed Alexander the Great to his face, ran around naked and lived in a barrel: the philosopher as comedian, in short, and also by the same actions a profound teller of truth. America once produced magnificent cynics. They have been superseded by toadies, associate professors, professional head-nodders, spokespersons for unspeakable bureaucracies, lovers of unanimity: in short, a full-scale onslaught of the noninappropriate.

If a philosophy is a set of doctrines or propositions—a set of positions about truth, beauty, justice, goodness—then cynicism is not a philosophy, though it might be several. But if a philosophy is also a stance, a posture, a mode of attentiveness or responsiveness to the world of the sort that would drive or underlie or motivate a system of philosophy in the propositional sense, cynicism as I'm going to describe it is certainly a philosophy.

It is routine to describe ours as a cynical time, when each person seems to be out only for herself, and no one trusts authorities and institutions as they ought. I think it is an amazingly credulous time where the most urgent question facing each person is what group she can join. It goes without saying, in the admission process, that you'll agree with everything the members of this group can convince themselves to believe after they've replaced the world with each other. Whether what they come to believe or say they believe is plausible or not, whether it displays any sort of rudimentary contact with reality: these are more or less irrelevant questions to social creatures such as ourselves; the question is how earnestly you can rehearse the catch phrases, how apparently passionate your commitment is to whatever fictions the group has constructed to enhance the self-esteem and pliability of its members. This is how both convenience store clerks and Harvard professors figure out what to believe; indeed, as many have argued, it is the very essence of the human. And that really is pretty hilarious when you think about it.

Here's one familiar outline of the history of American thought. America was a New World, an open horizon, a new birth of the human adventure. (True, true, there were some problems with the natives, etc.) The Puritans were sort of grim, holding that human beings were incurably depraved and had no free will, but they brought that with them from wherever it is they came from, and as time went on—and despite the fact that the total depravity of man and woman was proven decisively to them and by them every day—their descendants loosened up and got into a much more positive vibe, as befits "the American adventure." Franklin taught that we could make a good world by ingenuity, thrift, hard work, and conviviality. The Unitarians reversed the Puritans and said that human beings could achieve salvation through a free choice of the good, or even that all persons would be redeemed in the long run because we are all good deep inside. The characteristic American thinkers of the early to mid-nineteenth century were the transcendentalists, who declared American thought independent of Europe and articulated a philosophy of extreme openness and optimism, corresponding to America's apparently unlimited frontier. Emerson, the former Unitarian minister, always anticipated a transformed or redeemed humanity emerging from the American continent:

> Here stars, here woods, here hills, here animals, here men, abound, and the vast tendencies concur of a new order. If only the men are employed in conspiring with the designs of the Spirit who led us hither, and is leading us still, we shall quickly enough advance out

of all hearing of other's censures, out of all regrets of or own, into a new and more excellent social state than history has recorded.[1]

However, various things then occurred—the Civil War, robber baron capitalism, industrialization, growing political corruption and inequality, and so on—that must have made a skeptically inclined person or two wonder whether redemption was indeed nigh, or just another disaster. The frontier had closed, blahblahblah. It got hard in the late nineteenth century to think that things were just about to get much much better, and it might have occurred on a moonless evening even to an aging Emerson that we ourselves were no better than we needed to be, and no better overall than we were before. But Americans, as everyone knows, are an optimistic, forward-looking people. The next wave of great American philosophers, the pragmatists, maintained the positive thinking but had to temper the notion that redemption was at hand. They were meliorists rather than millennialists: they thought things could get better if we worked at it, and they did think that we'd work at it, and so things would probably get better as we went along. They embodied the American can-do, positive outlook, defining truth, in an allegedly quintessentially American moment, as what works.

That's a decent story, I suppose. But though John Dewey was an emblematic American intellectual of his era, so was H. L. Mencken, of the same era. Though Americans have been known to march hand in hand into a future bright with collective promise or something that sort of looks like that if you squint, there's that guy over there, watching the procession toward excellence, rolling his eyes and snickering. Americans might have a roll-up-our-sleeves can-do attitude. However, we've also produced amazing realists, skeptics, and cynics at every stage of our development. I don't think, putting it gently, that optimistic pragmatism intent on realizing a great collective future is any more characteristic of Americans than feet-on-the-ground realism, disaffection from our beloved and hypereffective institutions, hatred of power and pretense, and nasty extended jokes.

The strand of cynicism I'm talking about here developed contemporaneously with pragmatism, and is quite as characteristic (honestly, I think much more characteristic) of the American character, if any. My Charles Sanders Peirce, William James, and John Dewey, my Three Stooges of the apocalypse, are Mark Twain, Ambrose Bierce, and H. L. Mencken. These folks certainly have a claim on our attention as writers, but I think also, within limits, as thinkers. In that capacity they had a remarkable advantage over the prags: they squared up to reality. And they were funnier than the prags, which admittedly is not much of an accomplishment in itself. Well, James had a sense of humor, anyway.

In terms of candlepower, Twain was the sunniest, Bierce the darkest. Bierce saw brutal combat in the Civil War, which is the sort of thing that might sour you on America or humanity as a whole, and his Civil War stories are among the most intense and creative bursts of despair in the history of literature. Indeed, in a non-Civil War vein he wrote stories of unparalleled hilarious sickness, such as "An Imperfect Conflagration" (collected in a volume inspiringly titled *A Deodorizer of Dead Dogs*): "Early one June morning in 1872 I murdered my father—an act which made a deep impression on me at the time." Mencken was the broadest intellectual, and had an almost unbelievable facility with the written word. Twain was Twain, with quite a bit less hostility toward democracy, for example. He was a hero and to some extent the source of the approach of Bierce and Mencken.

I'm going to focus primarily on Mencken, and let me just mention that he was the first American translator of Nietzsche. He wrote *The American Language,* an amazing scholarly achievement representing a lifetime of devotion to the land and the language: a personal *OED* he tossed off while also editing magazines, covering political conventions, and drinking all night with Zelda Fitzgerald and Tallulah Bankhead. He produced philosophical/historical treatises upholding atheism and trying to develop a Darwinian account of ethics. He was certainly much more widely known and read than Dewey in his own lifetime. Mencken dropped out of Poly High School in Baltimore to work on newspapers, but he was, believe it or not, far more erudite than Dewey, as erudite as anyone this nation has ever produced: you can't believe at any given moment what the man knows, from the whole history of philosophy, religion, and literature to what music they're playing in the speakeasy down the street. At any rate, he should be taken seriously and unseriously as a thinker and as a central figure in American intellectual history, despite some drawbacks.

We might begin by considering one of Mencken's many synoptical treatments of "The National Letters." He starts out precisely by quoting famous bits of Emerson and Whitman on the astounding open infinite horizon of American literature and America in general. Mencken was an incomparable expert on the actual history of American lit, well beyond the first string. He writes:

> The dream of Emerson [as expressed in "The American Scholar"], though the eloquence of its statement is new and arresting, embodied no novel projection of the fancy; it merely gave a sonorous *Waldhorn* tone to what had been dreamed and said before. You will find almost the same high hope, the same exuberant confidence in the essays of the elder Channing and in the 'Lectures on American Literature' of Samuel Lorenzo Knapp, LL.D., the first native critic of beautiful letters—the primordial tadpole of all our later Mores, Brownells, Phelpses, Mabies, Brander Matthewes and other such grave and glittering fish. Knapp believes, like Whitman long after him, that the sheer physical grandeur of the New World would inflame a race of bards to unprecedented utterance.[2]

Mencken liked Emerson, or at least didn't merely hate him, though he definitely is lightly ridiculing him here, but he hated Whitman with a passion, regarding him as a gasbag. (Bierce: "Two things are *incompossible* when the world of being has scope enough for one of them, but not enough for both—as Walt Whitman's poetry and God's mercy to man."[3]) What Mencken wants to do is try to puncture the woolly pretensions of American greatness with a hard look at the actual mediocrity. He would replace Whitman's America with Edgar Allan Poe's, though he chastises Poe for his moments of optimism, which perhaps only Mencken could actually detect. But Mencken just piles on the realities in response: he mentions dozens of mediocrities from every era. He reminds us, as he often did, about actual Americans: "Knights of Pythias, Presbyterians, standard model Ph.D.'s, readers of the *Saturday Evening Post*, admirers of Richard Harding Davis and O. Henry, devotees of Hamilton Wright Mabie's "white list" of books, members of the Y.M.C.A. or the Drama League, weepers at chautauquas, wearers of badges, 100 per cent. patriots, children of God."[4] Such people were unknown to John Dewey, or at least did not figure explicitly in his inspiring vision of America.

"What ails [American letters], intrinsically," writes Mencken, "is a dearth of intellectual audacity and of aesthetic passion"[5], and it must be said that Mencken supplied these items in abundance. For this reason, he is no longer heard of.

> I often wonder what sort of picture of These States is conjured up by foreigners who read, say, Crothers, Van Dyke, Babbitt, . . . and the old maids of the Freudian suppression school. How can such a foreigner, moving in those damp asthmatic mists, imagine such phenomena as [Teddy] Roosevelt, Billy Sunday, Bryan, the Becker case, The I.W.W., Newport, Palm Beach, the University of Chicago, Chicago itself—the whole gross, glittering, excessively dynamic, infinitely grotesque, incredibly stupendous drama of American life?[6]

The University of Chicago is mentioned here, I believe, as a fraternal order on par with the Knights of Pythias. Now this was written by a man who saw America clearly, knew it as thoroughly as anyone, and loved it inordinately as it actually was. He is affirming and abusing *it*, not some idealized or fictionalized reconstruction or representation. But his is, precisely because of this, a real love, a real affirmation, whereas according to Mencken figures such as Emerson and Dewey loved an America that existed as an idea/ideal, so that you might wonder whether, after all, there was anything they actually did love.

Ambrose Bierce was known, even to Mencken, who was his friend, as "bitter Bierce"; his vision of humanity and of his native country was extremely bleak, as I've said. Twain supposedly but famously sank into bitterness toward the end of his life. Mencken's real metier as a writer was abuse: no one has ever turned more or better insults. Of course, this is not a rational consideration against their opinions, but they all did seem awfully hateful and negative. If so, then I think you need to work that element into your account of American thought and letters. "The American experience" has been extremely disaffecting for many people, even for many white men. But I actually would like to consider the place of American cynicism as being a lot more complicated than that.

I think that the humor has to be completely centralized in any true account of American cynicism. Here's Mencken's real orientation: He thought that, by and large, Americans were chumps who thought the most ridiculous yet banal crap, and thought it in herds. He despised democracy, pointedly, though perhaps not entirely sincerely, and not as much as Bierce did (though more than Twain); it is characteristic of him that he would take up positions to irritate you and see what happened. He was, in short, an anti-Dewey in virtually every respect. Also, Mencken was the most famous and effective and prolific public intellectual of his era. But the point is that Mencken was completely delighted by the stuff he hated. He relished every insult and every awful person and awful thing he insulted. He traveled around looking for things to despise and revel in. He got as close as he could to Aimee Semple McPherson or the Democratic Party. He ridiculed them mercilessly, as only he could. But he loved them inordinately: they were for him the very essence of his beloved, horrendous, ridiculous, delightful country. If nothing else, he loved American con men, from marketers of patent medicines to United States senators to lady novelists, who used the characteristic groupthink and gullibility of Americans to make their own way in the world.

There are many ways to try to affirm the world and your culture, even in a somewhat wised-up or chastened twentieth century. You might think that in the center of all the excruciating mediocrity and horrendous disasters there is a seed of genius. You might persuade yourself that despite certain appearances, we're in an amazing narrative of overcoming. But you might think: look how bad this all sucks! And then look at all the inflated ecstatic rhetoric flying around the grotesque usual human reality of self-aggrandizement and deep confusion. Seen this way, the whole country is a high burlesque. Isn't it great? It's hilarious! It's like America was sent here just to give writers like me, Henry Mencken, material. Thank God things aren't really as Emerson or Dewey represented them as being: then things would be all serious and important, and there'd be no scope for a good snicker. I don't think anyone has ever loved America as much as Mencken did, and what is remarkable was that he didn't love a myth, a story, or a better America to come: he loved America exactly as it actually was, or maybe even a little worse. He thought it was incomparable human spectacle, and he was at his best when he sank his teeth into its real details, as it were.

I think that this is true, though perhaps not always quite so clearly, of Twain and Bierce as well. They were evidently not merely bitter, because they were hilarious. They turned their own well-earned bitterness to account, put it to work in the hard task of seeing the truth and making fun of it. In that humor there lurks an amazing affirmation: a realistic affirmation, a love that overcomes well deserved hatred with a million jokes. In a way, the American cynics were Emerson's sons after all: wised-up, irascible sons of Emerson, to be sure, but Emersons who found redemption in every little moment of disappointment, corruption, debasement, and idiocy, because each little moment could be used to have fun. It wasn't the millennium Emerson expected, perhaps, but it was very amusing.

One thing that is centralized in the traditional narrative is progress, to which both transcendentalists and pragmatists were profoundly committed in somewhat different ways. Twain, Bierce, and Mencken were extremely skeptical of progress, feeling that the idea basically ignored the reality of what people are actually like. Bierce defined *degradation* as "One of the stages of moral and social progress from private station to political preferment." Mencken despised and loved reformers in particular, whom he constantly compared to criminals of various sorts, and against whom he thought every American should be heavily armed. Bierce really just ridiculed the whole idea of progress, defining *past* as

> That part of Eternity with some small fraction of which we have a slight and regrettable acquaintance. A moving line called the Present parts it from an imaginary period known as the Future. These two grand divisions of Eternity, of which the one is continually effacing the other, are entirely unlike. The one is dark with sorrow and disappointment, the other bright with prosperity and joy. The Past is the region of sobs, the Future is the realm of song. In the one crouches Memory, clad in sackcloth and ashes, mumbling penitential prayer; in the sunshine of the other Hope flies with a free wing, beckoning to temples of success and bowers of ease. Yet the Past is the Future of yesterday, the Future is the Past of to-morrow. They are one—the knowledge and the dream.[7]

This has a flippant air, but it is profound. What will the future be like? Well, we have plenty of means to judge in the many past futures that have actually occurred, such as the present.

Twain developed his own theory of evolution, in a number of texts.

> And so I find that we have descended and degenerated, from some far ancestor,—some microscopic atom wandering at its pleasure between the mighty horizons of a drop of water perchance,—insect by insect, animal by animal, reptile by reptile, down the long highway of smirchless innocence, till we have reached the bottom stage of development—nameable as the Human Being. Below us—nothing. Nothing but the Frenchman.[8]

The fun was also serious, of course: underlying the approach was a pointed disappointment with America or humanity in general and, at least in principle, an attempt to make it live up to its own idea, or at least to point up some of the myriad ways it didn't. There was a very serious critique of American culture and politics in their work, and a critique of their era in general, even from an Emersonian point of view. The Emersonian redemptive formula, of course, was precisely a formula for extreme alienation and disappointment: it just didn't happen the way he apparently thought it would, and, honestly, I could have told him it wouldn't. But the aspirations that Emerson articulated remained in the background for the cynics, I believe.

The pragmatists did inherit a lot from the transcendentalists, to whom they were pretty directly linked (for example through Henry James, Sr.). But they jettisoned a lot too, and much of what they jettisoned was cherished—albeit without a lot of hope for its preservation—by the cynics. I want to emphasize some of the elements that the cynics inherited from the transcendentalists: individualism, liberty as a political ideal, anti-authoritarianism, and a love (this might be the wrong word in Bierce's case) for the world as it actually is, and not as it might be if, unlikely as this seems, it could be profoundly transformed or steadily reformed. But in every case, the cynics are wised-up transcendentalists, and where I think Emerson or Alcott hoped to inspire people to be even better—more individualized, freer, bolder, more audacious and creative and honest—than they were, Twain and Mencken ridiculed or berated or teased them mercilessly for not being any of those things. But these might even be two ways toward the same result, a kind of good cop/bad cop routine, and the apparent hopelessness of the cynics might be incompatible with the intensity and ingenuity and focus of their ridicule: where the transcendentalists hoped to inspire a promising people, Bierce hoped to shame them into realizing that they were squandering that promise.

One thing that cynics retained that the pragmatists, as well as pretty much the entire emerging left-right political spectrum, had jettisoned was the particular individualism of Emerson, Thoreau, Fuller, Alcott. The cynics despised above all uncritical unanimity, and anything that seemed to express it: political parties, for example; bureaucracies; fraternal orders; religious denominations or fads; universities. Here's one aspect of individualism, centralized particularly in Thoreau: it is always possible for a single person to dissent from a consensus. This is a very good thing, because a consensus is liable to be false since it is unexamined from an external point of view. Also it shows that the agent of belief is lodged in particular human bodies, and not in collective agencies or consciousnesses.

Recall the last paragraph of "Civil Disobedience," compressing many transcendentalist themes:

> The authority of government, even such as I am willing to submit to—for I will cheerfully obey those who know and can do better than I, and in many things even those who neither know nor can do so well—is still an impure one: to be strictly just, it must have the sanction and consent of the governed. It can have no pure right over my person and property but what I concede to it. The progress from an absolute to a limited monarchy, from a limited monarchy to a democracy, is a progress toward a true respect for the individual. Even the Chinese philosopher was wise enough to regard the individual as the basis of the empire. Is a democracy, such as we know it, the last improvement possible in government? Is it not possible to take a step further towards recognizing and organizing the rights of man? There will never be a really free and enlightened State until the State comes to recognize the individual as a higher and independent power, from which all its own power and authority are derived, and treats him accordingly. I please myself with imagining a State at least which can afford to be just to all men, and to treat the individual with respect as a neighbor; which even would not think it inconsistent with its own repose if a few were to live aloof from it, not meddling with it, nor embraced by it, who fulfilled all the duties of neighbors and fellow-men. A State which bore this kind of fruit, and suffered it to drop off as fast as it ripened, would prepare the way for a still more perfect and glorious State, which also I have imagined, but not yet anywhere seen.

Now I think that Thoreau was actually just a bit more disillusioned than Emerson: hanging out with RWE and Bronson Alcott would make a lot of people seem more realistic in comparison, especially one so attuned to the details of the real world as Thoreau. The last sentence is not clearly readable as actually anticipating something better to come.

And in certain respects, Mencken gives voice to what Thoreau might be saying if he were transported to 1920, or had lived to be 103, and was ranting to a young, idealistic Warren G. Harding. Well look, after his first century, Thoreau had earned his irascibility. Sure was a hilarious shriveled old sod, though. It's not all funny, either; in the following the outrage swamps the cynicism; Mencken and George Jean Nathan are struggling to hold on to a detached and amused attitude. The manner of Americans, they write,

> is not incompatible with a certain superficial boldness, nor even with an appearance of truculence. But what lies beneath the boldness is not an independent spirit, but merely a talent for crying in the pack. When the American is most dashingly assertive it is a sure sign that he feels the pack behind him, and hears its comforting baying, and is well aware that his doctrine is approved. He is not a joiner for nothing. He joins something, whether it be a political party, a church, a fraternal order or one of the idiotic movements that incessantly ravage the land, because joining gives him a feeling of security, because it makes him part of something larger and safer than he is himself, because it gives him a chance to work off steam without running any risk. The whole thinking of the country thus runs down the channel of mob emotion; there is no conflict of ideas, but only a succession of crazes. In no other country in the world is there so ferocious a short way with dissenters; in none others is it socially so costly to heed the inner voice and be one's own man.[9]

In a piece—not necessarily overall his best outing—reflecting back on the decline and fall of the Connected States from the astounding year 4950, Bierce tries to explain to his readers, living under a completely dictatorial but benevolent monarchy, the principle of majority rule.

> Evidently, under the malign conditions supposed, it is the only practicable plan of getting anything done. A and B rule and overrule C, not because they ought, but because they can; not because they are wiser, but because they are stronger. In order to avoid a conflict in which he is sure to be worsted, C submits as soon as the vote is taken. C is as likely to be right as A and B; nay, that eminent

> ancient philosopher, Professor Richard A. Proctor (or Proroctor, as the learned now spell the name), has clearly shown by the law of probabilities that any one of the three, all being of equal intelligence, is far likelier to be right than the other two.[10]

In the event, this Professor Proroctor was perfectly real, but his correct name, so mangled by the historian, was Crispin Sartwell. Email him at crispinsartwell@gmail.com and he, or, looking at it the other way round, I, will ship you the proof.

I think even by the turn of the twentieth century, the actual political positions of Emerson and Thoreau, who were what we might think of as progressives of their own era (abolitionists, for example, and critics of capitalism), were considered to be reactionary, and have been ever since. Anyway, if they haven't been, they should be. This coincides with the rise of a world "collectivist" left, spearheaded by Marx of course. "Individualism" was a word that those folks used to mean reactionary, capitalist, "bourgeois," etc. The left, which could have agreed with more or less all of Emerson and Thoreau's actual political positions, were extreme enthusiasts for collective consciousness, probably more committed to that than to any particular political vision. Even the American right had moved strongly in this direction, in war-mongering nationalism, for example. Mencken despised them equally, but thought their palpable chumptitude, dogmatic certainty about harebrained schemes to improve the world, and epistemic slavishness presented great comical possibilities.

A pretty direct expression of all these themes is Mencken and George Jean Nathan's *American Credo*. Here's another sample:

> Ask the average American what is the salient passion in his emotional armamentarium—what is the idea that lies at the bottom of all his other ideas—and it is very probable that, nine times out of ten, he will nominate his hot and unquenchable rage for liberty. He regards himself, indeed, as the chief exponent of liberty in the whole world, and all its other advocates as no more than his followers, half timorous and half envious. To question his ardour is to insult him as grievously as if one questioned the honour of the republic or the chastity of his wife. And yet it must be plain to any dispassionate observer that this ardour, in the course of a century and a half, has lost a large part of its old burning reality and descended to the

> estate of a mere phosphorescent superstition. The American of today, in fact, probably enjoys less personal liberty than any other man of Christendom, and even his political liberty is fast succumbing to the new dogma that certain theories of government are virtuous and lawful and others abhorrent and felonious. Laws limiting the radius of his free activity multiply year by year: it is now practically impossible for him to exhibit anything describable as genuine individuality, either in action or in thought, without running afoul of some harsh and unintelligible penalty.[11]

As examples they give the Espionage Act and Prohibition. Now you may think Mencken and Nathan are basically hurling ridicule. True, true. But they are hurling ridicule at hypocrisy; the moral outrage that underlies the wit actually demands that Americans see the inconsistency of expressing the ideals of people like Thoreau while acquiescing, even enthusiastically, to tyrannical power and collective illusion. They see a nation that believes in liberty as the ultimate value and also enthusiastically connives in its own subordination.

All these figures not only endorsed various flavors of individualism, they enacted it on every page. They had extraordinarily distinctive authorial voices and a compulsive habit of attacking consensi. They lived quite eccentric lives, as you'll see if you read some of the biographies.[12] Above all, they gave themselves permission to speak as they pleased, perfectly freely. Mencken knew very well the emerging progressive consensus of the people he himself frequented in his capacity as literary wheeler-dealer and universal critic, and he permitted himself to tweak it in almost every sentence: he was continually saying what you were not supposed to say in the social circles which he himself frequented, using the words you were not supposed to use. But there is almost always a turn, a deflection, something you're not expecting, a kind-of-progressive undertow emitted, among other sources, by his contempt for authority. Bierce, in a perfectly routine gesture, defined *recreation* as "stoning Chinamen." This might have simply enraged people, and indeed Mencken came up for pc condemnation starting at latest in the 1980s: this took the form of a list of banned terms found in his writings. But in his own time, people knew him to be so utterly good-humored and charming, and such a fantastically excellent writer, that they managed to enjoy even material they thought was terribly wrong. He caught a break because he was Henry Mencken. But as the left and its educational wing, the academy, became ever grimmer and ever more committed to collective identities, it finally did extrude him, even from the American canon, the idjits.

To like reading someone or to love certain of their ideas and arguments is not to endorse the whole damn package lock, stock, and barrel. Never get into the business of making someone you love turn out right all the time. Or, Jefferson: that hypocrite! If you think that shows that his ideas about liberty or whatever it may be are actually false, you are really not a reliable reasoner. I don't fear being infected by the controversial opinions of sardonic, free-wheeling bastards of the 1920s, seriously. If there is at times a little anti-Semitic whiff or whatever, I repudiate that. Why would you let that deprive you of such good art and thought? Anyway, it's amazing how Mencken took on in the 1910s the persona of anti-pc provocateur from the 1980s. *The American Credo* consists of all and only the beliefs that all Americans share: all of them entirely false, of course. How about: (155) "That the extinction of the Indian has been a deplorable thing." (114) "That the editor of a woman's magazine is always a lizzie." (!) (105) "That a negro's vote may always be readily bought for a dollar." Or (79) "That a member of the Masons cannot be hanged." Every single one of these has a subversive reading precisely in its various transgressions and the ways they are shaped. But they are the words of a man who essentially controlled his own press and had given himself permission to say whatever he wanted to say, in whatever manner he deemed most amusing. That actually takes tremendous guts. Thoreau did the same in a different vein.

Mencken sort of supported the Kaiser in the run-up to American involvement in WWI, or at least expressed opposition to that involvement, and he was far too late hopping off the Nazis. (He definitely had an unfortunate or overweening Germanophilia going.) Actually, though, I don't think Mencken's politics were that problematic in other areas. I think he was reasonably good on race and gender, for example. But what you have to understand about Mencken: he was going to let himself say whatever he pleased, and he was trying to piss people off. Here's a typical bit:

> For who has ever heard of a Socialist who did not also believe in some other form of quackery? I have known all of the principal gladiators of the movement in my time, at least in America; I have yet to meet one who was not as gullible as a Mississippi darkey, nay, even a Mississippi white man. Didn't Karl Marx himself carry a

> madstone and believe in astrology? If not, then it was strange indeed. Didn't Debs believe that quinine could cure a cold? If not, he was not a genuine Socialist.[13]

Now if all you can see in that passage is the word "darkey," then you're precisely the sort of person Mencken set out to offend. And as you bristle, Mencken is thinking and writing rings around you. And I'll say this: banning or creating overwhelming social sanctions against certain words or thoughts would just make Mencken redouble his efforts to drive the banned material into your head with a hammer. He was trying to say what he was not supposed to say. Even some of the really actually wrong things he said were very much acts of intellectual and social courage, though they appeared as effortless expressions of his gigantic personality. He was trying to show people what it was really like to think and write freely, and so even or precisely his political transgressions were salutary acts of rebellion. Well, he wasn't as bad as Bierce about this.

So the politics of Twain, Bierce, and Mencken were highly problematic or regarded as anachronistic by the whole left. This made in particular Bierce and Mencken just seem like crazed reactionaries, and that is exactly the sort of persona that they would embrace. What Mencken needed was a committee of humorless progressives following him around muttering their slogans in solidaritical unison; he could destroy such a committee with unparalleled verve, and they wouldn't even know they'd been eviscerated, more or less because they didn't know anything at all; even though they were all thinking together as a class or something, none of them had had a moment of independent ratiocination since 1887, for principled reasons. This fact, along with their social positioning, has made it safe for the academy to ignore the cynics as, say, emblematic Americans, or as thinkers. It does also matter that, unlike Peirce, James and Dewey, Twain, Bierce, and Mencken were not professors.

One excellent way to crystallize the distinction between the pragmatists and the cynics is in their treatment of the question of truth and the nature of human access to reality. If James thought that "truth is what works in the way of belief," and later Rorty, with a slightly cynical undertow, defined it as "what your contemporaries let you get away with saying," the cynics regarded it as something terrible or bizarre or wild or unassimilable, and truth-telling as quite an antisocial social activity. Mencken and Nathan write as follows:

> Truth shifts and changes like a cataract of diamonds; its aspect is never precisely the same at two successive instants. But error flows down the channel of history like some great stream of lava or infinitely lethargic glacier. It is the one relatively fixed thing in a world of chaos. It is, perhaps, the one thing that gives human society the small stability that it needs, amid all the oscillation of a gelatinous cosmos, to save it from the wreck that ever menaces. Without their dreams men would have fallen upon and devoured one another long ago—and yet every dream is an illusion, and every illusion is a lie.[14]

Truth, for the cynics, was something to be *faced*, and once you did that you had access to an infinite source of critique of collective frauds and dreams and delusions, and an endless source of humor in the contrast between what people say and what they believe, how they think and how they live: the reality they inhabit and help create and the palaces of jive they build on top of it. But what I would like to emphasize is the first bit: *Truth shifts and changes like a cataract of diamonds.*

At any rate, there was moral seriousness underneath the great playfulness, and a reading of the American experience and American values. But it is rather sad, I admit, to defend excellent comedy on the grounds that it is serious after all, and even if it is, you should definitely not read the humor out, because that misses the love at the heart of the hatred, the redemption found in facing the truth. And what it really misses is the comportment at the heart, a kind of miracle of self-overcoming, the idea that, as bad as things suck, they are also really amazingly fun. So: let's play. This is not such a terribly serious matter, in that we're not going to be made over into angels or even good citizens any time soon. Well, that's a relief. Let's drink a beer, craft the greatest, most diabolical jokes ever told, and laugh from deep within, a sound to shake the whole body, now communicating itself from body to body until the whole place is guffawing joyously. I'm not sure, finally, that it gets any better or more American than that.

One lesson, I think, is that there could be many ways to narrate American intellectual history. If Mencken were sitting in that history where Dewey is now, the whole direction looks entirely different. I do think every story we tell about something like this—an incredibly vast terrain in which each of the myriad figures and texts and movements and moments could be inexhaustibly connected to indefinitely many others—is tendentious (also simplistic in relation to an infinitely profuse reality, and mostly false). It's going to have a lot to do with what you want to have been the case: you could narrate the whole thing around race, for example, or freedom, or progress, or unfreedom, or decline. The tension between the American pragmatists and the American cynics was in part precisely a struggle over how we should narrate our history and hence who we really are. But historical narratives, as the pragmatists did point out, tend really to be about the future: you establish a certain directionality and hence gain in your own head a certain argument about where we're going next, and hence (sic) about where we ought to go.

Now, one lesson of the cynics is that it would be wrong to conflate the direction of history, even if it could be reliably detected, with what you think ought to happen, and provide that as an argument that it really will happen. Marx committed this looping scribble of fallacies in a truly egregious way: what he thought should be, he identified as history's inevitable course. That was the *argument* that it ought to be. Then, remarkably and incomprehensibly, he and his followers tried to force it to happen. The pragmatists committed the fallacy more mildly: history was pretty progressive and all things being equal, later was better than earlier, and really the direction of America was democratic socialism; history was a progressive realization of the right theory. But the cynics avoided it. They thought people don't really get any better over time and the bigger the systems get, the more hugely, grossly human they become: just riddled with bullshit and nodding heads. Maybe they actually did have a notion of where we should go; we might call it Thoreauvian, ultimately. But that we ought to go there by no means entailed that we were headed in that direction at all. We weren't. We aren't.

Meanwhile, whatever happens, we should try to see if we can get any good, subversive jokes out of it, and thus, if only until the next one rolls around, redeem the world.

> Well, humor is the great thing, the saving thing, after all. The minute it crops up, all our hardnesses yield, all our irritations and resentments flit away, and a sunny spirit takes their place. . . . I remember exploding [an] American countermine once, under that grand hero, Napoleon. He was only First Consul then, and I was Consul-General—for the United States, of course; but we were very intimate, notwithstanding the difference in rank, for I waived that. One day something offered the opening, and he said:

"Well, General, I suppose life can never get entirely dull to an American, because whenever he can't strike up any other way to put in his time he can always get away with a few years trying to find out who his grandfather was!"

I fairly shouted, for I had never heard it sound better; and then I was back at him as quick as a flash:

"Right, your Excellency! But I reckon a Frenchman's got *his* little stand-by for a dull time, too; because when all other interests fail he can turn in and see if he can't find out who his father was!"

Well, you should have heard him just whoop, and cackle, and carry on! He reached up and hit me one on the shoulder, and says:

"Land, but it's good! It's im-mensely good! I'George, I never heard it said so good in my life before! Say it again."

So I said it again, and he said his again, and I said mine again, and then he did, and then I did, and then he did, and we kept on doing it, and doing it, and I *never* had such a good time, and he said the same. In my opinion there isn't anything that is as killing as one of those dear old ripe pensioners if you know how to snatch it out in a kind of a fresh sort of original way.[15]

XVI

"Don't Mean Sheeit"

On the Necessity and Impossibility of Meaning for Life

2010

We want to know the meaning of life, to begin with, in the face of death. We confront, as H. L. Mencken—the Sage of Baltimore—put it, "the harsh fact that on such and such a day, often appallingly near, each and every one of us will heave a last sigh, roll his eyes despairingly, turn his face to the wall and then suddenly change from a proud and highly complex mammal, made in the image of God, to a mere inert aggregate of disintegrating colloids, made in the image of a stale cabbage."[1]

Now this might make it appear that Mencken's highly unedifying confrontation with the abyss is caused by his naturalism. Caught in a world of dead gods, a material, Darwinian, sciencey world, Mencken despairs and resolves to confront the truth: face up; don't mean sheeit, as Mr. Natural put it back in the day.[2]

You may have heard about Mitchell Heisman, who in September [2010] shot himself in Harvard Yard in front of a tour group. He left behind a two-thousand-page manuscript titled *Suicide Note*, in which he constructed a philosophical system according to which his suicide made sense. Heisman's philosophy was more or less the philosophy of Richard Dawkins, for example: materialist, scientistic, atheistic, and so on.

The *Boston Globe* quoted and summarized *Suicide Note* as follows:

> "The death of my father marked the beginning, or perhaps the acceleration, of a kind of moral collapse, because the total materialization of the world from matter to humans to literal subjective experience went hand in hand with a nihilistic inability to believe in the worth of any goal," he wrote. He saw his emotions as nothing more than a product of biology, as soulless as the workings of a machine, making them in essence an illusion. "If life is truly meaningless and there is no rational basis for choosing among fundamental alternatives, then all choices are equal and there is no fundamental ground for choosing life over death," he concluded.[3]

For a suicide note, that's remarkably lucid, and perhaps we could frame the problem of the meaning of life as the demand to "produce a fundamental ground for choosing life over death."

One way the problem of the meaning of life arises is from the demystification of the universe and in particular the destruction of the ideas that it has a comprehensible moral order and that we are immortal. On the other hand, we might wonder whether immortality would really relieve our ennui; I think, reading Dante or something, that you could say it did not actually relieve the ennui of the believers. Indeed death lends to living shape and urgency, and it is very hard to tell the exciting full story of an immortal being. If living in the next world is anything like living in this world, or if we are anyone there like who we are here (and if we're not, then what does it mean to say we are immortal?), eternity is way too long. What life means is not answered by saying it's interminable. "What is the meaning of a life unending?" is just a longer version of the question "What is the meaning of life?"

One good thing about a life unending: in it, someone is going to tell you what life means. Of course in the situation we're in now, we can't know what it is we don't know. But we will know it there. In the next life God the sage will tell us why we're there and why we were here. God is the Buddha, Lao Tzu, Socrates, Jesus, the Dalai Lama, the Pope, Mr. Natural: he'll tell us and then we'll know. Well, that's nice, especially if it's true, but it doesn't actually solve the problem we face right now. The notion that we might someday know what we do not know now does not help us know anything now, in the midst of our existential crisis. Not only that, but this seems like a mere yearning after authority, an enthusiastic precapitulation. Once God tells me the meaning of life, I reserve the right to ponder whether whatever he just said makes sense.

If the universe displays a comprehensible moral order, we are not now in a position to assess its content: the basic dilemma of a little-bitty creature in a big old world. It doesn't seem to, actually, from here. And indeed, we might point out that various systems that have attributed to the world a comprehensible moral order—from Papal Bull to Sam Harris scientism—have also produced a certain anxiety, in that they tend to display us as failures within that order. And if you think that the doctrine of original sin, or the notion that evolution produces intelligence, or the idea that we are put here as stewards of the earth is edifying, then I say you aren't sufficiently alert to your own massive failures by the standards thus articulated. You haven't sufficiently contemplated your own future burning in eternal hellfire or in a carbon-rich atmosphere.

Speaking of hellfire, when Augustine wanted to contrast Christians and pagans, he said that pagans turned toward the self, while Christians turned toward God. Turning toward the self was, for Augustine, the essence of sin: "To live according to oneself is sin, and to sin is to lose God."[4] On this ground he condemned what we call the "Hellenistic" philosophies: skepticism, epicureanism, and stoicism. All turned from the grand metaphysical and political questions of Plato and Aristotle into philosophy as a way of life, philosophy as a way to achieve tranquility in the individual soul. Indeed skepticism and epicureanism were at best agnostic about the existence of the gods, and stoicism's god as reason and nature cut across the religious tendencies of the times, neither pagan nor Christian.

So one way to phrase this idea is that to live for oneself is evil, but to live for something greater than oneself is good: or, the meaning of life has to be found in something greater than the self. Here we face a number of options: the thing greater than the self might be God, or it might be nature as envisioned by Thoreau, for example. It could be the universe as a whole. Or it could be as close to you as your neighbor: we live to help each other, for social justice, or for the alleviation of suffering.

However, this appears merely to defer the question. If each of us has no meaning as a mere individual, it seems hard to explain the meaning of all of us together. If we are just another species of mammal, rushing like most species the world has ever produced toward extinction, then all of us together appear in a Heisman or Mencken structure to be just as meaningless as each of us. Living for nature conceived as a mechanical system of atoms swirling in a void appears no more sensible than inventing a God and living for him, or on the other hand, if God is real, capitulating to his incomprehensible imperatives.

Now one of the things that seemed to be bothering Heisman was his "inability to believe in the worth of any goal." And that is yet another way to read the demand for the meaning of life: produce the goal of human life, like a rabbit out of a hat. Aristotle thought the goal was happiness or flourishing. This purpose, like so much for Aristotle, is built into our nature as a brute fact; indeed all things for Aristotle are filled with purpose: that's ours.

But first of all, if life has a goal, I personally don't know what it is. And second, the goal would itself have to be meaningful: it can't make life meaningful recursively unless it has some meaning to lend. In other words, even if life had some obvious goal, or even if you gave yourself a goal of whatever sort, it would make sense to ask whether the goal was meaningful, and hence whether a life lived in its service was meaningful. Many life goals, such as big cash money, a BMW, and a job in investment banking, seem to have a problem in this regard. Even "happiness," a kind of blank into which we can pour whatever goal we imagine, seems to come up wanting. Perhaps it is a brute fact about us that we want to be happy, whatever that means exactly. It does not follow that happiness is the meaning of life. And if we consider a goal of life as something that could be reached at a certain moment—a culmination of us, as it were—still we would wonder about the merely instrumental value of all the activity that led to its achievement, while wondering what the hell to do next, and why, once we've arrived.

It's been a popular position that life is a kind of story or narrative. This would make it meaningful in a relatively comprehensible way: it is meaningful in the way a novel or a fable or a tragedy is meaningful. Now one thing about this is that novels consist of actual words; they are meaningful in the sense that the words signify. A novel is a linguistic item and has meaning in the sense that language has a semantics: the words don't just mean their own shapes or sounds, they mean a setting or a character or a plot.

Indeed it is with regard to such items as novels or paintings that the term *meaning* is fundamentally appropriate or something like literal. The *Boston Globe* piece on Heisman is meaningful in a relatively clear way: it refers to something beyond itself in a certain manner; it has sense and reference.

It is a description or exploration of something beyond itself, or beyond its own syntax: namely, Mitchell Heisman and his writings. I think perhaps the demand for meaning in life is a demand for each of us to interpret ourselves and others as though we were texts or pictures: items with a semantics, with reference to a level of reality beyond themselves. We want to know what we signify or symbolize. But though we are things that use symbols, we are not, I think, ourselves symbols. A person can be used semantically, and perhaps Martin Luther King symbolizes justice. But that means that, for us, King has become a word or a picture; he is a symbol of justice only insofar as his existence as a flesh-and-blood human being is dessicated. It helps that our experience of King is exclusively itself an experience of words and pictures: the flesh-and-blood organism is not itself a semantic item. Martin Luther King, whatever he was, was no picture, not to insult the man.

I just want to point out that our lives are not stories, and are nothing like stories. You could tell a story about your life, but most of it is lived in completely irrelevant detail, as if the story-teller were an excruciating parody of Proust, leaving you in the midst of an infinite enumeration of entirely incoherent and useless routine. So, last night after a long day I felt kind of dazed. I watched part of a baseball game but couldn't really pay attention. I ate a sub. I pissed three times. I stubbed my toe on the fucking top stair again. As a climax, I brushed my teeth. Every day is like this, more or less: an infinite tedium of mundane details, shaped into a coherent narrative only by total falsification. Indeed, that's precisely why we wish our lives were stories, or why we try to reconstruct them into something with directionality, plot, character: because our actual lives are lived at the level of continuous plodding everydayness.

Of course, you could try to settle the question of the meaning of life for yourself one way or another. Indeed I suppose that that is one possible answer, and perhaps it is well suited to our eclectic cultural moment in some ways: each of us must provide meaning for her own life. There is no reason to think that a single answer would satisfy everyone, and there is no reason it should. It's a kind of existentialist approach a la Sartre: each of us must be the creator of himself, and this creation includes making sense of your own life, telling your own story, giving yourself your own values, finding your own god or attributing to yourself your own immortality if any, and so on.

But the interminability of the question is not adequately snipped by locking it up inside your head or by decisively pretending you've answered it. Goals are revisable. If we were living stories, they'd suddenly fly off in a different direction, or end and begin again somewhere else. Perhaps you can decide to believe in God, but even if so, you can decide to silence all doubts about that belief only by a rigid regime of self-censorship. In other words, you're going to keep losing the thread, and if you're a reflective existentialist, you'll realize that your answers are essentially arbitrary and always subject to revision in the face of experience or a breakdown.

The question as it confronts the self-inventing individual (or as it would confront self-inventing individuals if there were any) is precisely as ambiguous and interminable as it is for whole societies or religious traditions or for the species as a whole. In fact, if you are aware that you're inventing your own meaning, then I don't think it can actually function as meaning; we want to know our place in a wider context, and we want our answers, if any, to conform to the reality outside our own subjectivities, or else we are aware that the world we are constructing is false. That you feel some sort of directionality or momentum in virtue of something you heard or made up—that, for example, you made up the idea of your own immortality, or science, and then committed yourself to it utterly, but arbitrarily, is nice. On this view, of course, there is nothing to choose between committing yourself to social justice or Jesus, and committing yourself to racial supremacism or Satanism. Subtract the actual world and find meaning in your head, and you're no longer engaged in the meaning of this life, but in the meaning of a fantasy.

I think that what these various rather casual observations suggest is that the demand for the meaning of life is multiply ambiguous and completely unsatisfiable. It is not at all clear what we could possibly mean by "the meaning of life"; it is not at all clear what we are asking for or what could ultimately satisfy us: a story, a goal, a god, living forever, dying right now, an ethical theory, pleasure without pain, and so on. These answers are not only in competition with each other, they are not even related to each other in any very clear way. They do not settle into a single dimension in which they might rightly be thought to be answers to the same question. This leads me to suspect that there is no question. Certainly there is no coherent single question being framed when one asks for the meaning of life.

And indeed, perhaps people live better or more clearly or more simply or more in reality when they just stop asking this question, or never get to the point of asking it at all. At any rate, this semester I am teaching Intro to Philosophy to forty undergraduates at Dickinson College. As professors often observe to one another, classes differ in their personalities, and this one is just a wee bit nonlively. Maybe it's me, or maybe it's them. Anyway, we're reading Plato or Epictetus when in a moment of pedagogical ecstasy I confront them with the momentous question: What does it mean to you that you yourself—*you,* Cody, Jessica, Zach—are going to die? How do you grapple with the overwhelming fact of your own mortality? Well, in response they stare blankly at the wall, or roll their eyes, or concentrate on texting. Someone will put up a hand and say: Is this going to be on the exam? Now admittedly, y'all are the products of an amazing standardized testing regime in which such questions cannot arise. You are the products of a profoundly authoritarian educational system in which thinking is heresy, and the profoundest form of individual expression permissible is the five-paragraph essay, graded by computer.

There's a lot to be said for this, which is one version of the unreflective life against which philosophy is supposedly juxtaposed. Reflection, as the previous paragraphs have shown pretty clearly, can leave you in complete puzzlement and possibly—as in the case of Mitchell Heisman—abject despair. Reflecting on one's own identity, as I believe I know as well as anything can be known by anybody, can induce nausea. Not only that, but thinking too hard about anything kind of hurts, and that is a form of pain that the average American undergraduate can avoid with ease and even a certain insouciant joy.

We philosophy professors think that when we frame such questions we are getting at the fundamental dilemmas and conditions of our own lives and those of our students; we flatter ourselves that no one should get through life without pondering them. Well, why not, exactly? We keep raising questions without answers, and if we don't give up because we are diseased in some way, it doesn't follow that everyone has to follow us down our road to nowhere. If you're focused not on what your life and death mean but instead on what's happening at tonight's kegger . . . well, we don't actually have any answers to the questions we are raising, but the kegger will actually occur. While we speculate our way into layers of reality that bear on nothing practical, and the existence of which is sheer speculation, people go on living just the same. And if they feel no demand for meaning, that doesn't seem to be any less rational than feeling no call to jump over the moon; not trying is a perfectly good approach. It's hard to quibble with the observation that going to the party is preferable, all things considered, to shooting yourself on the quad as a tour group strolls by.

However, there is also something touching in the cow who aspires to jump over the moon. At any rate, cows—like philosophy professors—have an excruciatingly limited behavioral repertoire, and you might find a cow who just can't quit jumping, no matter what. Perhaps the cow could be treated with medication. Or perhaps, after jumping again and again and again, the cow breaks a leg, or just gives up, or croaks and thenceforth jumpeth not. More likely, she simply declares, falsely but to her own immense satisfaction, that she has succeeded, that she's cleared the moon, or close enough. Thus the introduction to Kant's *Critique of Pure Reason*, or Hegel's *Phenomenology of Spirit*, or Schopenhauer's *World as Will and Idea*, in this wise: "For millennia, philosophers have puzzled over this and that. As you know, I am the culmination of the human species, and I have answered all these questions once and for all or just as good as, as any rational person will have to agree after reading this book. You'll be grateful to me because you no longer have to read my predecessors or idiotic rivals, think for yourself, and so on."

At any rate, as I say, philosophy might be a disease, but it is a poignant disease: touching, ironic, like the deafness of Beethoven. We cultivate unsatisfiable aspirations, ironic aspirations, tragic aspirations: infinite aspirations: aspirations that could be satisfied only by omniscience, or not even by omniscience. We ask questions so large and so obscure that every single possible answer is inadequate. Nothing could help us: not God, not immortality, not a nice clear goal or a beautifully coherent reconstruction of our lives into stories.

Beauty is the object of longing. And longing is unsatisfied or unsatisfiable desire. Indeed, it is worth saying that eternal beings could not experience beauty at all, that beauty is opened up as a possibility by our time-boundedness, by the fact that our losses are irremediable. We are always in the condition of losing everything we have, including ourselves if we have ourselves. Or put it another way: it's the loss of or lack of meaning, or even the fact that we don't actually have any idea what we're looking for as we go on looking, that makes our lives potentially beautiful, in a world that is potentially beautiful. It is our radical meaninglessness that opens up life as an arena of intense or eternal or infinite desire.

Now perhaps this sounds like I'm asserting that the meaning of life is aesthetic, or is a quest for beauty. And even though I actually would entertain that notion, at least for myself—even though if I were making my own meaning I might start with beauty—I don't propose it as an answer. Beauty is just as equivocal, questionable as a value, liquid, and contingent as anything else that might be proposed as the meaning of life. But what I'm saying is that beauty points us toward our meaninglessness in a worthwhile way, or is a way of revealing our condition.

Creatures, we might say, want. They are turned toward the satisfaction of desire. But creatures can get into a position of desire without object or surcease. Desire is more than a way to get you shoving food in your face; it is a habit of mind, the posture of a finite creature in a challenging environment. What do we yearn for when we yearn to be loved, for example? Well, we yearn toward some kind of perfect affirmation of ourselves, an ecstatic "yes" to everything we are. Love perhaps has a perfectly sensible object; maybe it's an epiphenomenon of our sexual desire, in turn an epiphenomenon of our condition as creatures who must reproduce, which would not be necessary if we were immortal. But the point is, in desiring an infinite or perfect affirmation of ourselves, we desire what we cannot deserve and what no person can give us. Even if we got it, it might be oppressive or disconcerting, or a mere hallucination on the part of the person loving us. Even if someone were capable of affirming me utterly and entirely, I don't think that that would actually fix me or cure me. Indeed, it might just irritate me.

However, the desire to be loved like that is irremediable. You can see that in everything from *General Hospital* to the Christian idea of God's perfect, infinite love, which is easy to say but hard to understand or square with reality, or with, for example, God's justice. But what I am saying is: the spectacle of people who need a love they can't even describe sensibly is a touching spectacle, or even a beautiful spectacle. That supposes precisely its conceptual impossibility, its infinity in the face of a constant confrontation with finitude, its contradictoriness and incomprehensibility, its excess to anything we could actually believe or experience. Somewhere I think even Dickinson College undergrads feel both that aspiration and its futility. And I want to say that it is only comprehensible as an aspiration on the condition of its futility. Even the quest for pleasure or sex or extinction through beer is a little node of the dilemma: you can't get drunk enough without puking and passing out; you cannot get through beer what you seek in beer. And yet you keep right on gulping toward ecstasy or unconsciousness, seek through living an end of living.

Religion is, as a series of assertions, a terrible crock. The promotion of Jesus to godhead is, it seems to me, no more sensible than the promotion of Haile Selassie: it's essentially arbitrary, and the huge quasi-intellectual edifices built on top of it are in a way pitiful, or at least entirely fantastic. But religion is also beautifully human in that it captures in crystal the dilemma of finite creatures with infinite aspirations. It marks our desire to know what cannot be known, as well as a need for moral certainty, and perfect love, and immortality. These needs, I am suggesting, have never been met and cannot be met. But they cannot cease; they are a site of the poignant expression of a useless, infinite longing.

Now I could come off of this and suggest that the meaning of life is precisely this aspiration. That it is unrealizable should give one pause, of course; it identifies the meaning of life with a kind of total futility, a futility by definition, a futility that cannot be solved or fixed. But what I am suggesting is that if this aspiration were to be met, it would, like any satisfied desire, cease, and we would cease to be recognizably human or animal; we would cease to be real creatures or finite things of this world. What you have to understand is that the need is comprehensible only in the face of its unsatisfaction. The need itself, in its irremediability, can drive you crazy or make you feel that life is meaningless. But if it were to be satisfied, it likewise would not yield what we are looking for; when meaning is satisfied it ceases to be meaning and becomes reality; when it stops having a reference to anything outside itself, it ceases to mean anything, or recedes into sheer objecthood.

So how would I counsel Mitchell Heisman, the philosophical suicide? I don't think I could really help, but I'd try something like this. The demand for meaning, for the meaning of your own emotions, for example, is an unsatisfiable demand. It's not exactly your materialism that drives you to despair; it's the fundamental conditions of life. But perhaps in the midst of this contradictory or impossible situation, you could find some lightness of touch, some distance from your own need for meaning. The very futility of the project opens it up as an arena of play. There could be a kind of joy in committing yourself to an answer. Or there could also be a kind of joy in a release from significance, a sense of the universe as radically open or indeterminate. Meaning is a burden as well as a satisfaction, and release from that burden might be conceived as a liberation. I think, however, that such joys are mixed with falsehoods: either that we have the answer or that we can actually achieve satisfaction without an answer. But the truth is that we cannot stop seeking and cannot find what we are seeking. In one way this is an extremely unsatisfactory situation, but in another way it is a lovely dilemma, without which we would cease to be anything like what we are.

So I suppose I am and I am not trying to answer the question of the meaning of life. It would hardly be too much to say that the meaning of life is that it has no meaning, or that its meaning is its meaninglessness, which opens it up as an arena of unsatisfied desire, longing, beauty, and play. We face death, and yearn uselessly for immortality; we want an infinite amount of money and money doesn't repair the hole in our souls. Nothing can cure or fix us, and we cannot stop needing to be cured or fixed. This is a terrible and terrifying situation. But it is also highly comical. If anyone read all two thousand pages of Mitchell Heisman's suicide note, it wasn't me. But the stuff I looked at was notably humorless. The question might not be what the meaning of life is, but how we comport ourselves in the face of its meaninglessness. Sick comedy is certainly not the meaning of life. Rather it is a way of affirming a condition that is at the same time fundamentally intolerable.

Human beings, we might say, are in a comedy of inadequacy, of noble-ish futility, like a schlumph played by Will Farrell or Fatty Arbuckle. Or we face the predicament of the immortal Howard the Duck: "trapped in a world that he never made." Mencken says of "man" that he always aspires, and adds: "Always he imagines things just over the skyline. This body of imaginings constitutes his body of beliefs, his corpus of high faiths and confidences—in brief, his burden of errors. And that burden of errors is what distinguishes man, even above his capacity for tears, his talents as a liar, his excessive hypocrisy and poltroonery, from all the other orders of mammalia. Man is the yokel *par excellence*, the booby unmatchable, the king dupe of the cosmos."[5]

The grand cynicism of a Diogenes, or an Ambrose Bierce, or a Mencken as represented, for example, in that thing about stale cabbage, is a way of welcoming the universe, an attitude of dark good humor, the only laughter that isn't ultimately hollow. Face up to the world squarely, more or less, and try to respond with a gracious, mordant wit, a slightly light touch, a disillusioned but nevertheless bitter resolution to keep your distance, or hop right in, snickering.

Appendix

Art History Lexicon

Abstraction. Form without representational content. There was no intentional pure abstraction at high levels of fine art painting and sculpture until around 1911–12 in the West. In retrospect this seems odd, or maybe not at all. It does show how thoroughly art was conceived to be mimetic in the West. Hilma af Klimt (1862–1944), Frantisek Kupka (1871–1957), Giacomo Balla (1871–1958), Arthur Dove (1880–1946).

Aestheticism. The movement, associated with figures such as Walter Pater (1839–1894) and Oscar Wilde (1854–1900), who made a religion of beauty or of art for the sake of art, and by extension any similar movement or tendency of any period. Pre-Raphaelite painting is related. A late or ultimate flowering of romanticism or, in Wilde, a tip into modernity or pomo. One of a number of proto-Bohemias of the nineteenth century.

Art.

> Let me tell you what art is. Art is process. Or, to give you a more official definition, a work of art is the product of a process engaged

> in for its own sake, and not merely for the sake of the product. Art is immersion in making; a work of art is the product of an immersion in making. The various forms of art are defined by the processes they involve. Painting is the process of applying pigment to a surface, for example, and if you engage in the process with devotion to the process itself, if you are absorbed in the process of applying pigment to a surface, then what you're painting is art. If you want to know whether something is art, and, if so, what sort of art it is, then you have to focus on the process that leads up to what you see. ("Presence and Resistance")

Avant-Garde. Concept drawn from military affairs and centralized in aesthetics by Clement Greenberg (1909–1994) with regard to modernism in "Avant-Garde and Kitsch," indicating the group of artists who were furthest out into the future at a given moment, namely, the postcounter-Fauves. Rosalind Krauss (b. 1941): *The Originality of the Avant-Garde and Other Modernist Myths.*

> The avant-garde arts are peculiar to the West, and Western-influenced cultures elsewhere, since the mid-nineteenth century, or roughly since Manet. They proceed by a series of radical innovations, or looking at it the other way round, through a series of radical rejections of the past: a series of negations. Overcoming or destroying the past is a mark of genius, and avant-garde arts consist of an ever accelerating series of movements, each defined in part by its destruction or negation of the previous movement: impressionism/fauvism/cubism/dadaism, for example, or expressionism/pop/minimalism/conceptualism. ("Beatles vs. Stones")

Baroque. In traditional art-historical periodization, the period that follows the Renaissance, or which follows mannerism which follows the Renaissance, and that segues on the other end into the rococo. Well, 1580–1710 in painting, perhaps, different in different places and in different arts. Characterized by elaboration, profusion, distortion, painterliness. Rubens (1577–1640), El Greco (1541–1614), Bernini (1598–1680), Caravaggio (1571–1610), Rembrandt (1606–1669) (the last two are signals of something else, however). Wölfflin makes the "Classical/Baroque" pair a recurring general structure for understanding various segments of art history, in which approach I tend to follow him: neoclassical/romantic, or early/late Beatles, for example.

Beauty. The object of longing.

Bluegrass. American traditionalist music codified in the late 1940s by Bill Monroe (1911–1996) and the Bluegrass Boys, including Earl Scruggs (1924–2012) on banjo. Characterized by the use of acoustic instruments—primarily guitar, bass, mandolin, banjo, fiddle, and Dobro, often played at high speed by virtuosi—and harmony vocals often showcasing a high tenor male singer. *Newgrass* and *Progressive Bluegrass* are subgenres or related genres explored by artists such as the Seldom Scene and Newgrass Revival, who tested some of the constraints of the form.

Blues. African-American popular music codified in the Mississippi Delta or East Texas or Georgia or somewhere else entirely or all at once early in the twentieth century. Many different styles were played, often centering on guitar and revolving around a twelve-bar AAB structure with a characteristic turnaround. Or: featuring piano and foghorn female vocals, a la Bessie Smith, or dueling electric guitars a la Duane Allman and Eric Clapton. Fundamentally constructive of jazz, rock, gospel, country, reggae, and other forms of twentieth-century popular music all over the world. Blind Willie McTell (1898–1959), Muddy Waters (1913–1983), Stevie Ray Vaughan (1954–1990).

Bop or Bebop. Jazz style codified in the late 1940s and early '50s by figures such as Charlie Parker (1920–1955) and Dizzy Gillespie (1917–1993), emerging from swing and moving toward free jazz at the end. As opposed to swing, a dance music often played by big bands, bop was an art music that abandoned many blues elements and demanded close listening. The top players were extreme technical wizards. Favorite of beatniks everywhere.

Classical. A style of all the arts and a conception of beauty originating in the Greek classical era (circa 500–200 BCE) and recurring throughout much Western, and even African and Asian culture ever since. As a general proposition, it asserts that beauty can be characterized as something like a compound ratio of uniformity and variety, or in terms of the relation of integral parts to a whole, sometimes conceived in mathematical terms, as in pillars and pediment in a classical temple. The greatest revival of the classical was the High Renaissance.

> The central idea of the Italian Renaissance is that of perfect proportion. In the human figure as in the edifice, this epoch strove to achieve the image of perfection at rest within itself. Every form developed to self-existent being, the whole freely coordinated: nothing but independently living parts. . . . In the system of a classic composition, the single parts, however firmly they may be rooted in the whole, maintain a certain independence. It is not the anarchy of primitive art: the part is conditioned by the whole, and yet does not cease to have its own life. For the spectator, that presupposes an articulation, a progress from part to part, which is a very different operation from perception as a whole.[1]

The term also refers to music of the period of neoclassicism in painting and politics, such as the works of Haydn (1732–1809) and Mozart (1756–1791). More widely, it is popularly applied to most "serious" or "art" music of the sort taught at Juilliard or whatever it may be.

Constructivism. Russian art movement (circa 1919–1925) paradigmatic of modernism, associated with such figures as Alexander Rodchenko (1891–1956) and Naum Gabo (1890–1977). Either effortlessly absorbed or ruthlessly repressed into various socialist realist modes, depending on whom you ask.

Country. A style of popular music drawn from and feeding back into various forms of music in the rural South, including blues, black and white gospel, rockabilly, bluegrass, soul, and rock; a dominant commercial form or format or market, circa late 1920s to the present. Instrumentation shifts but characteristically features something like a rock band, possibly with fiddle and pedal-steel guitar, at various stages of electrification. Often characterized by highly emotionally charged solo vocal performances; waltz times. There are many substyles, such as honky-tonk, Texas swing, Americana, and so on. Jimmie Rodgers (1897–1933), Hank Williams (1923–1953), Tammy Wynette (1942–1998), Taylor Swift (b. 1989).

Cool. An aesthetic orientation or attitude, perhaps partly African and African-American in origin, denoting self-containment, terseness, and masculinity: Miles Davis (1926–1991); the Man With No Name as portrayed by Clint Eastwood (b. 1930). An example of a gendered/orientated aesthetic concept or role. (See *Fabulous.*)

Disco. Interracial and interorientational dance-oriented pop music, initially dominant in the mid-'70s, with connections to soul and funk, but also adding, for example, glittering string sections. Nile Rodgers should be mentioned as a fundamental producer. Later, the term is used loosely for various outbreaks of dance music.

Dub. Musical form or technique invented by King Tubby (1941–1989) in Kingston in the late 1960s, fundamental for the practice of popular music ever since. Tubby drew many versions out of a single recording, adding echo and dub effects, and working tracks in and out to create a wide variety of soundscapes. Scientist (Hopeton Brown, b. 1960), Adrian Sherwood (b. 1958).

Eidetic. Used here to indicate the mode of representation characteristic of idealizing, especially neo-Platonic styles of depiction, associated with thinkers such as Plotinus (circa 205–270 AD) and Shaftesbury (1671–1713), and having as great paradigms Greek classical sculpture and High Renaissance painting.

Emo. Originally a punk subgenre incorporating elements of hardcore ("screamo") with emotive lyric content and changes of tempo. I believe I first heard the term applied to the band Rites of Spring in the mid-'80s. Later, almost any rock band featuring skinny or sensitive boys was an emo act. Fall Out Boy.

Fabulous. Used here as a complement/opposite of "cool," representing an aesthetic orientation of over-the-top expressiveness, loudness, and drenchedness in light and color. (See *Cool.*)

Fauvism. "Beastism": a movement of the first decade of the twentieth century, often associated with Henri Matisse (1869–1954) and André Derain (1880–1954), distinguished by unusual color choices, often applied in broad segregated areas, to delineate forms. Early and paradigmatic modernist mode: an avant-garde movement par excellence, radical and short-lived.

Flourish. In the world of conjuring, a flourish is an explicit display of skill that is what it appears to be, as opposed to a *sleight*, for example. Card fanning is an example of human flourishing.

Funk. A multivalent term of aesthetic taxonomy and appreciation. Might initially refer to a funky smell; then to a style of African-American music emerging out of soul, emphasizing extreme repetition of a syncopated beat and horn riffs. The innovators are James Brown's (1933–2006) bands of the late '60s; later the paradigm of the form is provided by Parliament-Funkadelic and its spinoffs. Funk tracks are the most sampled in hip hop (by genre).

Glam. Form of rock music beginning in the early 1970s featuring male performers in heavy makeup, sequined outfits, extreme coiffure, and the like. Associated above all with a certain phase of David Bowie's (b. 1947) stage shows. Also influential on punk through the New York Dolls and others, and on later "hair rock." A moment in the straightgirl/gayguy alliance.

Gospel. The term can refer to a number of styles of American religious music, including (primarily) African-American and rural white Southern styles, often performed by a preacher/singer with choir. Thomas A. Dorsey (1899–1993) was a key figure in codifying a canon of black church music as a popular genre. One way to describe the emergence of soul music is as a secularization of gospel, for example in Sam Cooke (1931–1964), first of the Soul Stirrers gospel group and then a solo artist.

Gothic. One of the many contrasts or complements of the classical: associated with "Germanic" styles of the medieval period, especially in cathedral architecture, characterized by pointed arches and extreme ornamental or narrative embellishment. Often reviled and often revived, for example by John Ruskin (1819–1900) in the nineteenth century.

Hip Hop. African-American and subsequently world popular music style beginning in the Bronx in the mid-1970s, making use of Jamaican DJ culture brought to New York by DJ Kool Herc (b. 1955). A dominant black pop style through the present, characterized by foursquare beats, sampling of previously recorded material, and lyrics that are spoken or chanted rather than sung (rapping). More widely, an arts culture encompassing graffiti, deejaying, emceeing, and break dancing, as well as fashion and design. Grandmaster Flash (b. 1958), Public Enemy, Eminem (b. 1972).

Idealism. The term is used with several meanings, but especially for the philosophy of Plato and neo-Platonists, and then in the related developments of German idealism in Kant (1724–1804), Schelling (1775–1854), Fichte (1762–1814), Hegel (1770–1831), and Schopenhauer (1788–1860). Used here, among other things, to characterize the theories of beauty in these movements. (See *Eidetic.*)

Impressionism. It's difficult to recover the radicalness of Manet (1832–1883) and Monet (1840–1926) from their subsequent demotion to pretty, but the impressionists are a good place to begin an account of modernism, the first avant-garde movement in painting, perhaps. Well, not exactly—realism and others would have such a claim—but at any rate fundamental to modernism.

Kitsch. A term of abuse, of spurious import and provenance, used to express a combination of aesthetic, political, and class attitudes. Associated with the work of Clement Greenberg (1909–1994), the high-modernist art critic, where kitsch is opposed to art of the avant-garde. (See *Avant-Garde.*)

Linear. "Linear" and "painterly" are features that Wölfflin makes central to the transition between classical (Renaissance) and baroque. Characterized by an emphasis on form, draughtsmanship, composition, and (of course) line. "Linear sees in line," says Wölfflin, "painterly in masses."

> If we wish to reduce the difference between the art of Dürer and the art of Rembrandt to its most general formulation, we say that Dürer is a draftsman and Rembrandt a painter. . . . [A] decisive readjustment of the eye took place everywhere [from the sixteenth to the seventeenth centuries]. The painterly mode is later and cannot be conceived without the earlier, but it is not absolutely superior. The linear style developed values that the painterly style no longer possessed and no longer wanted to possess. They are two conceptions

of the world, differently orientated in taste and in their interest in the world, yet each capable of giving a perfect picture of visible things.[2] (See *Painterly.*)

Mannerism. Properly, the period immediately following the High Renaissance in Italy in the second third of the sixteenth century, including works by such painters as Vasari (1511–1574) and Parmigianino (1503–1540), characterized by a perverse or even humorous distortion, testing of the limits of idealized form. No matter what anyone says, an air of self-conscious decline hovers over the period. Generalized, the term picks out any period that both labors under the power of what preceded it and comments on it with a derivative irony. *Mannered* also simply means conventional or academic.

Mimetic. Imitative. Greek theories of art focused on *mimesis* or imitation, or more broadly on the representational, semantical, and reproductive function of the arts. Plato, in Book 10 of *The Republic,* compares works of art to mirror images.

Minimalism. Properly, a dominant style of two- and three-dimensional arts beginning in the 1960s, associated for example with the work of Donald Judd (1928–1994). Later a design style favoring brushed steel and good concrete. More broadly, is sometimes used for any aesthetic style that resists ornament or gravitates toward simplicity, for example the abstracts of Mondrian (1872–1944) or the furnishings produced by the Shakers.

Misdirection. In stage and parlor magic and elsewhere, the process of guiding the attention of an audience to extraneous or deceptive matters as the real work is accomplished. Such figures as Dai Vernon (1894–1992) and Slydini (1900–1991) are famous close-up masters of misdirection. Check out the latter's "paper balls over the head," for example.

Modernism. Any drawing of dates is bound to be simplistic. Let's try 1870–1960, bounded on one end by romanticism and on the other by postmodernism (well, you could have figured that part out). Characterized in painting by a de-emphasis on craft skills, ever intensifying emotional expression, visual experimentation including the invention of abstraction, and concepts such as the avant-garde, an intensification of the romantic concept of the artistic genius, and an ever greater emphasis on originality. In painting, Manet, Gauguin (1848–1903), Picasso (1881–1973), Pollock (1912–1956).

Neoclassical. Refers properly to painting of the late eighteenth century, especially David (1748–1825) in France, associated with the classical revival that also led to American republicanism, for example the architecture of Jefferson. The classical is always what has been lost; it is always in revival, as in the Roman Republic or the American founders.

Neo-Platonism. Movement in philosophy associated anciently with Plotinus, Porphyry (circa 234–305 AD), and certain church fathers, later with Marsilio Ficino (1433–1499) and the Italian High Renaissance as a whole, for example in the paintings of Botticelli (1445–1510) and the sonnets of Michelangelo (1475–1564). Plotinus argues that the whole universe "emanates" in something like a spiral from a purely spiritual or abstract center: the Form of Goodness and Beauty, a kind of inert God. The closer any thing is to this Idea, the more beautiful it is; the more formed according to an Idea, the better; the ugly is the merely material, like a sack of shit, say. Neo-Platonism runs underground in amazing ways through Western intellectual history, always associated with "esoteric" erotic-educational ideas, through German idealism, romanticism, aestheticism, and Leo Strauss (1899–1973), for example.

Painterly. Contrasted by Wölfflin with "linear" as characteristics of baroque and classical (or High Renaissance) painting: articulating objects through internal mass rather than outline. (See *Linear.*)

Pop. As an art movement, beginning in the '60's, associated with such figures as Andy Warhol (1928–1987) and Roy Lichtenstein (1923–1997), characterized by the use and reuse of imagery from other parts of the culture. Pop is often held to be the fundamental turning point between the modern and the postmodern eras: genius to celebrity or originality to appropriation. Presented in "Divas etc." as an important moment in the gayguy/straightwoman aesthetic alliance. The most commercial form of music at a given moment, often associated with dance and a certain radio format.

Popomo. Short for *postpostmodern:* what comes next, a new dawn of human hope and of its wholesale suppression.

Postimpressionism. One of the first of the "posts." Cézanne (1839–1906), Gauguin, and van Gogh (1853–1890) moved further into the pure visuality of the painted object in distinction from its subject matter.

Postmodernism. In the visual arts and elsewhere, the period from the 1960s right up until popomo abruptly halted its career, or up until the present and some time to come, characterized by ironic or knowing appropriation from myriad sources, stylistic eclecticism, theoretical sophistication, and information technologies. Andy Warhol in visual arts and King Tubby in music must be mentioned as fundamental sources; often associated in intellectual history with such figures as Lyotard (1924–1998), Baudrillard (1929–2007), Foucault (1926–1984), and Rorty (1931–2007). It raids historical vocabularies at will and liquefies everything into an informational multiverse, or something along those lines. It is a matter of some controversy whether the postmodern period, with its simulacra and multiple valances, is an extension and intensification of trends in modernism or a wholesale reversal. Both, in different ways and moments, no doubt.

Psychedelic. A politico/cultural style associated with hallucinogenic drugs and mystical religious experiences, characteristic of some music and visual expression of the 1960s, such as the Beatles, Jimi Hendrix (1942–1970), Peter Max (b. 1937), Timothy Leary (1920–1996). Featuring bright colors, phase shifters, influences of pop and surrealism.

Punk. Musical, graphic, sartorial, etc. movement founded in New York in the mid-1970s by groups such as the Dictators, Dead Boys, Richard Hell and the Voidoids, and the Heartbreakers. Transported to London, where it grew into a generational fad or identity. Sex Pistols and Clash. Raw, fast guitar-based rock. Partly a reaction against smooth corporate rock and dance music of the late 1970s. Later superseded by a lurching, bellowing style known as *hardcore*, especially centered in LA and DC.

Realism. A multivalent term that has been applied to a number of specific art movements, especially in the circle of Courbet (1819–1877) and Proudhon (1809–1865) in the mid-1800s, and the literary movement associated with Balzac (1799–1850) and Flaubert (1821–1880). Used here primarily to indicate various outbreaks of attempts at verisimilitude or accuracy in picturing as an aesthetic program, for example in Dutch art of the seventeenth century and the Philadelphia school of the late nineteenth century. Eakins (1844–1916), Harnett (1848–1892.)

Renaissance, High. The momentary re-realization of the classical, especially in early sixteenth-century Florence, paradigmatically in Leonardo da Vinci (1452–1519), Raphael (1483–1520), and Michelangelo.

> Indeed, the High Renaissance is often represented in sketches of art history as an almost instantaneous or infinitesimal moment of perfect equipoise. The stretch between Leonardo's emergence from the Early Renaissance and Michelangelo's falling off into mannerism is pretty short, and shrinks up shorter the harder you look. Have you ever jumped off a swing? First you rise, then you fall and land or crash. But there's that instant in the air when you at least have the illusion that you are quite still and weightless: that's the High Renaissance. Well, it's been a long fall since that momentary culmination. Hardly had art reached perfection before people grew weary of perfection and started pulling it apart or distorting it quite intentionally: a mannerist and baroque distortion and excess and whimsicality break out in your pristine ideal universe, almost at the moment you've finally got it cleaned up. ("Holding on for Dear Life")

Rhythm and Blues. Dominant black pop style of the '50s and early '60s, emerging in part from jump blues and electrified Chicago blues, overlapping with or fundamental to other forms of the period, including rockabilly, rock 'n' roll, and doo wop. Louis Jordan (1908–1975), the Dominoes.

Rock. Blues-oriented pop form, dominant at least from the late 1950s through 1980. A thousand permutations and crossings to other forms were tried. Chuck Berry (b. 1926), Rolling Stones, Led Zeppelin, Bo Diddley (1928–2008). Dion and the Belmonts, the Ramones, Turbonegro. Characteristic rock band includes drums, electric bass and guitar, and vocals/showman.

Rock Steady. Supposedly the summer of 1966 was the hottest on record in Jamaica, and people couldn't bounce to ska. Rock steady is a slowed-down and stripped-down ska moving toward a rock band configuration: bass, drums, keyboard, guitar, with possibly a small horn section. Vocalists such as Marcia Griffiths (b. 1949) and Bob Andy (b. 1944) influenced anew by American soul. The underlying record begins to split and hybridize in this era, giving rise to DJ and dub versions.

Rockabilly. Propulsive melding of country and rhythm and blues in the early 1950s into an early form of blues-and-boogie-based rock. Carl Perkins (1932–1998), Buddy Holly (1936–1959).

Rococo. Often held to be the baroque, grown ever more frivolous, hedonistic, and sensual. A style associated with the French court in the buildup to its beheading by the Revolution. Fragonard (1732–1806), Boucher (1703–1770).

Romanticism. Is somewhat aptly painted as a kind of extension and rejection of the Enlightenment. Emerging from what many understood to be a period of scientism and skepticism in the eighteenth century, as well as the rather arid aesthetic canons of neoclassicism, thinkers, poets, and artists agitated a more emotive, unpredictable, and proto-Bohemian world of Gothic darkness, or nature-loving pantheistic ecstasy, or wild syntheses of all known truth in a mating of reason and feeling. Schiller (1759–1805), Coleridge (1772–1834), Caspar David Friedrich (1774–1840), Walt Whitman (1819–1892).

Roots Reggae. Form of Jamaican popular music emerging from rock steady by around 1968; the distinction between the two styles is haphazard. Emphasizing Rastafarian themes, drum parts influenced by Nyabinghi ceremonial, and the use of cannabis. Bob Marley (1945–1981) is of course the form's transcendent star.

Ska. The first indigenous pop music of Jamaica, taking form by 1960 and segueing into rock steady in 1966. A lurching, horn-oriented dance music: slow down its reversed beat, play with it, hold it off, and it is everything in Jamaica and much of the world ever since. The Skatalites and Toots and the Maytals. A young Bob Marley started as a ska artist. In continuous revival ever since, as in the "two-tone" movement of the late '70s in the UK and the Bay Area scene around the band Rancid.

Sleight. In conjuring, a sleight is a deceptive move, or "the work," in a trick or routine: the bit that is not what it appears to be, for example the bit in a card trick (which may be constructed as some sort of story or narrative) in which the selection is controlled.

Socialist Realism. Blanket term for a variety of official and propaganda art within communist regimes and parties, generally produced after the Russian Revolution, often heroically/absurdly depicting the working class. Some moments or related developments are aesthetically interesting on anyone's account, such as the murals of Diego Rivera (1886–1957) or work for the WPA in the USA.

Soul. Emerging in particular from African-American gospel (many of the classic artists, such as Aretha Franklin (b. 1942), started in churches), but replacing God with earthly love, soul was the dominant African-American popular music from, say, 1963 to 1972, when it made various transitions to funk and disco. Characterized by emotive vocals and with instrumentation commonly a rock unit (drums, bass, guitar, keyboard) and horn section. Used at various times in wider senses to mean black pop in general or almost any style framing very emotive singing.

Texas Swing. Syncretic dance music popular especially in Texas, Louisiana, Oklahoma, and other parts of the West and Southwest, featuring swing band, with pedal steel and vocals. Bob Wills (1905–1975) and the Texas Playboys.

Notes

I. How to Escape, 2006

1. Quoted in John Ogilvie, *History of the Attempted Assassination of James A. Garfield* (New York: Ogilvie, 1881), 129.

2. Michel Foucault, *Discipline and Punish: The Birth of the Prison*, trans. Alan Sheridan (New York: Vintage, 1977).

3. Quoted in *The Origin, Progress, and Conclusion of the Florida War* by John Titcomb Sprague (New York: Appleton, 1848), 86.

4. And of course, Osama did not escape either, though where is the corpse?

III. Beatles vs. Stones: An Aesthetics of Rock Music, 2011

1. I hate Elton John on innumerable grounds, thoroughly and in every respect. The shit is as musically and lyrically empty and deracinated, gutless, and pointless as, say, Andrew Lloyd Webber. When God condemns me to hell for eternity for my . . . shortcomings, he will pipe these recordings in to show me that I have not really understood the meaning of suffering. Listening to Elton John or Andrew Lloyd Webber is the price we pay for being white, for having exploited and raped the world. You come out of a few centuries of that and you just aren't really anything anymore: your art is a fungus of some kind. "I Guess That's Why They Call it the Blues" is

a typical Elton Melody, which is too boring to be really irritating, but lyricist Bernie Taupin, the master of meaninglessness, shoves the idiocy down your throat like force-feeding a hunger striker. Um, why do they call it the blues, as opposed to the pinks, or the New York Stock Exchange or Big Mikey? They call it the blues 'cause it's really sad. I'll teach Elton John what they actually do call the blues and why, if you give me an MP3 player and some duct tape: he'll be listening to Son House or Howlin' Wolf records until we cure him of the disease that is his art. Perhaps Elton's greatest moment is "Sad Songs Say So Much": it's not itself a sad song, and it doesn't say anything at all; it merely asserts of itself that it is sad and that it says something, as though I ran out of stuff to write about and just wrote about how amazing this very piece of writing I'm now doing really is.

IV. Reactionary Progressivism: Bluegrass and Political Philosophy, 2009

1. Tom Ewing, ed., *The Bill Monroe Reader* (Urbana: University of Illinois Press, 2000), 117.

2. Neil Rosenberg, *Bluegrass: A History* (Urbana: University of Illinois Press, 2005), 10.

3. Borges, Jorge Luis: "Pierre Menard, Author of *Don Quixote*," *Ficciones* (New York: Grove Press, 1962), 51.

4. Ibid., 53.

5. Sören Kierkegaard, *Fear and Trembling* and *Repetition*, trans. Howard and Edna Hong (Princeton: Princeton University Press, 1983), 149.

6. Ibid., 132.

7. Ewing, *Reader,* 117.

8. Rosenberg, *Bluegrass*.

9. Ewing, *Reader,* 71.

10. Ibid., 37.

V. Philosophy of Punk, 2002

1. From a 1999 interview: http://www.avclub.com/articles/ian-mackaye,13598/

2. Roland Bainton, *Here I Stand: A Life of Martin Luther* (Peabody, MA.: Hendrickson: 1950), 105.

3. Josiah Warren, *Equitable Commerce* (1852), republished in Crispin Sartwell, *The Practical Anarchist: Writings of Josiah Warren* (New York: Fordham University Press, 2011), 78.

4. Ibid., 85.

5. For much much more, see Crispin Sartwell, ed., *The Practical Anarchist: Writings of Josiah Warren* (New York: Fordham University Press, 2011).

6. Examples selected circa 2002.

7. As of 2002, i.e., in the Before Snowden (B.S.) era.

8. We would?

VI. Technology and the Future of Beauty, 1998

1. George Santayana, *The Sense of Beauty* (New York: Scribner's, 1896).

2. Perhaps not.

VIII. I Was a Teenage Terrorist, 2005

1. Selections from Kinkel's journals have appeared, for example, at http://www.pbs.org/wgbh/pages/frontline/shows/kinkel/kip/writings.html

IX. Detritus, 2008

1. Really, seriously, I am doing much better as of this writing: divorced and six years sober, reasonably happy on a good day, and publishing a volume of selected essays. One thing I wrote it for: to remember the bottom if I ever came up for air. Now it is hard, hard for me to read. But it keeps faith with its moment in my experience. Thanks to people who expressed concern when I put this up on crispinsartwell.com, and thanks to the amazing variety of people who wrote me to tell me that this essay was important to them. They had a role in changing for me the reality that the essay describes.

X. Tangled: What If Aesthetic Properties Were Real?, 2009

1. Ralph Waldo Emerson, "History," from *Essays: First Series*, in *Emerson: Essays and Lectures* (New York: Library of America, 1983), 254.

2. See, for example, Bruno Latour, *Reassembling the Social: an Introduction to Actor-Network Theory* (Oxford: Oxford University Press, 2007).

3. Frances Hutcheson: "What we call Beautiful in Objects, to speak in the Mathematical Style, seems to be in a compound Ratio of Uniformity and Variety; so that where the Uniformity of Bodys is equal, the Beauty is as the Variety; and where the Variety is equal, the Beauty is as the Uniformity." *An Inquiry into the Original of our Ideas of Beauty and Virtue* (Indianapolis: Liberty Fund [originally 1725]), 29.

4. Henry David Thoreau, "The Maine Woods," in *Thoreau* (New York: Library of America, 1985), 646.

XI. Holding on for Dear Life: The Value of Realism in Art, 2012

1. Alberti, *De Statua,* quoted, for example, in Moshe Barasch, *Theories of Art 1: Plato to Winckelmann* (New York: Routledge, 2000), 123.

2. Leonardo, *Trattato della pittura*, no. 411, trans. by J. S. Peake in Erwin Panofsky, *Idea* (New York: Harper and Row, 1960), 47.

3. Giorgio Vasari, *Lives of the Artists*, trans. George Bull (London: Allan Lane, 1978), 46.

4. Cicero, *Orator ad Brutum*, II, 7, quoted in Panofsky, *Idea*, 12.

5. Svetlana Alpers, *The Art of Describing: Dutch Art in the Seventeenth Century* (Chicago: University of Chicago Press, 1984), 30.

6. Francis Bacon, from "The Great Instauration," in *The Works of Francis Bacon* (London: 1857), vol. 4, 32–33.

7. Christiaan Huygens, *Treatise on Light*, trans. Silvanus Thompson (Chicago: University of Chicago Press, 1912), vii.

8. Friedrich Schelling, from *Ideas for a Philosophy of Nature*, quoted in Dale Snow, *Schelling and the End of Idealism* (Albany: State University of New York Press, 1996), 72.

XII. Presence and Resistance: Process in Graffiti Art and Crime, 2002

1. James Murray and Karla Murray, *Broken Windows: Graffiti NYC* (Gingko Press, 2002), unpaginated.

2. Ibid., still unpaginated.

3. Stephen Powers, *The Art of Getting Over: Graffiti at the Millennium* (New York: St. Martin's Press, 1999), p. 143.

XIII. Beauty, Sex, and the Banality of Pleasure, 2000

1. George Santayana, *The Sense of Beauty* (New York: Scribner's, 1896).

2. I am perhaps a bit concerned that parts of this have a quality of pseudo-profound claptrap. Some bits, especially toward the end, are examples of one of the ways I was writing in the mid-to-late-nineties: I was trying to write philosophical treatises completely improvisationally, as quickly as I could type, without even being too aware of what I was writing as I wrote, and then going with the result. I feel, however, that I was also trying to stupefy people with lightning strikes of dazzling brilliance that aren't on reflection all that dazzling, or even compatible with what I believe, exactly. So, anyway, sorry!

XIV. Guns, Dub, Technique, 2008

1. Michael E. Veal, *Dub: Soundscapes and Shattered Songs in Jamaican Reggae* (Middletown, CT: Wesleyan University Press, 2007), 78.

XV. Cynicism: The Characteristically American Philosophy, 2013

1. "The Young American," from *Nature*, e.g. in *Emerson: Essays and Lectures* (New York, Library of America, 1983), 230.

2. H. L. Mencken, *Prejudices: First, Second, and Third Series* (New York: Library of America, 2010), 154.

3. Ambrose Bierce, *The Enlarged Devil's Dictionary* (New York: Doubleday, 1967), 151.

4. Mencken, *Prejudices,* 158.

5. Ibid., 159.

6. Ibid., 161.

7. Bierce, *Devil's Dictionary,* 214.

8. Mark Twain, "Man's Place in the Animal World," in *What Is Man? And Other Philosophical Writings* (Berkeley: University of California Press, 1973), 87.

9. George Jean Nathan and H. L. Mencken, *The American Credo* (New York: Knopf, 1920), 41–42.

10. Ambrose Bierce, "Ashes of the Beacon," in *The Collected Works of Ambrose Bierce, Volume 1* (New York: Gordian, 1966), 26.

11. Nathan and Mencken, *Credo,* 4.

12. I'd especially recommend Sara Mayfield's *The Constant Circle: H.L. Mencken and His Friends* (New York: Delacorte Press, 1968), in which characters from Zelda Fitzgerald and Tallulah Bankhead to Sinclair Lewis and Alfred Knopf figure in one of wildest tales of partying and intellect ever told.

13. "On Faith" from *Prejudices: Sixth Series* (Library of America volume 2), 417.

14. Nathan and Mencken, *Credo,* 3.

15. Mark Twain, "What Paul Bourget Thinks of Us," *Collected Tales, Sketches, Speeches, & Essays, 1891–1910* (New York: Library of America, 1992) 178–79.

XVI. "Don't Mean Sheeit": On the Necessity and Impossibility of Meaning for Life, 2010

1. H. L. Mencken, "Exeunt Omnes," *Prejudices: First, Second, and Third Series* (New York: Library of America, 2010), 256.

2. Quote from R. Crumb, *Mr. Natural No. 2* (San Francisco: San Francisco Comic Book Company, 1971), cover: "Mr. Natural! What does it all mean??" "Don't mean sheeit . . ."

3. <boston.com/news/local/massachusetts/articles/2010/09/27/book_details_motives_for_suicide_at_harvard/?page=3>

4. Saint Augustine, *The City of God*, trans. Walsh, Zema, Monahan, and Honan (New York: Doubleday, 1958), 300–301.

5. Mencken, *Prejudices*, 371.

Appendix: Art History Lexicon

1. Heinrich Wölfflin, *Principles of Art History: The Problem of the Development of Style in Later Art,* trans. M. D. Hottinger (Mineola, NY: Dover, 1950), 9–10, 15.

2. Ibid., 18.